PORTRAIT
OF A
DECADE

The Second American Revolution

RANDOM HOUSE   NEW YORK

PORTRAIT
OF A
DECADE

The Second American Revolution

ANTHONY LEWIS

AND

𝕿𝖍𝖊 𝕹𝖊𝖜 𝖄𝖔𝖗𝖐 𝕿𝖎𝖒𝖊𝖘

TO LINDA

Who understood before any of us.

Contents

PORTRAIT
OF A
DECADE

The Second American Revolution

Chapter 1

The Revolutionary Decade

*"How many years can a mountain exist
before it is washed to the sea? . . .
How many roads must a man walk down
before you call him a man? . . .
How many ears must one man have
before he can hear people cry? . . .
The answer, my friend, is blowin' in the wind,
the answer is blowin' in the wind."*

In his great study of the Negro in the United States, *An American Dilemma*, Gunnar Myrdal wrote: "When we say that there is a Negro *problem* in America, what we mean is that the Americans are worried about it. It is on their minds and on their consciences." The book was published in 1944, and at the time many would have thought Myrdal unduly optimistic. Racial discrimination burdened the consciences of some white Americans, but not enough. Most never thought twice about the fact that in one-third of the states their fellow citizens with dark skins were excluded from most decent schools and restaurants and public parks, were confined to the rear of buses and to separate railroad cars and could not vote in the meaningful elections, the primaries; that, North and South, they were largely limited to menial employment; that they were forced to serve in segregated units of the armed forces of the United States; that, eighty years after the Civil War, they could not sit down at a drugstore lunch counter or see a movie in downtown Washington, D.C., the capital of the country.

A decade later some of that picture had brightened: President

Truman had ordered an end to segregation in the armed forces, and a Supreme Court decision had started to break down the barriers in Washington eating places and theatres. But as the year 1954 began, schools remained segregated in seventeen southern and border states and the District of Columbia—areas with forty per cent of the country's public-school enrollment. In voting, in employment, in transportation, in all the amenities of a civilized life, the Negro suffered rank discrimination. Most important, the conscience of America was still not deeply touched by the fact of racial injustice. The subject had hardly been mentioned in the election campaign of 1952. Congress had not passed a civil-rights act for seventy-five years. And the lack of political action reflected relative indifference on the part of the public.

Now another ten years have passed, and the landscape is beyond recognition. Congress has enacted three new civil-rights laws, bringing federal power to bear on a host of discriminations against the Negro. Segregation in buses and railroads has virtually ended, everywhere. Every southern state has been forced to face the issue of school desegregation. Negro political power has sharply increased, in the South and the North. A colored skin remains an enormous handicap in the United States, but masses of Americans—Negro and white—are engaged in the struggle for racial equality and justice. Militant Negro students are marching in the South, and at the great northern universities white students are singing "Blowin' in the Wind" and signing on to help Negroes register in Mississippi. No one could doubt that the conscience of America has been seized by the injustice of unequal treatment because of the color of a man's skin. At the same time, the acceleration of the drive for equality has brought new tensions and turbulence, in the North as well as the South. The strident tactics of Negro campaigns for better jobs and housing and schools in the great northern cities has aroused white resentment—the "backlash"—and this white reaction has intensified as tensions have broken into violence. At the least, now the country recognizes that its great internal problem—socially, economically, politically—is the problem of race.

It has been a revolutionary decade, 1954 to 1964. The most far-seeing of men, standing at the beginning of the period, would have been quite unlikely to predict that at the end of it the stereotype of the apathetic, satisfied Negro would forever have been destroyed; that the indifference of white America would have given way to sympathy and to admiration for and some fear of the fervor and courage of the new Negro; that the Federal Government would have abandoned a hands-off attitude of eighty years' standing and come to the point of total commitment against racial segregation in schools and streetcars and at lunch counters.

How did it happen? Change does not just begin at a point in time; it builds on history. There were many factors working before 1954 for change in American race relations: the industrialization and urbanization of the South, bringing with them social anonymity and security; the weakening of regional differences in this country through the impact of television and other mass media of communication; compulsory service in unsegregated armed forces; a slow growth in legal and political protection for the Negro. But revolutions require a spark, a catalyst. For the revolution in American race relations this was the School Segregation case, decided by the Supreme Court on May 17, 1954.

Men live by symbols, and school segregation was a special symbol to the white southerner. That racial separation should carry more emotional weight in schools than elsewhere was understandable: Attendance was compulsory, and in school children of an impressionable age were exposed to a culture. Intermingling of the races could not help but affect their outlook. Putting it another way, any breakdown in school segregation necessarily endangered the perpetuation of the southern myth that the Negro is by nature culturally distinct and inferior. And there was the fear—surely felt deeply by many in the South, however others regarded it—that school integration was a step toward racial intermarriage.

It was these reasons that led Hodding Carter, one of the most enlightened voices in Mississippi, to write a year before the School decision that a Supreme Court ruling against segregation would be "revolutionary" in character. Carter, the editor of the *Delta Democrat-Times* in Greenville, Mississippi, wrote in the *New York Times Magazine* on April 5, 1953:

> Abolition of the segregated school represents for them [white southerners] too sudden and complete a break with the past and even the present. The Negro's status is changing, and the barriers raised against his first-class

citizenship are crumbling here and there. But it is a
sporadic sloughing off. Some among the white southerners say it is happening too fast, some among both races
say it is happening fast enough, some—and almost all of
them are Negroes—say it is happening too slow. They all
agree that the acid test of how fast it can happen will
come if the Supreme Court holds against the segregated
school.

When the decision came, the white South reacted as Hodding
Carter had foreseen. There was bitterness, and racism flowered
in ugly new forms such as the Citizens Councils. Politicians swore
defiance of the Constitution and passed threadbare statutes in
futile efforts to preserve the past. Southern police and even
judges misused their power and manipulated the law to repress
the Negro. There was mob violence.

Yet these years of purgatory, however painful and destructive, began to teach the South what it had to know about itself
and the United States. The South learned that the Supreme
Court's interpretation of the Constitution, when it had the support of the rest of the country, could not be resisted indefinitely.
It learned that change was inevitable in race relations, that there
was a powerful momentum behind the movement against discrimination. It learned that the South cannot stand alone, that
it needs and is part of a larger country, and that the United States
is part of a world in which men with white skins are outnumbered by the black and brown and yellow. Of course not every
white southerner learned all or any of these things. In the rural
counties the acceptance of change is still miniscule, and there
is intransigeance in cities and towns, too, from Birmingham and
Albany to Shreveport and Jackson. But in most of the South
old ways are giving ground, and the strength of the moderates
—those who will accept change—is growing.

The School Segregation decision was a catalyst for the Negro,
too. Perhaps more than anything it gave him hope. The Supreme
Court of the United States, the pinnacle of the white establishment, had somehow understood at last the inequality of segregation. The law was on the Negro's side—often a faraway law, it
is true, offering little immediate protection against the local pressures of white supremacy, but still giving hope of ultimate justice. Hodding Carter had said in 1953: "I cannot believe that in
the event of a favorable Court decision any concerted effort will

be made by Negro parents to enroll their children in the white schools, at least not in Mississippi and the other states of the Deep South." But the Negroes did make that effort, even in deepest Mississippi before the decade was out. It was an effort that cost many parents dearly, in lost jobs and threats and fear; the burden was even greater for the children. Margaret Anderson was a white teacher in the Clinton, Tennessee, high school. In the *Times Magazine* of November 2, 1958, she wrote about the first two years of desegregation there:

> The few Negro children, trying to learn under fear, and sustained by a great American courage, in their more than two years in our school have endured every possible form of torment from the smallest harassment to threats of murder. "If you come back to school, I'll cut your guts out!" could be heard in the halls. Eggs smashed on their books, ink smeared on their clothes in the lockers, knives flourished in their presence, nails tossed in their faces and spiked in their seats. Vulgar words constantly whispered in their ears.
>
> There is one incident I think I shall never forget. A young Negro girl, whom I shall call Victoria, sat in the back of the auditorium among some 150 white students in a study hall. Tension was so high at the time it would have taken a policeman to maintain order. Without my knowledge, the girl was persecuted by vile language in whispering tones. She left the auditorium. Spontaneously, the students applauded as if they had scored a great victory.
>
> That night, I could not sleep. I wondered how I could call myself a teacher, knowing that a child, any child, had been persecuted under my supervision. I called her. It was with reticence that she related the events which had led to her leaving the auditorium.
>
> Victoria told how white students had whispered filthy names. "But I could take that," she said. "They kept on, and one boy looked like he was going to touch me, and I—left." I told her how ashamed I was. She answered, "I understand. I don't want to cause no trouble."
>
> The next day, my conscience demanded that I explain to my students the fundamentals of American

citizenship and constitutional law. We talked about the moral and Christian view that no human being has a right to harm another. We discussed "No man is an island, entire of itself" and the Golden Rule. I tried to think of all the things I had ever read or learned about our American heritage, so that I might in some way make these young people understand there is no freedom under anarchy and mob rule.

Some were no doubt moved. They apologized and hastened to exonerate themselves. They were sorry they had been glad when Victoria left. And some looked back at me, young men and women in their teens, with blood in their eyes, and whispered, "Nigger-lover."

Recently, I talked to a Negro girl about her college entrance requirements. There was a failure on her record—or, rather, she had chosen not to complete a course. She said, "I could have passed that course, only I was so upset; you know how it was." I think she could have passed, too, under normal circumstances. This was in the second year of integration.

Only today's Negro children really know what happens to them inside. I gather they are reconciled to making martyrs of themselves for their race. We hope the future will justify their sacrifice. And they do make a sacrifice, even when all appears normal, for there are more ways to show hate than by violence and harsh words.

Some days, I have looked at a Negro child in my classes, and I have wondered what it would be like to sit a whole year in a class and not have a living soul, except the teacher, speak to me. I have wondered what it would be like not to have anybody you could ask for a sheet of paper or a pencil. And what it would be like to have a new dress, and not a single person say, "How pretty you look today."

The courage of the little children who were the pioneers of school desegregation inspired other Negroes. The struggle to carry out the Supreme Court's decision created a climate that encouraged the Negro to protest against segregation on buses, to demand coffee at a lunch counter, to stand in long, patient lines waiting to take a biased test for the right to vote. It was easy to say, as many observers did during the decade, that it would be more logical for Negroes in the South to concentrate on obtaining the ballot because political power would open the way to all other rights. But that was only true in the abstract. In the real world the right to vote was too remote an idea to arouse the Negro of the South from apathy and fear. It took the drama of school desegregation, and then of the protest movements, to make the possibility of freedom come alive; then Negroes began demanding *en masse* the ballot to which the law had said they were entitled.

The most important effect of the School decision and its aftermath may well have been the awakening of northern opinion to the meaning of racism. Most Americans in the North had gone through their lives without thinking about how it would feel to have black skin. Then there were those scenes at Little Rock, where white youths outside Central High School shouted, "Niggers, keep away from our school, go back to the jungle," and a mother just kept screaming "nigger." Or the mob in New Orleans, in the fall of 1960, shouting "nigger-lover" at a Catholic priest who helped to bring a white Methodist minister's five-year-old daughter to a newly integrated school in the face of a white boycott. No northerner who saw any of those or many similar scenes on television, or read about them in the papers, was likely to miss the unreasoning hatred and not be frightened by it. Professor Alexander M. Bickel of the Yale Law School accurately described in his book, *The Least Dangerous Branch*, the impact on the North of Little Rock and New Orleans and other disturbances:

> Compulsory segregation, like states' rights and like "The Southern Way of Life," is an abstraction and, to a good many people, a neutral or sympathetic one. These riots, which were brought instantly, dramatically and literally home to the American people, showed what it means concretely. Here were grown men and women furiously confronting their enemy: two, three, a half-dozen scrubbed, starched, scared and incredibly brave colored children. The moral bankruptcy, the shame of the thing, was evident.

The Negro has "about one half as much chance of completing high school . . ."

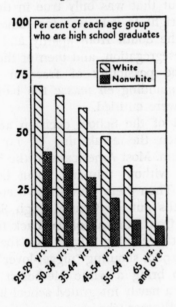

Per cent of each age group who are high school graduates

White
Nonwhite

25-29 yrs. 30-34 yrs. 35-44 yrs. 45-54 yrs. 55-64 yrs. 65 yrs. and over

The Negro has "one third as much chance of becoming a professional man . . ."

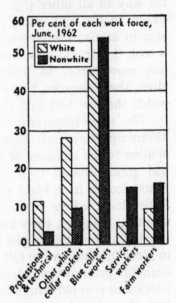

Per cent of each work force, June, 1962

White
Nonwhite

Professional & technical / Other white collar workers / Blue collar workers / Service workers / Farm workers

Quotes are from President Kennedy's nationwide broadcast, June 11, 1963. He compared the opportunities open to a Negro child in the U.S. with those open to a white child.

One observation to be made about the course of the racial issue between 1954 and 1964 is that the cause of equal rights often made its most significant progress as the result of racist excesses in the South. As Professor Bickel observes of the school riots: "The southern leaders overplayed their hand. Mob action led to the mobilization of northern opinion in support of the Court's decision—not merely because the mob is disorderly, but because it concretized the abstraction of racism." Extremism in the South did more than arouse northern opinion; it aroused the Federal Government. The Eisenhower Administration had done nothing to encourage acceptance of school desegregation, and was planning to do nothing, until Governor

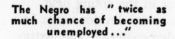

The Negro has " twice as much chance of becoming unemployed..."

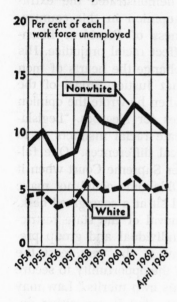

The Negro has "about one seventh as much chance of earning $10,000 a year . . ."

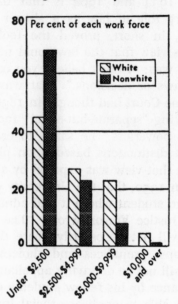

Faubus and the mob at Little Rock forced the federal hand.

Nor was this phenomenon confined to the school area. The brutal assaults on the freedom riders in Alabama in 1961 were met by federal intervention and then led to the promulgation of a new Interstate Commerce Commission rule barring segregation in all bus- and railroad-terminal facilities. The pictures of dogs assaulting Negro demonstrators in Birmingham in 1963 shocked the nation and the world; the police excesses there were instrumental in inducing President Kennedy to propose the broadest civil-rights legislation ever conceived; and, in his address of June 11, 1963, to identify the Presidency more completely than ever before with the cause of racial justice. The crude tactics used to bar Negro voters—the disqualification of college graduates for "mispronunciations," for example—led to the passage of the Civil Rights Act of 1957 and thus to the commitment of the Federal Government's power in the voting field.

A second important point about the racial developments between 1954 and 1964 is that they demonstrated the extraordinary role of law as a shaper of opinion in this country. Events, in short, proved the foolishness of President Eisenhower's view that the law could not affect racial prejudice. His phrase was: "I don't believe you can change the hearts of men with laws or decisions." That was what Justice Brown of the Supreme Court had thought in 1896, when he wrote the opinion permitting "separate-but-equal" facilities for Negroes. "Legislation is powerless," he said, "to eradicate racial instincts or to abolish distinctions based upon physical differences." One fallacy in that view was exposed by a later Supreme Court when it held, in 1950, that the University of Oklahoma could not make a Negro student whom it had admitted sit at a segregated desk. Chief Justice Vinson wrote: "The removal of the state restrictions will not necessarily abate the individual and group predilections, prejudices and choices. But at the very least the state will not be depriving appellant of the opportunity to secure acceptance by his fellow students on his own merits." Law may not be able to eradicate racial instincts, but it can either encourage or inhibit prejudice.

Moreover, laws and decisions (using the Eisenhower phrase) do affect patterns of external conduct, slowly forcing people to conform that conduct to new standards. And over a period of time, habits may affect beliefs. Dr. Martin Luther King, Jr., wrote in the *Times Magazine* of August 5, 1962:

There are always those who will argue that legislation, court orders and executive decrees from the Federal Government are ineffective because they cannot change the heart. They contend that you cannot legislate morals. But while it may be true that morality cannot be legislated, behavior *can* be regulated. The law may not change the heart—but it can restrain the heartless. It will take education and religion to change bad internal attitudes—but legislation and court orders can control their external effects. Federal court decrees have, for example, altered transportation patterns and changed social mores—so that the habits, if not the hearts, of people *are* being altered every day by federal action. And these major social changes have a cumulative force conditioning other segments of life.

But if law was a powerful force working against racial discrimination between 1954 and 1964, those years also taught that law alone is not enough. Americans characteristically think not only in legal but in moral terms. The pace of change was as revolutionary as it was because the American conscience was finally touched. More and more the country's churches became active opponents of discrimination, preaching and lobbying and sending workers into the field. The use by the civil-rights movement of the technique of non-violent resistance—one of the most remarkable developments of the decade—combined the American religious tradition with the revolutionary spirit of Gandhian protest. The young students sitting quietly at lunch counters as they were verbally and physically abused brought a needed spiritual content to the movement for racial justice. They ended the possibility of anyone's taking seriously the South's traditional claim that *its* Negroes were contented—that it was outside agitators who were causing all the trouble. The peaceful protestors caught the imagination and sympathy of the North, attracting widespread support that showed dramatically in the intermingled white and Negro faces at the March on Washington in August, 1963.

As the decade ends, one danger is that increasing Negro militancy will lose that necessary white sympathy and support. Disruption of supermarkets to make the stores hire more Negro employees, blocking of the Triborough Bridge in New York to dramatize slum conditions, school boycotts to support demands for bus transportation of pupils to distribute them evenly by race—tactics such as these began in 1964 to alienate northern whites. The northern primary votes for Governor George Wallace of Alabama, a man embarrassing even to most southern politicians, first demonstrated northern racial fears in concrete political terms. At least some of the force behind the Republican party's nomination of Barry Goldwater for President lay clearly in the white blacklash. The decade closed with the threat of race as a national political issue hanging over the country.

Some Negro leaders have started to point out the risk involved in alienating white support: Negroes are, after all, only some 22,500,000 of the 192,000,000 Americans—twelve per cent. But others think the time has passed for caring about the sensibilities of white men; they think aggressive tactics are called for whether the whites like it or not. Thus, at the end of this decade of change, the Negro faces a choice. He can go on following the course that has brought him so far in what seems to others so short a time—the course of reason and restraint. Or he can give way to impatience with what naturally seems to him too slow a pace and listen to the counsels of disorder, of anarchy. For those who now threaten to take over the Negro movement from the responsible leaders are essentially anarchists: They have given up on our system and would as soon destroy it.

For the white majority there is a choice, too. It can react to increasingly militant Negro demands with hatred and fear. Or it can react with understanding, meet the legitimate grievances and try to end the cycle of poverty and ignorance stemming from so many years of discrimination.

Hardly any revolutions in history, however noble their origins, have gone without a spilling-over of hatred and irrationality. The race-relations revolution in the United States has so far been a unique effort to join a society rather than to overthrow it. We are about to find out whether Americans, white and Negro, will permit the revolution to continue on that course.

Myrdal wrote in 1944: "The Negro problem is not only America's greatest failure but also America's incomparably great opportunity for the future. If America should follow its own deepest convictions, its well-being at home would be increased directly. At the same time America's prestige and power abroad would rise immensely. The century-old dream of American patriots, that America should give to the entire world its own freedoms and faith, would come true. America can demonstrate that justice, equality and cooperation are possible between white and colored people. . . . *America is free to choose whether the Negro shall remain her liability or become her opportunity.*"

The choice is still before us.

Chapter 2

The School Segregation Cases

*We boast of the freedom enjoyed by our people above
all other peoples. But it is difficult to reconcile that boast
with a state of the law which, practically, puts the brand
of servitude and degradation upon a large class of our
fellow citizens.*

—JUSTICE HARLAN, dissenting in
Plessy v. Ferguson, 1896.

The official southern myth sees
the School Segregation decision of 1954 as a sudden and unjusti-
fied break with history, a misuse of the judicial power, a departure from the Constitution itself. The myth rests on several
assumptions: that our constitutional history placed hallowed
sanction on the custom of providing separate-but-equal facilities
for Negroes; that the South, in faithful observance of that rule,
created substantial equality for the Negro in schools and other
public facilities; and that the Supreme Court relied on sociology,
not law, in overruling the segregation doctrine.

But the assumptions are false, and the myth is no more than a
myth. The separate-but-equal doctrine does not go back to some
distant constitutional fount; it was read into the Constitution by
judges at a fairly recent date, in what historians would call a
political act. Through most of its history the doctrine drew only
lip service from the South; there was separation but no equality
whatsoever. The Supreme Court's abandonment of the rule was
anything but sudden, the step being taken with the greatest care
and only after many previous decisions had pointed in that direc-

tion. Nor was it unusual for the Court to overrule what it regarded as its own mistake, in the light of experience, and return to the true spirit of the Constitution.

History has to be explored at least briefly in any meaningful discussion of the 1954 decision. For it was no isolated event but the climax of a lengthy historical process—the rise and fall of racial segregation imposed by law. It is a rich history, combining strands of war and politics and economics and the special role of judges in this country.

Many of the forces that still move race relations in the United States were loosed in the Civil War. Not that the racial issue was the dominant cause of the war; most historians have concluded otherwise. But by the end of the war the Union was altogether committed to the abolition of slavery and the uplifting of the Negro from his degraded status. The Thirteenth Amendment, prohibiting slavery, was adopted in 1865, immediately after the war. The southern states responded by enacting the Black Codes, which restricted the rights of the newly freed Negroes and effectively made them serfs. Some of these laws, for example, forbade Negroes to own land outside towns or do any work but farming without a special license. Congress, dominated by the so-called Radical Republicans, set about to overcome the southern schemes for keeping the Negro submerged. Some of the Radicals doubtless had motives of revenge or plunder, but others were moved by sincere egalitarianism. Whatever the motive, the post–Civil War Congresses assuredly did march under the banner of Negro rights.

In 1866 Congress passed the first Civil Rights Act. Specifically designed to wipe out the disabilities imposed by the Black Codes, it provided that Negroes should have the same right as white men "to make and enforce contracts, to sue, be parties and give evidence, to inherit, purchase, lease, sell, hold and convey real and personal property, . . . and shall be subject to like punishment, pains and penalties, and to none other, any law, statute, ordinance, regulation or custom to the contrary notwithstanding."

President Andrew Johnson vetoed the bill, saying that it attempted to legislate in areas where Congress had no power—matters of "internal police and economy" that the Constitution reserved for the state governments. Congress passed the act over the President's veto, but doubts remained about its constitutionality. To provide a broad constitutional basis for federal action insuring individual rights in any aspect of life, Congress proposed the Fourteenth Amendment later in 1866. It was ratified in 1868.

The Fourteenth Amendment began by declaring that all persons born or naturalized in the United States were citizens. This overruled the Supreme Court's decision in 1857 in the Dred Scott case, holding that Negroes could not be citizens. Then came the spacious language that has been the subject of so many lawsuits and so many political debates:

"No State shall make or enforce any law which shall abridge the privileges or immunities of citizens of the United States; nor shall any State deprive any person of life, liberty, or property, without due process of law; nor deny to any person within its jurisdiction the equal protection of the laws."

The one thing tolerably clear, as a matter of history, is that the primary, original purpose of the amendment was to protect the newly freed slaves. A contemporaneous Supreme Court so held. In 1873 a butchers' monopoly granted by the Louisiana legislature was attacked as a violation of the Fourteenth Amendment. In the Slaughterhouse cases, decided in 1873, a five-to-four majority of the Supreme Court held that the amendment did not extend to such an economic restriction unrelated to race. Justice Samuel F. Miller, for the majority, said the amendment's "pervading purpose" had been to secure the rights of the Negro and protect him "from the oppressions of those who had formerly exercised unlimited dominion over him." The dissenters did not disagree about this purpose of the amendment but thought "the mischief to be remedied was not merely slavery and its incidents and consequences."

The classic exposition of the Fourteenth Amendment by judges who had lived through its birth came in 1880. West Virginia law excluded Negroes from serving on juries. The Supreme Court, with only two dissents, held the law unconstitutional. Justice William Strong, for the majority, said the Fourteenth Amendment had been "designed to assure to the colored race the enjoyment of all the civil rights that under the law are enjoyed by white persons." Quoting the language of the amendment, he went on:

"What is this but declaring that the law in the States shall be the same for the black as for the white; that all persons, whether colored or white, shall stand equal before the laws of the

States, and, in regard to the colored race, for whose protection
the amendment was primarily designed, that no discrimination
shall be made against them by law because of their color? . . .
The very fact that colored people are singled out and expressly denied by a statute all right to participate in the administration of
the law, as jurors, because of their color, though they are citizens,
and may be in other respects fully qualified, is practically a brand
upon them, affixed by law, an assertion of their inferiority, and a
stimulant to that race prejudice which is an impediment to se-
curing to individuals of the race that equal justice which the
law aims to secure to all others."

But that was the end of an era. By that time northern politicians had lost interest in the cause of justice for the Negro.
The Republican party was dedicated not to human egalitarianism
but to laissez-faire economics and the growth of industrial em-
pires that dominated the last part of the nineteenth century. The
disputed Hayes-Tilden election of 1876 marked the political wa-
tershed. The award of the Presidency to Hayes was a bargain that
historians have summarized as giving the Republicans control
of the national government and economy while letting the
whites of the South do as they would with the Negro.

The South began taking advantage of the bargain in the late
1880's. Jim Crow statutes segregating Negroes in railroads and
streetcars were enacted by the southern legislatures. A poll tax
was levied and restrictive qualifications adopted to keep Negroes
from voting; the white primary completed the process of disenfranchisement. Ironically, poor whites and Populism hastened
the subjugation of the Negro. Recent research has uncovered a
body of upper-class southern opinion at the end of the century
that wanted to absorb the Negro into society.

As the political situation changed, so did the Supreme
Court's interpretation of the Fourteenth Amendment. The justices, like the country's business and political leaders, became
more interested in economics than in race relations. The protection of economic rights that the Court had refused to see in the
amendment in the Slaughterhouse cases was now found. The
Court redefined the "persons" protected by the language of the
amendment to include corporations and found various state regulations of business invalid.

As for the meaning of the Fourteenth Amendment to Negroes, that was redefined in *Plessy v. Ferguson* in 1896. Louisi-

ana had enacted a Jim Crow transportation law in 1890. When Homer Adolph Plessy, who was one-eighth Negro, entered a railroad car reserved for whites, he was arrested. He challenged the constitutionality of the statute. The Supreme Court, by a vote of seven to one, found it valid.

"The underlying fallacy" of Plessy's argument, wrote Justice Henry B. Brown for the majority, was its "assumption that the enforced separation of the two races stamps the colored race with a badge of inferiority. If this be so, it is not by reason of anything found in the act but solely because the colored race chooses to put that construction upon it."

Justice Brown did not cite any legal authorities for that proposition. Nor could he, for it was nothing but a psychological or sociological thesis, doubtless widely accepted in his day but not universally even then. There is nothing wrong with the Supreme Court's interpreting language as broad as "equal protection of the laws" in light of the best contemporary understanding of human behavior. Indeed, there is nothing else the Court can do. But it is somewhat ironic to realize the purely sociological basis of *Plessy v. Ferguson*, a decision so admired by the same southerners who used "sociology" as a term of derision against the Court when it overruled Plessy in 1954.

The dissenter in *Plessy*, Justice John Marshall Harlan, did not accept the majority's premise. "The destinies of the two races in this country are indissolubly linked together," he wrote, "and the interests of both require that the common government of all shall not permit the seeds of race hate to be planted under the sanction of law. What can more certainly arouse race hate, what more certainly create and perpetuate a feeling of distrust between these races, than state enactments which in fact proceed on the ground that colored citizens are so inferior and degraded that they cannot be allowed to sit in public coaches occupied by white citizens? That, as all will admit, is the real meaning of such legislation as was enacted in Lousiana. . . . The thin disguise of 'equal' accommodations for passengers in railroad coaches will not mislead anyone, or atone for the wrong this day done."

Certainly the spirit of Justice Harlan's dissent was much closer to what the Court had said sixteen years earlier, in *Strauder v. West Virginia*, about laws affixing upon Negroes "a brand . . . , an assertion of their inferiority, and a stimulant to that race prejudice. . . ." The Supreme Court in 1896 had simply turned its back on the aspirations of that earlier day. It had introduced the new thesis that the Constitution's demand for equal protection of the laws could be met by legislation treating whites and Negroes as separate classes of people.

Plessy v. Ferguson was necessarily prophecy in good part. Justice Brown said: "A statute which implies merely a legal distinction between the white and colored races . . . has no tendency to destroy the legal equality of the two races." Justice Harlan, in contrast, predicted that the *Plessy* doctrine of separate but equal would "stimulate aggressions, more or less brutal and irritating, upon the admitted rights of colored citizens."

As a prophet Justice Harlan prevailed. *Plessy v. Ferguson* did help to stimulate the proliferation of segregation laws in every corner of life, from cradle to grave—literally, for Negroes were barred from both white hospitals and white cemeteries. Nor was there any real pretense at equality in the decades following the *Plessy* decision. In 1915 South Carolina spent $23.76 on the average white child in public school, $2.91 on the average Negro child. As late as 1931 six southeastern states (Alabama, Arkansas, Florida, Georgia, North and South Carolina) spent less than a third as much per Negro public-school pupil as per white child. Ten years later spending for the Negro had risen only to forty-four per cent of the white figure. At the time of the 1954 decision the South as a whole was spending $165 a year for the average white pupil, $115 for the Negro.

Other public facilities, such as hospitals, were just as inferior for the Negro as schools. Nor was this physical inequality the only result of the climate fostered by segregation. Negroes were purged wholesale from the voting rolls. They were rigorously excluded from almost all except menial jobs. Their very lives were at the hazard of terror and mass injustice; and by the turn of the century more than one hundred Negroes were being lynched every year.

Through the early decades of this century it became clearer and clearer to any detached observer that segregation was part of a deliberate pattern to degrade Negroes and deprive them of the rights they had been given after the Civil War. The Supreme Court was not blind to this change in the informed understanding of society. Slowly but with growing inevitability it eroded the foundations of *Plessy v. Ferguson*.

In 1917 the Court held unconstitutional a Louisville ordinance forbidding Negroes and whites to move into houses on city blocks occupied mostly by the other race. The opinion said: "It is urged that this proposed segregation will promote the public peace by preventing race conflicts. Desirable as this is, and important as is the preservation of the public peace, this aim cannot be accomplished by laws or ordinances which deny rights created or protected by the Federal Constitution."

In 1927 the Court held that state laws barring Negroes from voting in primary elections violated the Fourteenth Amendment. Justice Oliver Wendell Holmes said: "States may do a good deal of classifying that it is difficult to believe rational, but there are limits, and it is too clear for extended argument that color cannot be made the basis of a statutory classification affecting the right [to vote]."

Then, beginning in 1938, there came a series of cases in the field of higher education. The first held that Missouri could not meet the test of separate but equal by offering to pay the tuition of a Negro applicant for the Missouri Law School at an out-of-state school. Chief Justice Charles Evans Hughes said the state had to provide equal facilities itself. The decision drew a dissent —the last in any major Supreme Court decision on racial segregation. Justice James C. McReynolds wrote:

"For a long time Missouri has acted upon the view that the best interest of her people demands separation of whites and Negroes in schools. Under the opinion just announced, I presume she may abandon her law school and thereby disadvantage her white citizens without impairing petitioner's opportunities for legal instruction; or she may break down the settled practice concerning separate schools and thereby, as indicated by experience, damnify both races."

Professor Paul A. Freund of the Harvard Law School has made a perceptive comment on the McReynolds dissent. "It is of course dangerous," he said, "to accept a dissenting opinion as an objective guide to the meaning of a decision. But in this instance Mr. Justice McReynolds saw which way the winds of doctrine were blowing, and he did not like what he saw. What he saw was a steady, unmistakable progression on the part of the Court in applying the guarantee of equal protection of the laws to a series of issues: the right to serve on juries, the right to vote in primaries, the right to choose a place of residence without a legal color bar, the right to be considered for admission to a state professional school without discrimination because of race. The Court was recognizing the developing consciousness of the country that equal protection of the laws was to be given a full and not a qualified meaning."

In 1950 the Court held that a new law school set up by the State of Texas for Negroes did not provide equal protection of the laws because, as Chief Justice Fred M. Vinson put it, "the University of Texas Law School [for whites] possesses to a far greater degree those qualities which are incapable of objective measurement but which make for greatness in a law school. Such qualities, to name but a few, include reputation of the faculty, experience of the administration, position and influence of the alumni, standing in the community, traditions and prestige. It is difficult to believe that one who had a free choice between these law schools would consider the question close."

When such intangible factors were placed in the scale, how could any separate school ever be termed "equal"? In the *New York Times* the day after the Texas Law School decision Arthur Krock said the separate-but-equal doctrine was now "a mass of tatters."

It was in that context that the Supreme Court came to the great issue of public-school segregation—the context of a legal history showing a developing momentum againt the separate-but-equal rule. But it was not an easy next step. For here, unlike voting or juries or graduate education, there was involved the compulsory association of children day after day and year after year, and it was just such association that southern whites most feared.

Moreover, the Court was dealing with a practice that covered a large part of the country. Seventeen southern and border states and the District of Columbia, with forty per cent of the country's public-school enrollment, required segregation in the schools. (The states were Alabama, Arkansas, Delaware, Florida, Georgia, Kentucky, Louisiana, Maryland, Mississippi, Missouri, North Carolina, Oklahoma, South Carolina, Tennessee, Texas, Virginia and West Virginia.) There were some segregated schools also in three other states whose statutes permitted the practice: Arizona, Kansas and New Mexico.

The Supreme Court, fully aware of the delicacy of the issue, handled it with exceptional care and deliberation. It should also be pointed out, as Professor Freund reminds us, that the Court

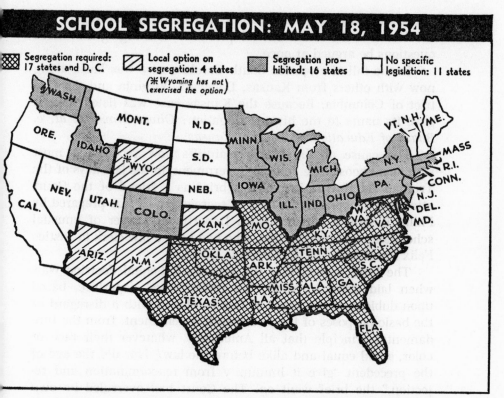

did not go out looking for the school-segregation issue. It was brought there by Negro individuals and civil-rights groups desperate to improve Negro educational opportunities. Originally in fact, in the 1930's, the N.A.A.C.P. had proposed lawsuits to attack only the inequality of Negro school facilities and teachers' salaries; but the victories in the graduate-school cases inevitably led to a direct assault on the institution of segregation.

The first school case came to the Supreme Court in 1951, from Clarendon County, South Carolina. A three-judge federal district court had upheld the constitutionality of segregated schools by a vote of two-to-one, but ordered prompt action to correct the admitted inequality of the Negro schools. (The dissenter, Judge J. Waties Waring of South Carolina, was virtually driven out of the state by ostracism for his courage.) On January 28, 1952, the Supreme Court acted to avoid an early constitutional decision in the case. It sent the matter back to the lower court to get its views on a report filed by the school board concerning the program to equalize facilities. Justices Hugo L.

Black and William O. Douglas dissented, saying the report was "irrelevant to the constitutional questions" and urging that those questions be argued at once.

In the fall of 1952 the South Carolina case was back, along now with others from Kansas, Delaware, Virginia and the District of Columbia. Because the Kansas case was listed first, it gave its name to the historic litigation: *Oliver Brown et al. v. Board of Education of Topeka, Kansas.*

The cause of the Negro plaintiffs now received a most significant boost. The Federal Government, in the last days of the Truman Administration, filed a brief as a friend of the Court attacking the constitutionality of segregation. It was prepared by Philip Elman, a career Justice Department lawyer of unusual scholarship and imagination, who had been a law clerk to Justice Felix Frankfurter of the Supreme Court.

The brief argued that the separate-but-equal doctrine was, when laid down in 1896, "an unwarranted departure, based upon dubious assumptions of fact combined with a disregard of the basic purposes of the Fourteenth Amendment, from the fundamental principle that all Americans, whatever their race or color, stand equal and alike before the law." Nor did the age of the precedent "give it immunity from re-examination and rejection," the brief went on. The Court had overruled its own decisions dozens of times. In 1944 it had said: "When convinced of former error, this Court has never felt constrained to follow precedent. In constitutional questions, where correction depends upon amendment and not upon legislative action, this Court throughout its history has freely exercised its power to re-examine the basis of its constitutional decisions."

The conclusion was that the Court should, if it reached the ultimate question, overrule the separate-but-equal doctrine. "Compulsory racial segregation is itself an unconstitutional discrimination." But this was not the only significance of the brief. Perhaps even more vital was a suggestion advanced as to the procedure for carrying out any decision against school segregation. The government said the Court would not have to order all segregation ended everywhere at once. Instead, the Court should send the cases back to the district courts so that those local tribunals could work with local authorities to devise plans for desegregation. The brief said the Court might even want to issue no final decrees with its decision but order a further argument on the question of implementation. In short, the government put forward a moderate approach that recognized, as it said, "the practical difficulties" in ending a custom with such deep roots.

What made that suggestion so significant was that the practical difficulties were just what concerned some of the members of the Supreme Court. The deliberations of the justices have not been disclosed. But it is known that some deeply feared the reaction that might be aroused by an order for immediate, total desegregation. If that had been the only course open, they might well not have voted to declare segregation unconstitutional. They might, as one alternative, have said that the magnitude of the issue made it appropriate for resolution not by the Court but by Congress, which is empowered by Section Five of the Fourteenth Amendment to enforce its terms. In this regard the position of Justice Frankfurter is believed to have been critical. For while he was personally a dedicated opponent of racial discrimination, he had often expressed concern about the effect on the Court as an institution if it tried to go too far too fast in constitutional decisions.

The Court heard the cases and then, at the end of the term in June, 1953, put them over for reargument in the term beginning the following October. The Court posed a series of broad questions now, asking counsel to deal with them in their briefs and argument. First there was a historical inquiry: Had the men who framed and ratified the Fourteenth Amendment understood that it would prohibit segregation in public schools? Then, interestingly, the Court asked about the relative powers of Congress and the judiciary in interpreting the amendment: Had its framers contemplated that future Congresses might abolish segregation? Was it "within the judicial power, in light of [changed] conditions, to construe the amendment as abolishing such segregation of its own force?" The Court also took up the suggestion in the Justice Department's brief and asked whether, if it held segregation unconstitutional, it could properly allow "gradual adjustment" and whether the proper way to carry that out was to remand the cases to the district courts.

The Government answered those questions in a lengthy new brief the following November. There was political as well as legal import in the brief, for a new Administration had taken office since the first Government presentation. President Eisenhower himself took a hand in determining the position. In charge at the

Justice Department were Attorney General Herbert Brownell, Jr., and Assistant Attorney General J. Lee Rankin. Mr. Elman again did the major part of the drafting.

The brief examined in great detail the legislative history of the Fourteenth Amendment as proposed by Congress and ratified in the state legislatures. While there were some references to school segregation, the Government said, they were "too few and scattered to justify any definite conclusion as to the existence of a general understanding . . . as to the effect which the amendment would have on school segregation." But "the primary and pervasive purpose of the Fourteenth Amendment" was "to secure for Negroes full and complete equality before the law and to abolish all legal distinctions based on race or color."

And the fact was that the amendment had been framed in the broadest, most general language. It did not mention schools, a point often raised by southerners as if it had some relevance. But neither did it mention voting or housing or juries or corporations, all areas in which the Supreme Court had repeatedly —and with general assent—held that the amendment barred discriminatory state action. And of course the amendment did not contain the words "separate but equal." The framers might have written a detailed code of what was and was not permissible in race relations. But they wisely had not; they had followed the example of those who wrote the original Constitution in using expansive phrases that would be given contemporary meaning by each generation. As Justice Holmes said of another constitutional provision: "When we are dealing with words that also are a constituent act, like the Constitution of the United States, we must realize that they have called into life a being the development of which could not have been foreseen completely by the most gifted of its begetters. . . . The case before us must be considered in the light of our whole experience and not merely in that of what was said a hundred years ago."

The demand of the Fourteenth Amendment was for "equal protection of the laws." There was no talisman in the history of the amendment that defined those words for all times. The separate-but-equal doctrine had itself been a fresh interpretation, a departure in 1896 from the spirit of earlier decisions. It was in the great tradition of the Constitution, the Government said, to read the words now in light of conditions now. A provision such as the equal-protection clause expresses "broad principles of government, the essence of which is their vitality and adaptability to the progressive changes and needs of the nation."

Nor did the Government's brief see anything in the suggestion that Congress rather than the Court should deal with the issue. The Supreme Court had applied the Fourteenth Amendment in hundreds of cases without reference to Congress—in the racial field most recently in the graduate-school cases. What was posed now was "a question not of legislative policy but of constitutional power—and it is a question which under our system of government must ultimately be determined by this Court."

When the brief was filed, it puzzled some observers in one respect. It did not directly urge the Court, as the previous Administration's brief had, to hold racial segregation in the public schools unconstitutional. Instead the 188-page document was confined to what was termed "an objective non-adversary discussion" of the questions posed by the Court the previous June. The brief concluded, for instance, with a conditional statement: "If the Court holds that laws providing for separate schools are unconstitutional, it should remand the instant cases to the lower courts with directions to carry out the Court's decision as the particular circumstances permit."

Just how the brief emerged in this form is disputed. Some who participated in the drafting say that it contained a direct call for a finding of unconstitutionality when the draft was submitted to Attorney General Brownell, and that it was softened by either Brownell or President Eisenhower. But Brownell states that the draft "did not include any such conclusion . . . when it reached my desk and, so far as I know, never did include it. Mr. Rankin . . . and I agreed at all times that since the brief was filed in direct response to questions asked of the department by the Court, it should answer those questions solely." The truth is probably that Rankin and Brownell would personally have liked to include a direct statement on the unconstitutionality of segregation but did not believe President Eisenhower would approve it. The Attorney General did advise the President that Rankin, if asked by a member of the Supreme Court during the oral argument what the Justice Department's position was, would say that segregation should be struck down. The

President evidently made no objection, and the question was asked and answered as planned. In any event the thrust of the new brief, for all its lack of a firm conclusion, was plainly against segregation. It told the justices that they had the power and the duty to give the Fourteenth Amendment a contemporary interpretation. And it said that the import of decisions up through the graduate-school cases was to make it "unreasonable and unconstitutional . . . for a state to establish or enforce legal distinctions based on race or color."

When the cases were reargued, in December, 1953, fate had made a most important change in the Supreme Court. Chief Justice Vinson had died during the summer, and President Eisenhower had appointed in his place the Governor of California, Earl Warren. Only when some future historians have access to the judicial papers of that period will it be possible to state accurately the impact of the new Chief Justice on the School cases. But enough has been said or hinted to make it clear that the change of membership on the Court made a real difference in the way *Brown v. Board of Education* looks to history. Chief Justice Vinson's inclination was to carry on the approach of the Texas Law School case, further tightening up the standard of equality within the separate-but-equal doctrine. In short, he thought it was not the time to challenge segregation per se; the most he was likely to have done was to say that the Negro pupils here did not have real equality. The indications were that he might have carried one or more of his colleagues with him, and there is also reason to believe that at least two members of the Court were inclined to put the whole issue to Congress. There was certainly no unanimity of desire on the Court to face up to the ultimate question—whether segregation itself denied the equal protection of the laws. In all likelihood, as things stood during the Vinson period, the Brown case would have produced a collection of differing opinions.

Unanimity was the most striking aspect of the actual decision when it came down on May 17, 1954. Chief Justice Warren delivered the opinion; there was no dissent, not even a separate concurrence.

The opinion found the history of the Fourteenth Amendment "inconclusive" in relation to school segregation, as the Justice Department had argued. In any case, history could not give an adequate answer because public education was just beginning in the 1860's. "We cannot turn the clock back to 1868 when the amendment was adopted, or even to 1896 when *Plessy v. Ferguson* was written. We must consider public education in the light of its full development and its present place in American life. . . . Today, education is perhaps the most important function of state and local governments. . . . In these days, it is doubtful that any child may reasonably be expected to succeed in life if he is denied the opportunity of an education. Such an opportunity, where the state has undertaken to provide it, is a right which must be made available to all on equal terms. We come then to the question presented: Does segregation of children in public schools solely on the basis of race, even though the physical facilities and other 'tangible' factors may be equal, deprive the children of the minority group of equal educational opportunities? We believe that it does."

The Chief Justice noted the Texas Law School case and its emphasis on intangible differences in schools. "Such considerations," he said, "apply with added force to children in grade and high schools. To separate them from others of similar age and qualifications solely because of their race generates a feeling of inferiority as to their status in the community that may affect their hearts and minds in a way unlikely ever to be undone. . . . Whatever may have been the extent of psychological knowledge at the time of *Plessy v. Ferguson*, this finding is amply supported by modern authority." Here the opinion, in a footnote that has been much criticized, cited the writings of various social scientists, including Myrdal.

"We conclude," the Chief Justice said, "that in the field of public education the doctrine of 'separate but equal' has no place. Separate educational facilities are inherently unequal."

The Court ordered still further argument the next term on problems of implementing its decision. Simon E. Sobeloff, who had now become Solicitor General, submitted a brief for the Federal Government suggesting—as the Justice Department had earlier indicated—that the cases be remanded to the trial courts to work out local problems. President Eisenhower personally inserted a passage in the brief. Where it said that the Court had outlawed "a social institution which has existed for a long time in many areas throughout the country," he added "—an institution, it may be noted, which during its existence not only has had the sanction of decisions of this Court but has been fervently supported by great numbers of people as justifiable on legal and moral grounds. The Court's holding in the present cases that segregation is a denial of constitutional rights involved an express recognition of the importance of psychological and emotional factors; the impact of segregation upon children, the Court found, can so affect their entire lives as to preclude their full enjoyment of constitutional rights. In similar fashion, psychological and emotional factors are involved—and must be met with understanding and good will—in the alterations that must now take place in order to bring about compliance with the Court's decision."

On May 31, 1955, after what was surely one of the most exhaustive considerations it had ever given to any issue, the Supreme Court finally disposed of *Brown v. Board of Education*. Chief Justice Warren's opinion on implementation generally followed the line suggested by the Justice Department but was even more gradualist in one respect: The Court did not, as proposed by the department, direct the lower courts to make local school authorities present desegregation plans within a specified time. It said only that the lower courts must require "a prompt and reasonable start toward full compliance." The process of desegregation, the opinion concluded, must proceed "with all deliberate speed"—a phrase first used in the Supreme Court in 1911, by Justice Holmes, and often invoked in recent years by Holmes's great admirer, Justice Frankfurter.

One item especially in Chief Justice Warren's 1954 opinion was seized upon by southerners as proof that the decision did not rest upon "law." This was the footnote citing social scientists as "modern authority" for the statement that segregation generated feelings of inferiority. But the footnote was at worst pretentious superfluity. It took no reference to social scientists to know that state-enforced separation of human beings on account of their race was a calculated device to exalt one group and debase another. Justice Brown had simply been proved wrong in his sociological hypothesis, in *Plessy v. Ferguson*, that there was nothing invidious about segregation unless the Negro chose "to put that construction upon it." After Adolf Hitler the world knew, and the Supreme Court would have been blind not to see, that it was invidious to separate out one group in society, whether Negroes or Jews or some other. Justice Harlan had been right when he said that segregation "puts the brand of servitude and degradation" on the Negro. The Court had moved toward his dissenting view in *Plessy v. Ferguson*: "Our Constitution is color-blind, and neither knows nor tolerates classes among citizens." Segregation was not the equal protection of the laws.

Chapter 3

The South Reacts

Caution was the prevailing tone of the first southern reaction to the decision in *Brown v. Board of Education*. Even so stalwart a segregationist as James F. Byrnes, the Governor of South Carolina, called on his people to be "calm" and "reasonable." The day after the decision Governor Thomas B. Stanley of Virginia said: "We will consider the matter and work toward a plan which will be acceptable to our citizens and in keeping with the edict of the Court." After a meeting with officials of other southern and border states on June 11, 1954, to arrange a joint strategy to cope with the Supreme Court decisions, Governor Stanley said: "This was a very helpful and harmonious meeting, and no one had any thought of doing anything wrong. Everyone is just trying to find a solution for what they regard as a major problem."

In the border areas there were rapid steps toward desegregation. Such states as Kansas and Arizona, with relatively small Negro populations and a tradition of merely local option on segregation, found it relatively easy to move toward integration in the classroom. The District of Columbia, at President Eisenhower's direction, undertook a wholesale realignment of school districts to wipe out all racial lines. Baltimore, one of the largest metropolitan centers with school segregation, similarly made a complete assault on the custom. Altogether, in the years 1954, 1955 and 1956, several hundred school districts throughout the country abandoned racially segregated classes.

In those years there were also several dramatic tests in the South itself, as distinguished from the border states, and the principle of desegregation as laid down by the Supreme Court seemed in these cases to be prevailing over turmoil. Two of the most crucial tests came in Hoxie, Arkansas, and Clinton, Tennessee.

Hoxie, a town of fewer than two thousand souls, is in Lawrence County in the northeast section of Arkansas, about one hundred miles north of Little Rock. Less than two per cent of the county's twenty-one thousand inhabitants are Negroes. Eighteen thousand live on farms or in rural villages. It is one of the poorest counties in the nation, and the schools have terms in summer and at other odd times of the year to fit in with the rhythm of farm duties.

There were, in 1955, about eight hundred white children in several fairly modern schools and twenty-six Negro children who either went to a one-room Negro school or, in the case of high school students, were transported to a Negro school twenty-five miles away. On June 25, 1955, the Hoxie School Board announced that it would integrate the classes at the start of the summer term, July 11th. It described its decision as economically practical, legally required and "right in the sight of God."

On September 25, 1955, Cabell Phillips described in the *New York Times Magazine* what happened.

By most accounts, things went along smoothly for about two weeks after desegregation began. The eight hundred white and twenty-six colored children got along well enough together and there was no untoward reaction from the community. On Monday, July 25, someone brought into town a current issue of *Life*, which was passed as eagerly from hand to hand as a three-dollar bill would be. There was a two-page spread of "Integration at Work in Hoxie," showing white and Negro children self-consciously sitting and playing together in the Hoxie school.

It seems fairly certain that the magazine story not only triggered the latent discontent in Hoxie but also stirred up the white-supremacy forces elsewhere as well. Locally, the mutterings grew louder and centered mainly around City Hall and the persons of Mayor Mitchell Davis and farmer Herbert Brewer, two local and single-minded foes of integration. During the week, cheaply printed and mimeographed handbills bearing the imprint of White America, Inc., National Citizens Protective Association, National Association for the Advancement of White People, Pro-America, and similar organizations, and postmarked at Memphis, St. Louis, Dallas and Little Rock, showed up in people's mail and were stuck unaccountably under their doors or dropped on the seats of their automobiles. By the end of the week the town was beginning to seethe, and teachers reported signs of strain and restiveness among some of their pupils.

On Wednesday, August 3, Brewer, who had emerged as the local leader of the anti-integrationists, called a mass meeting at City Hall. About three hundred persons showed up, overflowing onto the sidewalks. The *Life* article was displayed, some of the white-supremacy leaflets were read, and there were some angry speeches. An overwhelming vote was taken to boycott the schools until the Negro pupils were removed. During the next two days from a third to a half of the white students stayed away and an informal "picket line" of parents took up positions on the school grounds.

On Wednesday, August 10, with the boycott still in effect, the School Board met (Brewer says they refused his request to attend) and voted not to abandon its stand on integration. The following Saturday, Brewer called an outdoor mass meeting that drew about five hundred persons. The chief speaker was Amis Gutheridge, a Little Rock lawyer and furniture dealer, who has long been a militant states' righter and is now state chairman of White America, Inc.

The invocation was pronounced by the Reverend Robert Watkins, pastor of a nearby Missionary Baptist Church (a Fundamentalist sect), who gave it as his opinion that God would condone violence in Hoxie if that were necessary to preserve the purity of the white race. The master of ceremonies was Mayor Davis, who proclaimed that though he was as good a friend of the Negro (in local dialect this is "Nigger" or "Nigra") as the next man, he wanted them kept in their place—"and this means in their own schools."

Public support for the School Board up to this point was as conspicuously lacking as it was conspicuously conferred upon the Brewer-Gutheridge group. "The better people in the town," one Board member said ruefully, "just clammed up. They were either afraid to speak out or they just didn't want to get mixed up in the thing. They let us stand alone." So, also, did the State Department of Education and Governor Orval Faubus, at Little Rock, from whom the Board earnestly sought guidance and support. The official reply was that integration of the Hoxie school was purely a local matter to be settled locally.

On August 17, the Board met at the request of Gutheridge. Presenting the petition with its 1,063 signatures, he called on the Board to resign and demanded their answer by the following Saturday. If they did not resign he promised legal action by state authorities to have them ousted.

Two days later, on Friday, Board members met in secret with William Penix, a young Jonesboro attorney whom they had retained to counsel them, and announced that while they refused to resign, they had voted to end the summer school session as of that day, two weeks ahead of the normal closing date.

There the matter stands, with the segregationists feeling that they have won the first round and confident that both the Lord and a majority of the people are on their side. Two subsequent developments have not changed this view, although they may have a significant bearing on the future course of events.

The first is an announcement, which the Board issued through Penix on September 7, declaring flatly that when the Hoxie schools reopen on October 31 they will continue to be integrated.

The second was a quiet invasion of the community two weeks ago by a squad of impeccably discreet Federal

Bureau of Investigation agents inquiring into possible violations of federal civil-rights statutes. This is largely a strategy of "counter intimidation" engineered by Penix, for the civil-rights laws applicable to the present case are notoriously fragile. But real live G-men in a town like Hoxie can stir up a lot of apprehension.

A good guess is that not more than twenty-five per cent of the residents in the Hoxie school district would vote to continue integration if the question were put to them in a secret ballot today. Regardless of their convictions in the matter, so many have become fearful of the consequences of prolonging the controversy that they would rather be rid of it than worry it through.

"I'm convinced we can win this fight if we can get enough of the right people to stand up and show some guts," Bill Penix said recently with an air of desperation. "A half a dozen sermons in the right pulpits in Lawrence County would do it, too."

Brewer has no such troubles on his side. Of zeal and righteous anger he has an abundance. He would like to know, though, just what those F.B.I. fellows are up to.

The Hoxie schools did reopen on an integrated basis that October, and they stayed integrated. The critical factor in the victory was a landmark case in the federal courts. The School Board sued for an injunction against Brewer, Gutheridge, et al., to keep them from interfering with the desegregation plan. There was much doubt in the minds of legal scholars, then, that school officials had the necessary legal standing to go into court for protection of the children's constitutional rights. But the United States Court of Appeals for the Eighth Circuit, in the case of *Brewer v. Hoxie School Board,* sustained the Board's right to sue and its right to an injunction against those who wanted to force a return to segregated classes. As for those F.B.I. men, the move the Federal Government made was to come into the case as a friend of the court, arguing on the School Board's side— the first time it had done so since the Supreme Court decision. Federal intervention helped, but the real lesson of the Hoxie case was what a difference a courageous school board could make.

An even more acute and emotional test for a school board and a whole town came the next year in Clinton, Tennessee.

In the *Times Magazine*, reporter George Barrett described what happened to Clinton in September, 1956.

At 11 P.M. on that Friday night, a man this town had never seen before entered one of the two telephone booths in the back corner of Hoskins Drug Store on Main Street. His knees pushing against the narrow wooden sides, his words flowing in soft undertone into the black mouthpiece, the stranger made several quiet calls to housewives, store proprietors, businessmen in this small community in the hills of eastern Tennessee.

"The niggers got to be pulled out of the high school," the voice out of the night said as community residents picked up their telephones. "We're calling a meeting— you'd better come."

One woman turned to her husband in alarm. He took the receiver, told the stranger to keep his dirty business to himself and stop disturbing decent people. Some in the town, and in the communities outside the town limits, gave the caller the same kind of advice.

But others did not.

Three weeks have passed since the Friday the stranger came to town, and those three weeks brought turmoil and terror to Clinton before peace and order returned.

The town fathers had decided that every possible step would be taken to guarantee a smooth and peaceful transition to school integration. From his desk, decorated with a big, black eight-ball, D. J. Brittain, Jr., the high school principal, directed a program of theme assignments and student debates to make the white youngsters aware of their own responsibilities on the issue.

Then John Kasper, a twenty-six-year-old northerner from New Jersey, whose confused hates include integration and "pink punks, freaks, golf players, poodle dogs, hot-eyed Socialists, Fabians, scum," came to town and began making phone calls.

When the stores opened Saturday morning for Clinton's big shopping day, Kasper began operating in the open, buttonholing passers-by. Sixteen-year-old redheaded Joe Millsaps, whose dad runs a dry-goods store in town, laughed in Kasper's face and said he was not going to school to fall in love with a Negro but to get an education.

But Kasper, organizer of something he calls the Seaboard White Citizens Council, was not to be readily rebuffed. The next day, Sunday, in front of the old, five-towered courthouse, before the spread-eagle war memorial for all the dead, color unspecified, who "gave their lives that freedom might live," Kasper held what might be called a prayer meeting against the Negro.

Kasper speaks softly. Listeners must sometimes strain to hear him. He said to the curious crowd gathering around him—a crowd including many teenagers—that he supposed they were Christians. A couple of "Amens" rang out. Good Christians. "Amen," again. Now the Communists, they were godless, they were not Christians, nobody could call them Christians. And the Communists wanted to see the colored man going to school with white boys and girls. Are you a Christian or a Communist? The crowd moved uneasily. Some listeners exchanged nods.

Mayor W. E. Lewallen was also uneasy. The Mayor, like just about everyone else here, is opposed to integration, but he was determined to try enforcing the laws, those he likes and those he doesn't like. The six-man Board of Aldermen met while Kasper talked, and decided to tell him to leave town. When he refused, Kasper was arrested for inciting a riot. Kasper refused to accept bond that day. He wanted the martyrdom of a night in jail. He got it.

The next day, Monday, school opened and practically the whole student body went through the doors of Clinton High School, including the twelve Negroes. Among them was fourteen-year-old Jo Ann Allen, who wants to be a doctor. Miss Eleanor Davis, the home-room teacher who also handles freshman English, asked Jo Ann to tell the class about herself and her hopes and ambitions.

Carol Peters, fifteen-year-old president of the high school's Future Homemakers of America Club, recalls how attentively the students listened to Jo Ann. Jo Ann was elected vice-president of the home room, and color or charity had nothing to do with it, Carol says.

"It's just that Jo Ann is so pretty and smart and has

such a wonderful personality," Carol declares. "Anyhow, she had to be good to get elected; she ran against a member of the football team."

But that was inside the school. Outside, Kasper was flicking at the segregationist nerve ends of Clinton's citizenry. Mr. Brittain had been up all night answering the telephone and listening to warnings that "nigger-lovers" would soon get theirs. Nevertheless, all eight hundred and six students were enrolled in high school; it was evident that parents did not feel strongly enough about segregation to send their children to another, all-white school, as they could have.

Kasper was enjoined by Federal District Judge Robert L. Taylor from interfering with Judge Taylor's own desegregation order. When he went right on haranguing a crowd after being served with a restraining order, he was charged with contempt and found guilty by Judge Taylor in a trial without a jury. He was sentenced to a year in prison but went free on bond pending appeal—and kept on agitating.

Clinton had a seven-man police force, including one constable who had not made an arrest in twenty years. Each day heightened the tension, each day the students had to run through crueler gantlets of insults, and each day fewer students dared to show up. Once, from a classroom window, a white boy watched while three of his new Negro classmates fled before a mob yelling, "Kill the niggers." The white boy recalls: "It was unreal—like watching a movie, only it hurt to watch."

One Saturday night tight clusters of people suddenly crystallized into a strange mob of three thousand shrieking, laughing, cursing, fun-making, blood-hunting men and women and youngsters.

It was a mob that turned hot, then cold, milling around the old courthouse, banging on one Negro's car as he turned accidentally into Main Street, slashing his tires, then suddenly putting friendly shoulders to the car to help him get it started again.

But it was whipping itself into emotional wildness, and up in the shacks on Foley Hill, behind the high school, the Negroes listened to the shouts on Clinton's streets. The

Negroes left their homes that night, some rushing in cars to another city, or parking quietly on some secluded road, others huddling all night—children and babies and crippled oldsters among them—in meadows far from the shacks.

Fear hung over the little town that Saturday night, but a small group of Clinton's citizens did not huddle in their homes, did not stare helplessly at each other. Buford Lewallen—the Mayor's son, a thirty-six-year-old Clinton attorney and former speaker of the State House—heard that his sixty-year-old mother was walking around the house toting a .45, and he rushed there and took the gun from her. His mother-in-law, a bitterly unreconstructed rebel who refers to the "alleged surrender of General Lee," ceremoniously handed him a pearl-handled shooting piece that was a family heirloom, with this command: "I want this used to bring law and order back to this town."

Leo Grant, Jr., a twenty-eight-year-old Florida-born lawyer who spent several boyhood years in Malverne, Long Island, is an old friend of Buford's. Leo was a company commander in Korea, carries a Silver Star and five bullet wounds, and doesn't like to see anyone get pushed around.

"I guess you might say we just up and formed a posse, good old-fashioned style," Leo says with a grin. "Forty-seven we rounded up in all, preachers, doctors, clerks—and most of us mighty scared, but also mighty provoked."

One seventy-one-year-old neighbor turned up, and Leo told him to go home. "Son," the old man replied, no quaver in his voice, "this is my town, this"—pointing to the street —"is my home." He stayed.

"You never saw such an unmilitary collection of weapons," Leo laughed. "A German burp gun some guy brought back from France; a fancy telescope-equipped single-shot rifle; plenty of twelve-gauge double-barreled shotguns; even a couple of derringers; old Colts and forty-fives and thirty-eights, and we got from the Mayor of Knoxville two machine guns and six tear-gas grenades."

Buford, looking as though he were going to a cocktail party, with his French cuffs and silver links, his silk tie and navy-blue jacket, climbed to the second-floor office of the tax assessors in the old courthouse and crouched behind a machine gun to cover the little marching army below. Leo picked up a gun and got a tap on the shoulder from a man with whom he had been feuding for years.

"Just wanted you to know, I'm only putting aside our fight temporarily, until this thing is over," the man said.

"Exactly how I feel," Leo replied. They moved forward together.

The volunteers formed a skirmish line, shoulder to shoulder, and moved toward the packed crowd to divide it into two parts. It was friend against friend, neighbor against neighbor, in many instances. The crowd swayed, then held ground as the volunteers came within a foot of the mob. Leo waved his line back a short distance, suddenly let fly with a gas grenade, followed it up with two more. The crowd broke up, then began to collect again, and Leo threw three more grenades.

"The whole thing was crazy; sometimes I think it was all a dream," Leo says. "As I was marching toward the mob, my gun up, a reporter jumps in front of me, walks backward toward the mob, his pad and pencil poised, and he asks me while I'm marching, 'What did you say your first name was, Mr. Grant?'"

A few moments later, about one hundred and fifty youths clustered together, bellowing, "Let's get the nigger-lovers." Leo recalls that a meek-looking, well-dressed man who was sitting on the courthouse lawn with a pretty girl when the fighting started, suddenly yanked away his tie and shouted: "Christians . . . white citizens . . . kill them."

"I didn't think we would have to fire our guns," Leo says. "But if it was necessary to fire I knew that the meek-looking Milquetoast was going to get my first bullet."

The grenades were enough. As the shouts to kill roared out, one hundred and ten state highway patrolmen rolled up with screaming sirens, and the crowd scattered. The next day the National Guard arrived, the 1911 Brockway Torpedo fire engine was rolled out and the recreation center was taken over to provide room for some of the troops.

Peace—still uneasy, still breakable—came to Clinton.

The students who stayed away are coming back to Clinton High, to mixed classes; only a few transferred to other schools, and probably some of them will rejoin their friends at Clinton as soon as they can do so without losing face.

There are solid signs that the determined show of resistance already made by Clinton's group of responsible and indignant citizens has stunned the attackers and has probably even brought them a touch of humility.

Some of the young men who were rounded up by the National Guard and put into jail during the rioting later politely sought out photographers whom they had earlier attacked, explaining that there had been a lot of misunderstanding all around. Some of them, proudly, had once been policemen and deputy sheriffs in their home towns and they were still visibly shocked by their first involuntary visit to a jail. One of them came quietly to this reporter to whisper that he was sorry about the whole mess.

"What happened to us is going to happen to a lot of communities when they try to integrate," one resident says. "Some towns down here are going to make mistakes that we—maybe just by accident—didn't make, and they are going to lose law and order, and back down before the mob."

If Clinton has demonstrated any lesson that can be learned by other states also accepting the challenge of integration, that lesson is: Keep a microscopic eye and strong arm on the professional agitator, and mobilize the responsible elements of the community, once the courts have made their decision, to stand up firmly to the race haters. Communities like Clinton have shown that a few resolute civic leaders can have much more combined strength than they may suspect.

Clinton's determination to stand against the John Kaspers of this world received important new support ten months later, when Kasper and his fellow agitators were tried by a jury in Knoxville, Tennessee, for another alleged violation of Judge Taylor's injunction. The jury found Kasper and six others guilty— a decision that some had doubted twelve white southerners would ever reach. It was a major victory for the integrity of the federal judicial system. In Clinton as in Hoxie a southern community had stood resolutely for the law despite its basic sympathy for racial segregation.

Unhappily, however, such reason and responsibility were not, in the long run, to characterize the reaction of the South to the Supreme Court's decision. The years ahead would be years of irresponsibility and hate and violence. Clinton itself is remembered today not for the resolute community leadership that it displayed in 1956 and 1957 but for the fact that a year later, on the night of October 5, 1958, its integrated high school was destroyed by three dynamite blasts. Clinton's attitude did not change; her people reacted with revulsion to the act of violence. But in much of the South the "good people" were not to be found on the side of the law. For during Clinton's torment communities elsewhere were ranging themselves against the federal Constitution and the courts. From the perspective of history it is clear that by 1956, after a first calm and responsible reaction to the Supreme Court decision, most of the political leaders of the South had come around to a position of defiance.

In this process of swinging from reason to violence a critical role was played by Virginia, traditionally the leader of the South. The decisions there were made by the state's Democratic patriarch, Senator Harry Flood Byrd. It is probably fair to say that no man could have done more to bring about peaceful compliance with the School Segregation decision; Harry Byrd's word carried special weight not only in Virginia but throughout the South. But his decision was for total resistance.

Governor Stanley, a faithful product of the Byrd political machine, indicated the chosen course just a few weeks after the School decision. His first reaction had been mild and constructive. But on June 25th, completely reversing his position, he said: "I shall use every legal means at my command to continue segregated schools in Virginia."

In 1955 Governor Stanley proposed an amendment to the state constitution to permit the payment of tuition grants from public funds for children in private schools. This was still a moderate program, one merely providing an escape hatch for parents so disturbed by integration that they would want to withdraw their children from the public schools. The plan assumed that there would be some public-school desegregation.

On January 9, 1956, Virginia voters approved the tuition grant plan in a statewide referendum by a two-to-one margin. But by then it was not strong enough medicine for Senator Byrd. He and the state administration called for Massive Resistance to desegregation. The proposal was for laws requiring an automatic end to state aid for any desegregated school, and indeed for closing of that school. The legislators gathered in Richmond that August cheered when Governor Stanley told them:

"Do we accept the attempt of the Supreme Court of the United States, without constitutional or any other legal basis, to usurp the rights of the states and dictate the administration of our internal affairs?

"Do we accept integration?

"Do we want to permit the destruction of our schools by permitting 'a little integration' and witness its subsequent sure and certain insidious spread throughout the commonwealth?

"My answer is positively 'No.' "

A month later Massive Resistance was on the statute books of Virginia. And of course Virginia was not alone. In Georgia, in Alabama, in Louisiana, in Mississippi, in South Carolina, even in less southern Texas, officials were breathing fire at the Supreme Court and its decision. But the most influential single document of defiance came not from political leaders at home in those states but from their representatives in Congress. It was the Southern Manifesto of 1956, signed by one hundred and one senators and members of the House from the eleven states that had made the Confederacy. The only southern senators not on the list were Lyndon Johnson of Texas and Estes Kefauver and Albert Gore of Tennessee.

"The unwarranted decision of the Supreme Court in the public-school cases," the Manifesto began, "is now bearing the fruit always produced when men substitute naked power for established law." The statement called the decision a "clear abuse of judicial power" that was being exploited by "outside agitators." It said "the Supreme Court, with no legal basis for such action, undertook to exercise their naked judicial power and substituted their personal political and social ideas for the established law of the land." It ended with a pledge "to use all lawful means to bring about a reversal of this decision which is contrary to the Constitution."

The Manifesto steered carefully clear of any call to illegality

or violence; it cautioned against "disorder and lawless acts."
But that advice hardly carried much weight against the central
message of the Manifesto, which was that the Supreme Court's
School decision was itself "contrary to the Constitution." If
the Court had violated the Constitution, how could any measure
to fight its decision be termed philosophically unlawful?

The true meaning of the Manifesto was to make defiance
of the Supreme Court and the Constitution socially acceptable
in the South—to give resistance to the law the approval of the
Southern Establishment. The first phase of the South's response
to the School decision ended in 1956 with statesmen sowing
the wind of defiance. The next year, at Little Rock, they reaped
the whirlwind.

Chapter 4

Little Rock

As the 1957-58 school year be-
gan, southern resistance to the Supreme Court decision was
proving highly effective. Voluntary desegregation, which had occurred in hundreds of school districts in the first three years
after the decision, had come to an almost complete stop. Legally,
southern devices to delay integration were proliferating. Politically, a unified southern voice was speaking out against the Court
and its ruling, while President Eisenhower and his Administration said nothing in their support.

The South's effort, putting aside the merits of racial segregation, was within an American tradition of resistance to dis-
liked judicial decisions. More than once in the past, criticism of
a Supreme Court decision had eventually persuaded the country
or the Court itself that the position was unsound; only a generation before, a Court that had held New Deal measures unconstitutional changed its mind within a few years. The South
was following a beaten path in attempting, as the Southern Manifesto said, "all lawful means to bring about a reversal of this
decision."

But now the South changed tactics. As Professor Alexander M. Bickel of the Yale Law School put it: "Having scented victory, the southern leaders, or at least a sufficient number of them, sought to assure it by turning from litigation and agitation to direct action by the use of mobs. Thus they abandoned the tradition in which they had been acting."

Few would have expected Little Rock, Arkansas, to be the testing ground for the new course of violence. Little Rock was a city of the New South, a middle-class, moderate town with an enlightened mayor (Woodrow Wilson Mann), congressman (Brooks Hays) and newspaper (the Arkansas *Gazette*, edited by Harry Ashmore). Arkansas had had some integration at the university level for years, and Governor Orval Faubus had never been a race-baiter; indeed, his election had been considered a liberal victory. The federal courts had approved a desegregation plan proposed by the Little Rock School Board and fought by the N.A.A.C.P. A most gradual plan, it was to begin with the senior high schools in the fall of 1957—specifically, with the admission of a few Negro children to Central High School on Tuesday, September 3, 1957.

On Monday night, September 2nd, Governor Faubus made an unexpected television address to the state. He said it would "not be possible to restore or to maintain order if forcible integration is carried out tomorrow" at Little Rock. He announced that he was therefore posting National Guardsmen outside Central High, to act "not as segregationists or integrationists but as soldiers."

The Guardsmen acted as soldiers on the side of segregation. They were there the next morning, two hundred and seventy of them, and on the advice of the School Board no Negro child appeared. The Board went before Federal District Judge Ronald N. Davies—serving in Little Rock temporarily on assignment from North Dakota—and asked what to do. He said he would take the Governor's word about the neutrality of the troops "at its face value," and he ordered the desegregation plan into effect "forthwith."

The next morning, Wednesday, September 4th, nine Negro children tried to exercise their legal right to attend Central High along with nearly two thousand white students. A crowd waited along with the soldiers. Suddenly the cry went up:

"A nigger! They're coming! Here they come!"

It was fifteen-year-old Elizabeth Ann Eckford, first of the nine that morning. She walked quietly up toward a school door, but a National Guardsman barred her way. Then, to leave the tense scene, she had to walk a hundred-yard gantlet of ugly gestures and jeers from the crowd. She finally reached a bench at a bus stop and sat down. A white woman went over to comfort her. "What are you doing, you nigger-lover?" someone yelled from the mob. The woman answered: "She's scared. She's just a little girl." The two finally got on a bus and left.

Just why Orval Faubus chose this path of physical defiance to federal law may never be known. Some militant segregationist leaders from Georgia had lately been in town and talked to him. The Governor himself never gave a straightforward explanation; he only repeated that he had acted to prevent violence. The result of his action was the mob.

The events in Little Rock were immediately recognized by almost everyone as a direct challenge to the Federal Government. President Eisenhower's first comment missed the point. At a press conference on September 3rd, the day the Guard was posted at Central High, he was asked about the news. He repeated his familiar contention that "you cannot change people's hearts merely by laws" and added the unfortunate remark that people in the South "see a picture of mongrelization of the race, they call it." But by the next day the Federal Bureau of Investigation had agents in Little Rock looking into the situation. Faubus telegraphed the President, who had gone to Newport, Rhode Island, for a vacation, to stop the "unwarranted interference of federal agents." He received a reply that marked by far the strongest position yet taken by Mr. Eisenhower on the school-segregation issue: "The only assurance I can give you is that the federal Constitution will be upheld by me by every legal means at my command."

Outside Central High School the mob stood watch. The Times's education editor, Benjamin Fine, who was covering the story, more than once found himself the object of taunts.

"You got a nigger wife?" a woman asked the reporter. She was identified later as a waitress in a Little Rock tavern.

Mr. Fine did not answer.

"Are you a Jew?" the woman shouted.

"Yes," Mr. Fine said.

On Monday, September 9th, the F.B.I. delivered a four-hundred-page report to Judge Davies on the causes for obstruction of the school-integration order. He asked the United States to enter the case—which was formally a lawsuit by the Negro school children and their parents against the School Board—as a friend of the court. The Government promptly asked the judge to enjoin Governor Faubus from interfering with the integration plan. A hearing on that request was set for ten days later.

At this point the use of force by the Federal Government did not seem a likely course. A Washington dispatch to the *Times* accurately reflected the mood when it said:

"It is all very well to discover a statute that would allow the President to send an army into Little Rock. But no responsible person in or out of government thinks this would advance peaceful acceptance of the Supreme Court decision in the South. The one certainty about the Administration's plans is that there is no desire for an open test of strength."

Instead, the theory went, the Administration would rally moderate opinion in the South and persuade Governor Faubus to climb down. But this was only a theory. President Eisenhower made no great effort to arouse the South, or the country, to the issues at Little Rock in those early days of the episode. Nor did he undertake any dramatic gesture such as going down to Little Rock and taking the Negro children into Central High School himself, as some had suggested. He did talk to Governor Faubus, in a meeting at Newport, and they both issued complimentary statements afterward. But the Governor did not remove the Guardsmen; he said later that he thought he was making some headway in arguing his case to Eisenhower until Attorney General Herbert Brownell intervened.

On September 20th Judge Davies granted the injunction against Governor Faubus. When school opened the following Monday, September 23rd, the Guardsmen were gone. The nine Negro children went into the school. What happened next was described by Benjamin Fine in a dispatch from Little Rock that evening:

A mob of belligerent, shrieking and hysterical demonstrators forced the withdrawal today of nine Negro students from Central High School here.

Despite a heavy turnout of local and state police to see that the Negroes were not molested in Little Rock's newest attempt to integrate the high school, city authorities bowed to the fury of about one thousand white supremacists. They ordered the Negro students to leave the school about noon. The integration attempt had lasted three hours thirteen minutes.

While fringe fights broke out and several persons were roughed up by irate segregationists, the mob shouted insults and obscenities against the "niggers" and "nigger-lovers." Groups of white students who had walked out of the school after the nine Negroes entered chanted: "Two, four, six, eight, we ain't gonna integrate."

Mayor Woodrow Wilson Mann charged that the violence outside the school had been stirred up by plan and "bore all the marks of the professional agitator." He said that detailed information on the events of the day would be turned over to the Department of Justice for whatever action the Federal Government considered warranted.

Many of those who milled in front of the school today were from out of town, some from communities two hundred miles distant. It was noted that one of those in the crowd of demonstrators was Jimmy Karam, Athletic Commissioner for the state and a close friend of the Governor.

Mrs. Daisy Bates, president of the Arkansas N.A.A.C.P. branch, said the Negro students "will not be out there again until they have the assurance of the President of the United States that they will be protected from the mob."

For a time this morning it appeared as though integration would take place smoothly in this city of 102,213 population. A few persons had arrived at the high school by six o'clock. By seven, with the sun just beginning to break through the clouds, only one hundred or so had gathered at both ends of the street leading to the two-block-long school. Wooden barricades, placed at either end of the street, stopped them at those points.

Eighty members of the local police force, some on motorcycles and in squad cars, but most on foot, were on the school grounds or in the vicinity. Fifty state troopers were in the area, ready to help if needed.

At eight o'clock it was evident that the violence that Governor Faubus had predicted would take place. By this time some five hundred persons had gathered. They appeared in a fighting mood.

"The niggers won't get in," members of the crowd said, time and again.

At eight forty-five the school buzzer could be dimly heard. School was in session.

"Where are the niggers?" one person asked another. "Let them try to get in . . ."

"We'll lynch them all," several yelled.

"Sure, and all you Yankee newspapermen with them," a gravel-voiced man shouted. This was met with a howl of approval.

The police tried to keep the crowd off the street. The surging angry mob kept pushing forward. "Please keep back, step back," the police said politely at first, then with more authority.

"Don't you dare lay your hands on me," one woman screamed as a police officer asked her to move away.

"Lady," he pleaded, "I'm not going to touch you. I'm just doing my duty."

Suddenly a yell went up: "There they are, they're coming."

The crowd rushed after four men who turned out to be Negro newspapermen. They were manhandled by the crowd, but managed to escape.

A man yelled: "Look, they're going into our school."

Six girls and three boys crossed over into the schoolyard. They had arrived in two automobiles and had driven to the side of the school. Mrs. Bates accompanied them.

Slowly, almost as though they were entering a normal classroom on a normal school day, the students walked toward the side door of the school. The boys, in open shirts, and the girls, in bobbysocks, joked and chatted among themselves. They carried armfuls of textbooks.

The crowd now let out a roar of rage. "They've gone in," a man shouted.

"Oh, God," said a woman, "the niggers are in school."

A group of six girls, dressed in skirts and sweaters, hair in pony-tails, started to shriek and wail.

"The niggers are in our school," they howled hysterically.

One of them jumped up and down on the sidewalk,

waving her arms toward her classmates in the school who were looking out of the windows, and screamed over and over again: "Come on out, come on out."

Tears flowed down her face, her body shook in uncontrollable spasms.

Three of her classmates grew hysterical and threw their arms around each other. They began dancing up and down.

"The niggers are in," they shrieked, "come on out of the school. Don't stay there with the niggers. Come on out. Come on . . ."

Hysteria swept from the shrieking girls to members of the crowd. Women cried hysterically, tears running down their faces.

"I'm going to get the niggers out," said Mrs. Clyde Thomason, recording secretary of the Mothers League of Central High, a segregationist group.

She started toward the school. Two policemen blocked her way.

"Please go back on the sidewalk," one begged quietly.

"Go on and hit me, just go and hit me," Mrs. Thomason, who had been enjoined by Judge Davies not to interfere with the integration program, said. She became hysterical.

A man walked over to the policemen who were struggling to restrain Mrs. Thomason. "This is my wife, officer," he said. "I'll take her with me."

An elderly man jumped upon the barricade. "Let's go over the top," he shouted. "Who's going over with me?"

"We'll all go," the crowd yelled.

Over the wooden barricade they went. A dozen policemen stood in the way. Slowly the crowd gave way.

The police were taunted by the mob, well out of hand by now. Instead of tapering off, as it had at previous morning demonstrations, the crowd grew in numbers. By ten o'clock it had grown to about one thousand.

"Turn in your badge," the crowd yelled at the police.

One of the policemen said, apologetically: "I'm only doing my duty. If I didn't I'd lose my job."

Another one, Thomas Dunaway, took off his badge and walked away.

"Hurray! Hurray!" the crowd cheered.

"He's the only white man on the force," a young man in a plaid shirt shouted.

"Let's pass the hat around," someone suggested.

In a moment several persons went through the crowd, collecting money. Dollar bills were tossed into the hat. It was estimated that about two hundred dollars had been collected for the policeman who gave up his badge.

The men and women, augmented by students, surged over the "off limits" line and spread into the street facing the school grounds. For a time it appeared as though the local police would be completely overwhelmed by the angry crowd.

"Come on out of school, come on out, the niggers are in there," the crowd yelled.

Four girls slowly walked down the side steps of the high school.

A tremendous cheer echoed through the crowd.

"They're coming out," was shouted time and again.

Soon a group of six left. The students began to leave the school at more frequent intervals. At first the police did not permit adults to enter the school. They were acting under order of Virgil T. Blossom, Superintendent of Schools.

"I'm going to get my child," one parent said defiantly.

"Sorry, you'll stay right here," the policeman answered.

Quickly this order changed. One by one, mothers and fathers walked up the school steps, and then returned with their children. Each time a student walked out of the school the cheers increased.

"Mother, come and get me," a girl telephoned. "They're fighting something awful here inside the school."

By twelve o'clock the mob had reached its greatest strength, and by now completely ignored the local police. The crowd remained behind the barricade, but it did not maintain order there. Several newsmen were attacked and beaten. A Negro reporter was kicked and manhandled.

Threats, jeers, and insults became more ominous.

"Let's rush the police," a ringleader shouted. "They can't stop us."

At noon the police received this message on their

short-wave radios: "This is the Mayor. Tell Principal Jeff Matthews [of Central High] that the Negroes have been withdrawn. Tell Mr. Matthews to announce that to the student body. I've talked with Virgil Blossom and Negroes have been withdrawn."

At twelve-fourteen Lieutenant Carl Jackson of the Little Rock police force stood on the school grounds facing the crowd. Over a loudspeaker set up on the sidewalk in front of the school the officer said, "The Negroes have been withdrawn from school."

"We don't believe you," the crowd yelled back. "That's just a pack of lies."

"Is there anyone whom you would believe?" he asked.

"I saw a nigger standing in the doorway just now," a woman yelled.

"Let's go in and see," another shouted.

"If you have any one person in the crowd you believe, he can go in and see, then report to you," Lieutenant Jackson said.

Mrs. Allen Thevenet, of the Mothers League of Central High School, stepped forward across the street.

"Will you accept Mrs. Thevenet's word?" the Lieutenant asked. The crowd gave a reluctant approval.

Accompanied by a policeman, Mrs. Thevenet went into the school. On her return she came to the loudspeaker and said: "We went through every room in the school and there was no niggers there."

The Negro students, meantime, had been taken out through a side door and escorted in two police cars to their homes. Despite the rumors that had been flying through the crowd that the students "had been beat up," they were not molested while in school.

"They were surprised when they were told to leave at noontime," Mrs. Bates said later.

"Nothing much happened at all," Thelma Mothershed, one of the nine Negro students, said.

"Nothing really happened," agreed Terrance Roberts, age sixteen. "We went to classes as scheduled. After the third period we were taken out and driven home. Some school officials came in to see us." He added: "I was pushed once but I wasn't hit. It was quiet after we got

into our classes. A few white students walked out."
Another of the girls, Elizabeth Eckford, said: "I was
the only Negro girl in my class."
Would they want to come back?
"Yes," they agreed, "if we can come here without
causing any trouble. The students will accept us once we
go with them for a while."

That evening President Eisenhower denounced what he called
the "disgraceful occurrence" at Little Rock and said a federal
court's orders "cannot be flouted with impunity by any individual
or mob of extremists." Invoking a statute with deep roots in
United States history, he issued a proclamation directing those
who had obstructed federal law "to cease and desist therefrom
and to disperse forthwith." But on Tuesday morning a crowd
still milled about Central High School. No attempt was made
to bring the Negro children in.

The President then took the ultimate action—one that on
July 17th he had called unthinkable, one that only three weeks
earlier few had considered a real possibility. For the first time
since Reconstruction, federal troops were sent into the South to
protect the rights of Negroes. Eisenhower ordered one thousand
paratroopers to Little Rock and placed ten thousand members
of the Arkansas National Guard on federal service to put down
the mob. The soldiers were under the command of Major General
Edwin A. Walker—the same General Walker who was removed
from his command in Germany in 1961 for spreading right-wing
extremist propaganda and who was to fulminate against federal
forces sent to the University of Mississippi by President Kennedy
in 1962.

The dispatch of troops brought the expected outcry from
the South and its friends. Senator Richard B. Russell of Georgia,
ordinarily a wise and cultivated man, sent the President a
telegram comparing the soldiers in Little Rock to "Hitler's
storm troopers." One of the main charges was that the use of
troops was illegal, an unconstitutional invasion of states' rights.
Except for the agitated political atmosphere, this claim would
doubtless have been laughed off as frivolous. For an explicit
statute on the books since 1792 permitted the use of federal
forces whenever federal law was obstructed. George Washington
had invoked the statute to put down the Whiskey Rebellion. Even

in the absence of such specific authority, many would have considered it the constitutional duty of the President to use all necessary force to protect the federal rights of American citizens against mob violence condoned or encouraged by state officials.

The nine Negro children re-entered Central High School on Wednesday morning, September 25th. The mob was dispersed, and twenty-four paratroopers patrolled inside the school to prevent incidents. Desegregation had been achieved—but at what anyone would admit was a heavy price. Some non-segregationist critics thought the Administration had jumped too quickly from no force to too much; they said federal marshals might have been tried first, for example. The Justice Department said that would have been ineffectual temporizing, and in any event the argument by hindsight could get nowhere. The troops were there, and now the problem was to get them out. That was a problem primarily in the assumption of responsibility by the moderates of Little Rock. The terrible dilemma they faced—one to be repeated in so many other southern communities—was described by Cabell Phillips of the *Times* in the *Times Magazine* of October 20, 1957:

> Central High School here was in its fourth week of continuous operation under military occupation when I went to keep an appointment, one evening recently, at the home of one of the city's top education officials. His handsome suburban house was dark when I arrived by taxi, and a hall light came on only after I had rung the bell. He admitted me, grim and unsmiling, turned off the hall light and led me to his study at the back of the house.
>
> "I hope you won't mind," he said, "if we have our talk in a hotel downtown. We are all packed and I am moving my family down there for the time being.
>
> "We have put up with quite a lot of threats and anonymous telephone calls. Of course, nothing serious has happened so far. But I have to be away from the house so much of the time, and there's talk of another flare-up at the school tomorrow, that—well, I'll just feel safer if they are not here by themselves."
>
> Why did one of the most respected citizens of this normally civilized community fear for the physical safety of his family? How is it that a fractional defiant minority

in a community of one hundred and fifty thousand, backed by a few scores of hoodlums and agitators, could obliterate the instinct for decency and public order of an overwhelming majority?

To understand, one has to recognize the fact that school integration is so uniformly unpopular in the South that even men of the most generous good will cannot conscientiously be its advocates. And when, as in Little Rock and Nashville, Tennessee, and Charlotte, North Carolina, there comes the ultimate, dreaded dilemma of either accepting Negroes in the white schools or condoning defiance of civil authority, the responsible citizen makes his choice for law and order reluctantly, and often fearfully. Even then, his motivation may not be wholly a concern for the integrity of civil authority; it may contain such subjective factors as "face" for his town or state, or awareness of the political or economic consequences of defiance.

There are, I believe, no whole-hearted, all-out pro-integrationists among the generality of white citizens of the South and none at all of substantial influence. The awareness of racial "difference"—*not* racial animosity, necessarily—strikes deeply into the subconscious mind, beyond the reach of introspection or reason or prayer. It is a fundamental coloration, an ineradicable trace element in the chemistry of the southern white's mind. One may tell himself that he has cast it out, but the mere fact that he reminds himself of his cleansing is a clue that its debris remains.

Thus, however right a southerner may believe the rule of integration to be in terms of legality or justice or inevitable social change, it cannot be a cause that arouses his fervor and devotion. If he nevertheless takes a stand for it, reason compels him, not his heart. This is the melancholy burden of the moderate.

Segregationists, on the other hand, have invested their cause with a searing emotional impact. It has been made to appeal to the most susceptible tribal impulses: patriotism, racial purity, religious dogma, group solidarity, status and personal pride. At the top, it has been given an intellectual and political gloss by introducing questions of

constitutionality and states' rights. What is more important, the segregationist has a tangible, human symbol for
his fears—the Negro. In the volatile, undisciplined lower
echelons of the movement these impulses fuse unpredicta-
bly and explosively into hatred and mob violence.

Thus, the temperate southerner who would weigh
justice and respect for the law against his native customs
and sensibilities is trapped between the cold sea of indecision and the zealot's fire. Not being quite sure what he
is *for*, he cannot effectively oppose what he is *against*. So
it is that there has emerged throughout the South the
pattern of silent assent among those who would be moderates in this superheated struggle. Bogged by irresolution
and taking a prudent heed of their own best interests,
they melt into the faceless anonymity of the sidelines and
let him who will carry the flag.

There are among them, of course, courageous ones
who are willing to stand up and be counted. But often
the articulate moderate can make himself heard only by
singing less stridently in the same key as the segregationist.

And so it is that we have had the spectacle, time
after time, where the segregation controversy has flared,
of the "good" citizens seemingly being cowed into impo-
tence while others defied the law or even resorted to
violence.

In Little Rock, as mobs faced troops across the barricades around the school, and the city ached with tension,
Governor Orval Faubus, the benignly ambiguous leader
of the insurrection, was showered daily with praise and
messages of encouragement from states' righters, segregationists and the lunatic fringe of "nigger-haters" all over
the South.

From the other side there was little but stunned silence. Little Rock's two newspapers, it is true, opened up
their editorial artillery; Mayor Woodrow Wilson Mann
made a futile grab to wrest control of the situation from
the Governor's hands; the Ministerial Alliance called resolutely for observance of the Golden Rule. But the great
mass of the "good" people of Little Rock—and their
spokesmen and leaders—played it safe.

A break in this wall of apathy came only after a month. Twenty-four of the city's outstanding business and professional leaders got together in the first week of October on a statement of principles that called for an end to violence and submission to legal authority. The following day forty ministers and rabbis adopted a similar resolution and launched a "ministry of reconciliation." Late in the same week, Winthrop Rockefeller, the state's most distinguished adopted citizen, said on a national television program that the whole episode was having a disastrous effect on efforts to rehabilitate Arkansas' sagging industrial economy. It began to appear at last that a counter-force of public opinion was being thrown against the defiant minority.

The tardiness with which Little Rock faced up to its crisis can be attributed to a number of factors.

One was the conviction that "it can't happen here." This is not a Deep South city and its record of race relations for the last quarter of a century is quite good. Furthermore, the general acceptance which seemed to have been accorded token integration allayed the fears of most people that there would be violent opposition at the last moment.

Another factor was the lack of rapport and communication between the city government and community leaders. For many reasons, Mayor Mann does not enjoy widespread confidence either among the public or within his own administration (eight of his ten aldermen aligned themselves with Governor Faubus). City Hall did not offer a rallying point for community action.

Little Rock has no bi-racial organization equipped to deal with abrasive community problems of this kind. The one possible exception is a chapter of the Urban League, which this year was frozen out of the Community Chest because it is "controversial."

And while Little Rock is not Deep South, it still is southern enough to be acutely attuned to southern Democratic mores. It is the trading center of the most intensely conservative region of the state, the rich farming counties of the Mississippi Delta. Eastern Arkansas is as Confederate—and pro-segregation—as Mississippi or Georgia, and it controls the legislature and the Democratic party in Arkansas. When Little Rock's merchants, bankers, brokers and other business leaders said (as many of them did) that they didn't want to stick out their necks to oppose Governor Faubus and the Citizens Council, they undoubtedly were thinking of the customers they do business with in the eastern counties.

Finally, there was the risk—or the fear—of reprisal. Mothers of carrier boys for the Arkansas *Gazette*, whose outspokenness has made it a prime target of the militant segregationists, were warned by telephone that their boys might be hurt in some way if they continued delivering the paper.

School Superintendent Virgil T. Blossom and other school officials were subjected to anonymous threats and harassment. Some merchants and professional men were threatened with boycotts. The father of a student leader at Central High refused to let this reporter interview the boy on sentiment in the school. "I do business with people on both sides of this issue," the father said, "and I can't afford to take any chances."

Such is the pattern of silent assent; it is true not only in Little Rock but wherever in the South the question of segregation plagues the conscientious citizen.

But in the wake of Little Rock the moderate well may wonder if silent assent is enough. Had he rallied sooner, marshaled public opinion, demanded with a voice as loud and insistent as the mob leaders' that solutions be found in law and not in violence—had he done these things in Little Rock, might not the catastrophe have been averted?

A good many responsible people in this town think so. They point to the example of Nashville, where an almost simultaneous eruption was put down in less than a week.

There are differences, of course. The Mayor and the Governor of Tennessee made it plain at the outset that they would tolerate no disorders over integration of the city schools. That gave the moderates solid political and legal backing. Furthermore, there had been for many years in Nashville an effective and realistic bi-racial community organization to prepare the citizens at all levels for the impact of social change. So, when violence flared on that first day of integration—Negro children were heckled, a school was dynamited—there was an explosive response of outraged public opinion backed up by a deter- mined police force.

The race issue is an agonizing one wherever it exists, in Philadelphia and Detroit as well as in Birmingham and Little Rock. But in the South it has an extra dimension, for many of the root causes of this tension are imbedded in the laws and customs of the states.

There should be no doubt in anyone's mind any longer that, wherever segregation is sanctioned, the might and majesty of the United States Government is now com- mitted to its eradication—not today or this year neces- sarily, but ultimately, and with bayonets if need be. Little Rock is more than an incident; it is a precedent.

There is no likely turning back from this course, and intelligent leaders of the South admit it, however privately and ruefully. If this reality is to be lived with, and with a minimum of bitterness and shock, the moderate will have to contribute something more to the effort than his silent assent.

The soldiers never did leave Central High during that school year. Four moderate southern governors—Luther H. Hodges of North Carolina, Frank G. Clement of Tennessee, LeRoy Collins of Florida and Theodore R. McKeldin of Maryland—tried to per- suade Governor Faubus to take over responsibility for maintain- ing order with the Negro children in the schools so the federal force could be withdrawn. But this effort collapsed when Faubus reneged on a promise to issue an agreed statement. The troops were gradually thinned out; the paratroopers left by the end of November, and a reduced force of Guardsmen on federal duty patrolled the school.

Inside Central High, school went on under difficult circum- stances, described on October 12th by Homer Bigart of the *Times*:

Subjected to tensions and pressures inconceivable to most Americans, the students have had to concentrate on a tough and exacting academic routine while the cries of adult white mobs and the tread of paratroopers' boots intruded from the streets outside.

Against this tumultuous background, teenagers tried to concentrate on algebra, or Latin, or perhaps on one of the "frill" courses of which Central is proud: music, water-color painting, costume designing, photography, commercial law, printing.

There was some trouble inside the school, too. Jeers, rebel yells and muttered threats were directed at the Negroes. The troublemakers were of a group of perhaps one hundred to one hundred and fifty students who came from "disturbed" homes. They had absorbed the racial hatred of segregationist parents who felt that their whole way of life was being threatened by "race mixing."

Some of the troublemakers boycotted school when the paratroopers came. They hung around near the street-corner barricades, taunting the soldiers: "Join the paratroopers and see Central High."

So long as the chief troublemakers stayed out of school, peace reigned in the classrooms. Not one of the student leaders, not one of Central's championship football team, joined the rebels. A fierce pride in their school helped them resist the slurs of "chicken" (coward) heaped on them by young agitators when they refused to join a walkout.

Even the most ardent segregationists could not stomach the end of Central High. "I'm not going to let nine Negroes keep my daughter from getting an education," said one mother. Common sense began to prevail as soon as passions cooled.

Fewer than sixty students participated in a planned walkout October 3rd. Attendance rose slowly from a minimum of 1,400 to nearly 1,800 at the close of this week. After the walkout failed, Governor Faubus tried to keep the parents in turmoil. He charged last week that paratroopers had committed "very grave indiscretions" by invading girls' dressing rooms. He refused to reveal any evidence to prove it. His charge was promptly denied by army officers and school officials. Students laughed at it.

Meanwhile students were getting a better understanding of the federal troops guarding their school. In a smart public-relations gesture, paratroopers and their of-

ficers attended school football games and cheered for the
Central High "Tigers." There was plenty to cheer about
—Central's big team has won twenty-six games in a row.

There have been no clashes between students and
troops. The student paper, the *Tiger*, carried in its latest
issue a page-one article deploring the taunting of soldiers. "They're somebody's husband, somebody's son,
somebody's boy friend, and they want to be friendly with
the students of Central High," said the paper. "They were
sent here to do a job with a minimum of force and as
quickly as possible." The paper urged a "sensible, peaceful neutrality," and that students should "accept the situation without demonstration."

As for relations between the majority of white students and the nine Negroes, they are cautious and correct. A small minority of troublemakers has tried to
jostle and insult the Negroes, and one Negro boy was
kicked and pummeled, but the Negroes, well prepared in
advance for this ordeal, have behaved with poise and dignity. Not one of the nine has "chickened out" by requesting transfer back to all-Negro Horace Mann High School.

The self-control of one of the Negro children did finally
crack. Minnijean Brown, sixteen years old, was unable to go on
enduring the segregationist students' taunts—and worse—without replying in kind. She was suspended briefly in December and
then again in February for getting into a fray. Persons in the
North then got up a fund to send Minnijean to a private school
in New York, the New Lincoln School, and she graduated from
there the following year. Before she left Central High, Minnijean participated in a remarkable interview conducted for the
National Broadcasting Company by a Norwegian correspondent,
Mrs. Jorunn Ricketts. Five other Central students were on the
program: three white girls—Sammy Dean Parker, Kay Bacon
and Robin Woods—one white boy, Joseph Fox, and one Negro
boy, Ernest Green. These excerpts from the transcript were
printed in the *Times* on October 14, 1957:

MRS. RICKETTS: Do you think it is possible to start
working this out on a more sensible basis than violent
demonstration?

SAMMY: No, I don't because the South has always

been against racial mixing and I think they will fight this thing to the end. . . . We fight for our freedom—that's one thing. And we don't have any freedom any more.

ERNEST: Sammy, you said that you don't have freedom. I wonder what do you mean by it—that you don't have freedom? You are guaranteed your freedoms in the Bill of Rights and your Constitution. You have the freedom of speech—I noticed that has been exercised a whole lot in Little Rock. The freedom of petition, the freedom of religion and the other freedoms are guaranteed to you. As far as freedom, I think that if anybody should kick about freedoms, it should be us. Because I think we have been given a pretty bad side on this thing as far as freedoms.

SAMMY: Do you call those troops freedom? I don't. And I also do not call free when you are being escorted into the school every morning.

ERNEST: You say why did the troops come here? It is because our government—our state government—went against the federal law. . . . Our country is set up so that we have forty-eight states and no one state has the ability to overrule our nation's government. I thought that was what our country was built around. I mean, that is why we fight. We fought in World War II together—the fellows that I know died in World War II, they died in the Korean War. I mean, why should my friends get out there and die for a cause called "democracy" when I can't exercise my rights—tell me that.

ROBIN: I agree with Ernest.

JOE: Well, Sammy, I don't know what freedom has been taken away from you because the truth there—I know as a senior myself—the troops haven't kept me from going to my classes or participating in any school activity. I mean, they're there just to keep order in case —I might use the term "hotheads"—get riled up. But I think as long as—if parents would just stay out of it and let the children of the school at Central High figure it out for themselves, I think it would be a whole lot better. I think the students are mature enough to figure it out for themselves. . . . As far as I'm concerned, I'll lay the whole blame of this trouble in Governor Faubus's lap.

SAMMY: I think we knew before this ever started that some day we were going to have to integrate the schools. And I think that our Governor was trying to protect all of us when he called out the National Guard—and he was trying to prepare us, I think.

ERNEST: . . . Well, I have to disagree. . . . I know a student that's over there with us, Elizabeth, and that young lady, she walked two blocks, I guess—as you all know—and the mob was behind her. Did the troops break up the mob?

ROBIN: . . . And when Elizabeth had to walk down in front of the school I was there and I saw that. And may I say, I was very ashamed—I felt like crying—because she was so brave when she did that. And we just weren't behaving ourselves—just jeering her. I think if we had had any sort of decency, we wouldn't have acted that way. But I think if everybody would just obey the Golden Rule —do unto others as you would have others do unto you —might be the solution. How would you like to have to . . . walk down the street with everybody yelling behind you like they yelled behind Elizabeth?

MRS. RICKETTS: Sammy, why do these children not want to go to school with Negroes?

SAMMY: Well, I think it is mostly race mixing.

MRS. RICKETTS: Race mixing? What do you mean?

SAMMY: Well, marrying each other.

MINNIJEAN: Hold your hand up. I'm brown, you are white. What's the difference? We are all of the same thoughts. You're thinking about your boy—he's going to the Navy. I'm thinking about mine—he's in the Air Force. We think about the same thing.

SAMMY: I'll have to agree with you.

ERNEST: Well, getting back to this intermarriage and all that. I don't know [where] people get all that. Why do I want to go to school? To marry with someone? I mean, school's not a marriage bureau. . . . I'm going there for an education. Really, if I'm going there to socialize, I don't need to be going to school. I can stand out on the corner and socialize, as far as that.

MINNIJEAN: Kay, Joe and Robin—do you know anything about me, or is it just that your mother has told you about Negroes? . . .

MRS. RICKETTS: . . . Have you ever really made an effort to try to find out what they're like?

KAY: Not until today.

SAMMY: Not until today.

MRS. RICKETTS: And what do you think about it after today?

KAY: Well, you know that my parents and a lot of the other students and their parents think that the Negroes aren't equal to us. But—I don't know. It seems like they are, to me.

SAMMY: These people are—we'll have to admit that.

ERNEST: I think, like we're doing today, discussing our different views . . . if the people of Little Rock . . . would get together I believe they would find out a different story—and try to discuss the thing instead of getting out in the street and kicking people around and calling names—and all that sort of thing. If . . . people got together it would be smoothed over.

KAY: I think that if . . . our friends had been getting in this discussion today, I think that maybe some of them—not all of them—in time, they would change their mind. But probably some of them would change their mind today.

SAMMY: I know now that it isn't as bad as I thought it was—after we got together and discussed it.

KAY: [Sammy and I] We both came down here today with our mind set on it [that] we weren't going to change our mind that we were fully against integration. But I know now that we're going to change our mind.

MRS. RICKETTS: What do your parents say to that?

KAY: I think I'm going to have a long talk with my parents.

The episode exposed the error in President Eisenhower's view that "you cannot change people's hearts merely by laws." It may be true that law cannot at once alter emotions. But by forcing a change in objective circumstances, law does alter patterns of conduct in ways that may, in time, change a human being's outlook. Had the law not brought Sammy Dean Parker and Kay Bacon into contact with Negro children, the racist preconcep-

67   LITTLE ROCK

tions imbibed from their parents would have gone undisturbed. The law, in short, can change one's experience—and experience changes hearts.

But it was not the time, in the 1957-58 school year, for this lesson to be learned in Little Rock. Federal force had not lessened the determination of the segregationists, from Governor Faubus down, to bring implementation of the Supreme Court decision to a stop there and then. In the face of the pressures, the School Board late in the school year asked the federal judge then on duty there, Harry J. Lemley of Arkansas, to suspend the integration plan for two and one-half years because of the "unfavorable community attitude."

On June 27, 1958, Judge Lemley granted the request of the School Board. The tensions in Central High, he said, were "intolerable," and enforcement of the principle of desegregation would have to wait.

The Lemley decision brought a second constitutional crisis to Little Rock. The first had been one of force—a physical clash of federal and state sovereignties. The second was one of law. The question was whether the Constitution had to give way when faced with community resistance.

Inevitably, that question had to be settled in the place where the law of the Constitution had originally been decided, in the Supreme Court of the United States. After some indecisive intermediate appellate proceedings, the Court met in special session on August 28, 1958, to hear argument of the Little Rock case, *Cooper v. Aaron*. (William G. Cooper was a School Board member, John Aaron one of the Negro pupils.) In the lofty marble courtroom that afternoon there was the air of a great occasion in that court different from all other courts, given final authority to distribute sovereign power in this country. At the end of the day James Reston wrote in the *Times*:

It was the Court, in all its majesty, that was in command today, dominating the proceedings, bringing the lawyers back to root questions, even managing to hush the normally noisy Washington crowds that rush after all great battles in the Capital.

The Court may not tame the South, but at least it does something no other branch of the government manages to do. It concentrates on great rather than small issues and it provides a calm and orderly forum for their disposition.

This is one of the great gaps elsewhere in the Capital. Both the executive and the legislative branches spend much of their time on trivial things that are debated in an untidy uproar. But not the Court.

It was appealing again today to "the universal constituency of reason and justice." It was dealing with the momentous issues of law, and education, and human reason and at least commanding unanimous respect, if not consent.

The Court did not decide the case that day; it asked for further argument two weeks later, on September 11th. But the questions from the bench gave ample clues to the justices' frame of mind. Their questions were directed most sharply at the lawyer for the Little Rock School Board, Richard C. Butler, who argued that the people of Arkansas were confused by Governor Faubus's attacks on the School Segregation decision as unlawful and that desegregation should be postponed until a clearer "national policy could be established."

"Why aren't the two decisions of this Court a national policy?" Justice Frankfurter asked.

Chief Justice Warren intervened. "Suppose every other school board in the South," he asked, "said the same thing: 'We'll postpone this thing until the law is clarified.' How would it ever be clarified? . . .

"Can we defer a program of this kind merely because there are elements in a community that will commit violence to prevent it from going into effect?"

The Chief Justice's question was answered by the Court itself on September 12th, the day after the second argument of the case. The answer was No: The law will not give way to violent resistance. The Court unanimously rejected Judge Lemley's order for suspension of the Little Rock desegregation plan. Its opinion, filed September 29th, said: "Law and order are not here to be preserved by depriving the Negro children of their constitutional rights."

Governor Faubus had one more string to his bow. He ordered all the high schools in Little Rock closed to prevent "impending violence and disorder." They stayed closed through the 1958-59 school term. White students went to private schools, moved

away, took correspondence courses—or gave up school altogether. Most of the Negroes enrolled in segregated county public
schools just outside Little Rock.

At first, events seemed to be moving with the Governor. In
the fall of 1958 voters ended the House career of Congressman
Brooks Hays, a moderate man who had tried to bring order out
of the school chaos; a write-in campaign chose in his place a
militant segregationist, Dr. T. Dale Alford. The legislature armed
Faubus with new weapons, such as the school-closing laws.
Three members of the Little Rock School Board took a pro-
Faubus view. But then the mood seemed to shift. Those three
School Board members were removed by Little Rock voters in a
recall election. A federal court found the school-closing laws
unconstitutional. During the summer of 1959 the School Board
decided to reopen the city's high schools, assigning three Negro
children to Central and three to Hall, another white school.

On August 12, 1959, Elizabeth Ann Eckford, who had
walked so bravely through the mob toward Central High School
two years earlier, made the trip again. Again there was a mob—
but this time the Little Rock police sternly maintained order.
The mob and the tension gradually faded, and token desegregation of the schools was peacefully accomplished. The battle of
Little Rock was over.

Chapter 5

Montgomery, Cradle of the New Negro

The Confederate flag was first unfurled there in 1861, and Jefferson Davis inaugurated. Montgomery was called the Cradle of the Confederacy. A century and many lives later, the city was still a monument to the southern white dream of a society ruled by whites and served by contented Negroes. Life in Montgomery was completely segregated —except in the homes of the well-to-do who had Negro cooks and maids and nurses. It was not a society of the *nouveaux riches* or the managers, like Birmingham. It was a genteel society, and all was serene.

Or so it seemed to the whites who made up a little more than half of Montgomery's population of one hundred and twenty-five thousand. To the Negroes life looked a little different. There was the difficulty in getting any but a dirty, low-paid job in an economy shifting from agriculture to industry. For the few who could get a decent education, there were the closed doors to professions; the city had, for example, only two Negro lawyers. There was the constant irritant of segregation in all public places.

These factors were common to Negro life in the South. What

was distinctive in Montgomery was the presence of a handful of intelligent, well-educated, young Negro leaders uncompromising in their opposition to segregation. Their leadership made the difference when the accumulated grievances of the Negroes were ignited by one incident—an incident no different, really, from what had happened at many other times and places.

On the evening of December 1, 1955, a forty-three-year-old Negro seamstress, Mrs. Rosa Parks, got on a bus in Montgomery to ride home. She was tired, and she took a seat near the front of the bus in the section reserved by custom for whites. When a white man came along, the bus driver ordered her to get up and give him the seat. Mrs. Parks, a leader in her church and in the local chapter of the N.A.A.C.P., refused. She was arrested, jailed briefly, then ordered to trial on December 5th on the charge of violating segregation laws.

The next night fifty leaders of the Negro community met to discuss the case of Mrs. Parks in the Dexter Avenue Baptist Church, a simple, handsome red-brick building at the edge of the State Capitol mall. The minister of that church was a twenty-seven-year-old doctor of divinity and of philosophy, born in Atlanta and educated in Boston, Martin Luther King, Jr. The leaders decided to organize a mass protest.

On December 5th, ninety per cent of the Negroes who ordinarily rode the buses of Montgomery stayed off them. That night there was a mass meeting. The Negroes there, jubilant at the day's events, appealed to "all the citizens of Montgomery" to stay off the buses until conditions were satisfactory to "all citizens." The great Montgomery bus boycott was under way.

At the beginning the issue could have been resolved by a compromise on segregation. The Negroes would have agreed to an arrangement under which they would be seated from the rear forward, whites from the front back, with no one having to give up seats when all were taken. But something went amiss in negotiations with city officials, and the latter gave up all attempts to settle. The Mayor and city commissioners publicly enrolled in the White Citizens Council.

And so the boycott went on into 1956, operating with astonishing success. Its leaders were Dr. King and other ministers—a natural development because for generations the ministry had been the only profession fully open to Negroes. The ministers influenced the whole nature of the Montgomery movement. Wayne Phillips, a *Times* reporter, explained:

> By emphasizing the Christian virtue of "love thine enemy," the boycott was made a mass movement of passive resistance—though it took months for the Gandhi similarity to be recognized. And by preaching the protests in their churches and mass meetings they gave it the dynamism of a religious crusade, bringing to bear the strongest emotional force in the Negro community.

Because most of the bus riders had formerly been Negroes, the boycott cut the bus company's gross income sixty-five per cent, forced it to raise fares and slice schedules and still had it operating at a loss. Most of the white people of Montgomery were not directly affected; they did not ride the buses. But the specter of Negro revolt began to bother them. They realized that something more was at stake here than bus segregation. The stubborn sacrifice and determination of the Negroes—the willingness of a laundress to walk to the white home where she was employed, the well-organized arrangement of car pools—signified an end to the subservient, satisfied mood that the whites always thought they had seen.

The words of Dr. King were disturbing, too, and not the less so for their emphasis on non-violence. No one could mistake the power in this characteristic statement of his:

"Integration is the great issue of our age, the great issue of our nation and the great issue of our community. We are in the midst of a great struggle, the consequence of which will be world-shaking. But our victory will not be a victory for Montgomery's Negroes alone. It will be a victory for justice, a victory for fair play and a victory for democracy. Were we to stop right now, we would have won a victory because the Negro has achieved from this a new dignity. But we are not going to stop. We are going on in the same spirit of love and protest, and the same dignity we have shown in the past."

White Montgomery retaliated on February 22, 1956, by indicting Dr. King and nearly one hundred other Negroes on the charge of conspiracy to conduct an illegal boycott. The Negro response came at a mass meeting the next night, which Wayne Phillips described:

> One after the other, indicted Negro leaders took the rostrum in a crowded Baptist church tonight to urge

their followers to shun the city's buses and "walk with God."

More than two thousand Negroes filled the church from basement to balcony and overflowed into the street. They chanted and sang; they shouted and prayed; they collapsed in the aisles and they sweltered in an eighty-five-degree heat. They pledged themselves again and again to "passive resistance." Under this banner they have carried on for eighty days a stubborn boycott of the city's buses. The boycott has brought criminal charges against Negro leaders; and tomorrow those arrested are to be arraigned in Circuit Court. The Negroes have been called on to stage at that time a "prayer pilgrimage day" —to give up the use of automobiles and taxis and walk the streets in protest.

"It is not expected that a single peace-loving Negro will turn the key in his ignition or turn the crank of his automobile or take a taxicab," the Reverend Ralph D. Abernathy told tonight's meeting. "And we know," he said, "that nobody will ride the buses."

Dr. Abernathy, twenty-nine years old, is the pastor of the First Baptist Church, where the meeting was held. He headed the negotiating committee that tried unsuccessfully to settle the boycott that was organized December 5. "We're not trying to impress anybody with our strength," Dr. Abernathy said. "We just plan to demonstrate to the people who do not have cars that we're willing to walk with them."

Sixty-five per cent of the city's bus passengers before the boycott were Negroes. Since the boycott, buses have plied the streets almost empty, while Negroes make their way to and from work in taxis, with the aid of a three-hundred-car auto pool, or on foot.

As the Negroes waited for the meeting to start they sang, picking up the hymns that sprang to mind. When the leaders appeared at the rear of the church the audience stood and shouted and whistled and waved and cheered. The program opened with a hymn—"Onward Christian Soldiers"—and a prayer to God "not to leave us in this hour." The scripture was from Corinthians 1—"If I have no love I count for nothing." And then they sang "O lift me up and let me stand on higher ground."

Reverend Martin Luther King, Jr., head of the Montgomery Improvement Association, which has directed the boycott, told the gathering that the protest was not against a single incident but over things that "go deep down into the archives of history."

"We have known humiliation, we have known abusive language, we have been plunged into the abyss of oppression," he told them. "And we decided to rise up only with the weapon of protest. It is one of the greatest glories of America that we have the right of protest.

"There are those who would try to make of this a hate campaign," the Baptist minister said. "This is not a war between the white and the Negro but a conflict between justice and injustice. This is bigger than the Negro race revolting against the white. We are seeking to improve not the Negro of Montgomery but the whole of Montgomery.

"If we are arrested every day, if we are exploited every day, if we are trampled over every day, don't ever let anyone pull you so low as to hate them. We must use the weapon of love. We must have compassion and understanding for those who hate us. We must realize so many people are taught to hate us that they are not totally responsible for their hate. But we stand in life at midnight, we are always on the threshold of a new dawn."

A month later, on March 22nd, Dr. King was convicted of leading the assertedly illegal boycott. He was fined five hundred dollars plus five hundred dollars for court costs; when he said he would go to jail instead of paying, the sentence was converted to 386 days. The other prosecutions were withheld pending appeal of his case. In the end, nothing came of this legal effort to squelch the boycott: Dr. King settled his case by paying five hundred dollars, and the other cases were dropped.

Far from injuring the Negro cause, the mass arrests and the prosecution of Dr. King fed the emotional support of the boycott. Buses still traveled the streets empty while Negroes went to and from work in car pools. And the legal action attracted the attention and sympathy of the rest of the country and even the world. This in turn lent a new impetus to the protest movement. No longer was it fighting for fairer segregation, or even to overthrow segregation. Now it was, in the words of Dr. King, "a battle for the oppressed people of the world."

While continuing their direct protest action, the Negroes of Montgomery also took to the law. Their case bore the name of Mrs. Aurelia S. Browder, who, like Mrs. Rosa Parks, had been arrested for refusing to move to the rear of a bus. She and three others filed a suit in federal court to challenge the constitutionality of state and local laws requiring segregation in transportation facilities. The question had not then been decided by the Supreme Court: The School decision of 1954 had been specifically limited to segregation in education, and the only rulings against segregation on buses and trains had involved *interstate* transportation and had rested on the federal power over interstate commerce. As to local transit, the separate-but-equal rule laid down in *Plessy v. Ferguson*—which was a transportation case—had not been officially overturned.

On April 23, 1956, the Supreme Court threw the legal situation into confusion with a cryptic ruling on a case involving bus segregation in Columbia, South Carolina. Miss Sarah Mae Flemming of that city had brought a damage suit against the bus company there, claiming that her civil rights were infringed by segregation. The federal trial judge dismissed her complaint, saying that *Plessy v. Ferguson* was still the law. But the Court of Appeals reversed, holding that bus segregation was unconstitutional and that Miss Flemming was entitled to a trial of her suit. The bus company then appealed to the Supreme Court. It was at that point that confusion entered.

The Supreme Court dismissed the appeal in a brief order that gave no explanation. It simply cited an old case that reporters, on a hasty reading, thought called for the dismissal of trivial appeals. If the bus company's appeal was trivial, segregation had been condemned. As a result, newspapers all over the country—the *New York Times* included—carried headlines the next day to the effect that the Supreme Court had held bus and streetcar segregation unconstitutional. A dozen cities in the South quickly ordered their transit facilities integrated, and the orders were carried out without incident. But it turned out that the Court had not meant to decide the issue at all in this case. Somehow explanations were leaked out, and corrective stories were written. That old case cited by the justices really stood for the proposition that the Supreme Court would not review nonfinal judgments. The Court of Appeals decision was not final, because Miss Flemming still had to go back and have a trial of her case. All the Supreme Court had said was that the appeal by the bus company was premature. Considering the delicacy of the issue, it might have said that a little more clearly.

The beleaguered bus company in Montgomery actually announced an end to segregation when the first, inaccurate account of the decision was received. But city officials said they would continue to enforce the traditional practice, and bus drivers were in danger of arrest themselves if they disobeyed. Segregation continued.

Then, on June 3rd, the case brought by Mrs. Browder in Montgomery made some progress. A three-judge Federal District Court, dividing two to one, held bus segregation unconstitutional and enjoined Mayor W. A. Gayle and other officials from enforcing the racial laws. The officials appealed to the Supreme Court, the city commission explaining that it must take "every step possible to prevent such a drastic change in the habits of the people." Meanwhile, the effect of the decision was stayed.

The Supreme Court ruled on November 13, 1956, and this time there was no mistake. In a brief order citing the School Segregation case it unanimously affirmed the District Court order that bus segregation violated the Constitution. Five weeks later, after routine procedural steps, the decision took effect.

At last the boycott could end—more than a year after it started. The *Times* carried an Associated Press story written from Montgomery the evening of December 20, 1956:

Jubilant Montgomery Negroes decided to end their long boycott tomorrow morning and ride buses again without the restrictions of racial segregation. The action came at a mass meeting of several hundred cheering Negroes, who were celebrating the United States Supreme Court's order banning bus segregation in Montgomery. The order went into effect earlier today.

Dr. Martin Luther King, Jr., urged the gathering to patronize the buses but warned against violence. "This is a time when we must evince calm dignity and wise restraint," Dr. King pleaded. "Emotions must not run wild. . . . If we become victimized with violent intents, we will have walked in vain and our twelve months of glorious dignity will be transformed into an eve of gloomy catastrophe."

A "laboratory institute period" in a church auditorium filled with singing, cheering Negroes followed Dr.
King's speech. Its purpose was to acquaint Negroes with
"some of the things that might be expected" when they
ride integrated buses. The Negroes have been schooled in
recent weeks in a non-violent approach with constant
emphasis on remaining peaceful "even if others strike
first."

A notice to drivers was posted at the office of Montgomery City Lines, Inc., which operates the city's only
bus service. It contained a copy of the injunction writ
along with instructions to bus operators to cease enforcing segregation laws. J. H. Bagley, the bus-company
manager, said it would be impossible to resume full service on all former routes immediately, but that would be
done "as fast as possible." Many drivers had been laid off
and routes through predominantly Negro sections of
Montgomery were discontinued during the boycott.

The next day the victory was tasted. George Barrett wrote in
the *Times*:

> The Negroes of Montgomery, victors in a year-long
> boycott to end segregation in public transit here, quietly
> and in determined numbers went back on the city's de-
> segregated buses today.
>
> For the first time in this "cradle of the Confederacy"
> all the Negroes entered buses through the front door.
> They sat in the first empty seats they saw, in the front of
> buses and in the rear. They did not get up to give a white
> passenger a seat. And whites sat with Negroes.
>
> As one of the oldest race barriers in this Deep South
> community fell this morning, following a formal order
> from the Supreme Court to abolish segregation in local
> buses, nothing happened to indicate that Montgomery's
> seventy-five thousand whites and fifty thousand Negroes
> looked upon the historic event as anything but a natural
> development. There were no special details of police on
> duty, nor were they needed. Despite alarms by city offi-
> cials and members of the White Citizens Council during
> the last year that bus desegregation in Montgomery
> would bring riots and bloodshed, only one minor inci-
> dent marred today's changeover from long-established
> custom.

A Negro woman who was one of the first to board the newly desegregated buses this morning was slapped in the face by a white youth as she stepped out of a bus into the street. She reported that her assailant then jumped into a car with an out-of-state license plate and sped away with a group of white men.

In a couple of instances, carloads of white men were seen to follow some of the buses, but no overt attempt was made to interfere with the bus company's decision to carry out the Supreme Court order.

Aboard the buses, as the Negroes and the whites for the first time sat where they both chose to sit, the talk was rarely about integration. At first there was no exchange between whites and Negroes as they took up the strange pattern of mixed seating. But often the stiffness gradually disappeared. A Negro turned in one bus to ask a white passenger sitting behind him—the mark of the new order—what time it was and got a courteous reply. A white man who had been sitting next to a Negro said later he did not understand what all the fuss and the difficulty had been about.

Two white men in one bus today found themselves sitting behind a Negro, and one of the men said, "I see this sure isn't going to be a white Christmas."

The Negro looked up, and smiled. He said, with good humor but firmness: "Yes, sir, that's right." Everybody in the bus smiled, and all rancor seemed to evaporate.

All did not remain perfectly peaceful in the weeks after the buses started running. Some whites tried to provoke incidents on the buses, and one Sunday Dr. King told his congregation, in the middle of routine announcements from the pulpit, that a shotgun blast had been fired through the front door of his house a few nights earlier. He said he would like to have met those who did the shooting to tell them that surely they must know they could not solve problems that way. Four days later a sniper fired a bullet into a bus, wounding a Negro woman. On January 10th bombs went off in four Negro churches and in the homes of two ministers who had fought segregation, one white and one Negro. Authorities stopped all bus service for a time, and the white citizens of Montgomery had to learn to make do without transit service, as the Negroes had. But emotions subsided, and unsegregated buses became just a part of life in Montgomery. George Barrett went back to Montgomery three months later to survey the aftermath of the troubles he had reported. In the *Times Magazine* of March 3, 1957, he wrote:

Not yet where the tar road ends and the mud ruts start, but far enough out to where the whites never go, a Negro seamstress looked for a moment in silence at the folds of velvet that divided the choir loft in her church from the front-row pews. The velvet was worn, very worn, and the threads holding it to the brass rings around the choir rail were broken in many places. Sections of the drapery yawed over, gave peephole views of the organ's pedal clavier. Abruptly, she pushed aside her sewing kit, began pulling away at the drapery. She talked as she pulled.

"Velvet, I'm sorry. But you're tired. And we've put up just about long enough with tired things. You gotta go." And down came the velvet. Then she turned the talk to Jim Crow, spoke without rancor, without defiance, without raising her voice: "I guess that's our answer. Jim Crow, he's more than one hundred years old, and real tired, and like you just hear me tell this velvet, we figure we've about put up long enough with tired things."

That seamstress, a fifty-seven-year-old grandmother who left school before the eighth grade and still refers to her employer as "my white lady"; her Negro neighbor, a handyman who says "Yes SIR, Boss" and spends his evenings drafting and redrafting an essay on the duties of citizenship so sound that the white man's election board will no longer dare to hold back his ballot; their community leader, the twenty-eight-year-old Reverend Dr. Martin Luther King, Jr., whose fusion of Christianity, Hegelianism and Gandhism has spurred Montgomery's Negroes and set back Montgomery's whites in the opening battle here to end racial segregation; indeed, each of Montgomery's 50,000 Negroes shares an identical distinction.

Each is the South's "new Negro."

When the white man—the northern white man—speaks, as he often does these days, of the "new Negro," he generally means the Dr. Kings, the Negroes who have left their back-hollow birthplaces, the "Jim Towns" and "Shanty Villages" in the Deep South and gone North to collect their master's degrees and their doctorates from integrated universities. He means the Negroes who have found their first day-to-day reality of racial democracy in the armed services and in foreign duty, and are now coming back to mobilize the stay-at-home Negroes for the big march against the bastions of the Old South.

When the white southerner speaks of the "new Negro" these days he means the same thing, except that if he's a reputable member of the community he will probably fiddle uneasily with a paper clip on his desk and say, "That communistic N.A.A.C.P. is sending them back down here to stir up our decent nigras." And if he is not so educated or prosperous he will spit at the dirt in angry silence, or he will say, with unprintable interpolations, "That communistic N. C. double-A. P. or whatever it's called is sending them back down here to stir up our niggers."

Example number one here in Alabama, in fact in the entire Deep South, is Dr. King, according to most of the southern whites who are fighting each new attempt to carry out the Supreme Court's mandates against segregation. They are convinced that the Dr. Kings—and particularly *the* Dr. King, who they are certain is regarded by most Negroes as a kind of latter-day Messiah—are basically causing All The Trouble.

But visit Negro night spots in Montgomery, attend midweek prayer meetings, go with them to their pep sessions, join them in their parlors: the "new Negro" is not only the Dr. Kings but the seamstress, the handyman; in fact, most of Montgomery's Negroes, who never went North. Negroes here who have traveled in the Deep South or have received letters from their friends and families in other southern states say that the forces that unified Montgomery's Negroes in the remarkable year-long bus boycott are emerging also in other areas across the southern tier.

The "new Negro," in fact, is a phrase that brings quick looks between Negroes here, then good-natured grins. A Negro mail carrier put it this way: "New Negro?

Dr (King => Gandhi
Passive Resistance
Alabama

It's just us old Negroes, the same old folks. It's not the 'new Negro'—it's the 'new times.' Only we know it, that's all, and the white folks here haven't caught on to it yet."

The "new times," of course, means today, the culmination of long years of better Negro education, of a fast-narrowing world with its ready exchange of ideas and closer living patterns, of the Negroes' emerging economic power, of spreading industrialization throughout the Deep South, of the day-by-day absurdities involved in sectional segregation in a nation tending naturally and swiftly toward integration on all levels, and finally of the Supreme Court's parade of bans against Jim Crow, which for the Negroes here meant, as a quietly jubilant Negro housewife said: "Before, we only thought we were right—now we know we are right."

From his pulpit Dr. King has warned softly those who have three times now bombed or shot up his home: "Kill me, but know that if you do you have fifty thousand more to kill!"

Most of the whites here, who see nothing unusual about a member of the board of trustees of Tuskegee working as a chauffeur for his living, have never got past the porches of Negro homes, except on occasional paternalistic visits to see if Cora is coming along all right. If they had, they would have discovered that in the past as well as in the present minister of the Dexter Avenue Baptist Church, in the Jasons and the Rubys, in the Anna Maes and the Sams who scrub their kitchen linoleum and change the oil in their cars, there has been for a long time a determined—if very quiet—resolve to get rid of Jim Crow.

"Funny thing," one Negro girl said recently after a prayer meeting, while other Negroes in the pews nodded in agreement, "our white families say to us it's such a terrible thing that a man like that Reverend King comes here and gets the colored people all stirred up, and we say, 'No, ma'am, the Reverend, he didn't stir us up, we've been stirred up a mighty long time.' But our white folks, they just don't seem to hear us, because later at the dinner table they'll be talking to their friends and saying what a terrible thing it is for that Reverend King to come in here and stir up all us colored people and how they were just that morning talking to their maid, only they never say what it was we answered. I guess they just don't hear us."

This religious conviction is the most quietly dramatic aspect of the Negro story in Montgomery. Dr. King has been correctly described as the man who introduced intellectual dynamism to the Montgomery Negroes, who has transcribed Hegel's philosophy of strength through struggle, harmony out of pain, in terms of the Negro living in the South, and thereby given the Negro a new awareness (and, therefore, a new strength). Many admit they don't always understand his words, but, as one of his own congregation put it, "We sure get the force of his meaning."

And he has won world-wide recognition for the way he has translated Gandhi's philosophy of passive resistance into Alabaman terms, an adaptation that has administered a solid defeat to the segregationists. The Negro churches still show old movies of Gandhi to demonstrate again and again how victory—real victory— comes from non-violence.

But it is as a man of God, a man as profoundly religious as he is philosophically knowledgeable, that Dr. King has been chosen by Montgomery's Negroes to lead the way to the "new times." This is the Bible Belt, and Fundamentalism survives. It is the land of rousing hymns and camp-meeting tunes, the songs that cry of the Negro's suffering and his struggle.

Enter a Negro church any Sunday. The minister reads the prayer, slowly, and a single finger, then a foot, tap out the rhythm, swiftly, the congregation picks up the crescendo: "Hear our prayer, O Lord!" But it's no longer the old-style religion, no longer the way of escape from terrible realities. There is a sound now more than a cry; there is the ring that is the ring of a deep conviction.

The words and the music are old—yet strangely new —as massed voices sing:

"Thou hast made us willing,
Thou hast made us free,

> *By Thy grace divine,*
> *We are on the Lord's side."*

And this is the remarkable strength of the Negro in Montgomery: his conviction, so vivid in his face, that he must at last win because he is on God's side.

From the preaching of Dr. King, the Negroes have learned in the last year the hardest of Christ's truths—how to love, how not to judge, how not to hate—and found these precisely through their refusal to strike back when white men spat in their faces, slapped them across the mouth, hurled dynamite at their homes and churches.

Clearly—and this is probably the most stirring experience for the visitor to Montgomery—the Negroes' day-by-day acceptance and practice of Christ's principles, applied to the struggle against Jim Crow, have brought them a calm that seems unshakable, a humility that is formidable, a love that shatters hate and prejudice. The combination can only mean the ultimate—and not so distant—defeat of the segregationist cause.

One Negro woman said: "Did you ever dream of getting a million dollars some day, and buying all the things you've wanted? For us, right now, it's like suddenly getting a million-dollar check from the United States Government. We've waited a hundred years for it, only its Friday afternoon and the bank won't open until Monday. It really doesn't matter if we don't get the cash until Monday. A weekend is not so long, now."

The Montgomery experience did a number of important things for the revolution in American race relations. It produced a major new leader in Dr. King, and really a whole new kind of leadership—young and indigenous to the southern Negro community, not tied to the funds and ideas of enlightened but necessarily remote northern whites. Montgomery raised the banner of non-violence for the first time in the Negro cause, and raised it for all the South and the country and the world to see. The experience demonstrated that the Negro could fight for his own rights with courage and dignity. Montgomery was the genesis of "direct action" as a technique in the movement for racial justice, and it was a great demonstration of the effectiveness of social protest.

But it is not always remembered that social protest did not win a victory unaided in Montgomery. In the end, the determined Negroes of Montgomery had help from the Supreme Court of the United States. The law and human expression of discontent had worked together to produce peaceful change. That these two techniques of social change were complementary was a lesson sometimes forgotten during the succeeding years of the racial revolution.

Chapter 6

Non-violent Direct Action

Freedom Riders

On January 31, 1960, a Negro college freshman in Greensboro, North Carolina, Joseph Mc-Neill, tried to get something to eat at the bus terminal in downtown Greensboro. Like other Negroes at other lunch counters throughout the South and through much of the border area, he was turned down: We do not serve Negroes. But the humiliation that so many others had experienced for so long this time set off a spark.

That night, in his dormitory, McNeill asked his roommate, Ezell Blair, Jr., "What can we do?" Then he answered his own question: "Let's have a boycott. We should go in and ask to be served and sit there until they do."

The next day McNeill, Blair and two of their classmates, David Richmond and Franklin McCain, sat down at the lunch counter in Woolworth's. When they were not served, they continued to sit there. When they finally left after several hours, they had still not had a cup of coffee, but they did not feel let down. McNeill told the others that he thought the idea would spread.

The four students drew no national attention that first day. But when they returned to Woolworth's the next morning, the wire services began to take notice. The *New York Times* carried this United Press International story:

A group of well-dressed Negro college students staged a sit-down strike in a downtown Woolworth store today and vowed to continue it in relays until Negroes were served at the lunch counter.

"We believe, since we buy books and papers in the other part of the store, we should get served in this part," said the spokesman for the group.

The store manager, C. L. Harris, commented: "They can just sit there. It's nothing to me."

He declined to say whether it was the policy of the store not to serve Negroes.

The Negroes, students at North Carolina Agricultural and Technical College here, arrived shortly after ten A. M. and sat at two sections of the lunch counter. At twelve-thirty P.M., the group filed out of the store and stood on the sidewalk in this city's busiest downtown area. They formed a tight circle, threw their hands into a pyramid in the center and recited the Lord's Prayer.

The spokesman said that "another shift" of students would carry forward the strike and it would continue "until we get served."

By the fourth day the four young men were joined by other students, Negro and white, men and women, from the Greensboro area. And outside of Greensboro the power of what they were doing began to be recognized. Other students sat at other lunch counters, and a movement was born. It was an extraordinary movement, displaying as really nothing else had the suffering in the soul of the Negro. When young people, without money or influence, risked literally everything to demonstrate for equal treatment as human beings, it was impossible for the South to talk convincingly about "outside agitators" or northern politicians or the Supreme Court as the source of the "trouble."

The sit-ins were an immediate success. In some of the more cosmopolitan communities of the southern and border states only a small psychological push was needed to topple segregation at lunch counters. It took just six months to open the counter at Woolworth's in Greensboro to all races. Hundreds of other stores began serving Negroes by the end of 1960 and hundreds more in succeeding years. Demonstrations also focused on other targets—hotels, movie theatres, amusement parks. And the sit-ins gave rise to a companion movement against segregation in transportation, the freedom rides.

The country learned about freedom riders in the spring of 1961, when for the first time the non-violent protest movement was met by violence so serious that the Federal Government intervened. Whites and Negroes associated with a major arm of the movement, the Congress of Racial Equality, filled two buses that were driven into Alabama to protest segregation at terminals. At Birmingham and Anniston the riders were savagely beaten, stomped on the ground, slashed with chains. One bus was stoned and then burned. News pictures of the savagery went out to the world.

The next week a bi-racial group of students left Atlanta and headed for Montgomery, Alabama, to protest bus-terminal segregation. Dr. King, who was in Atlanta, was also going to Montgomery to make a speech. The mood in Alabama was tense, and the Attorney General of the United States, Robert F. Kennedy, feared bloodshed. He did not wait until after violence and legal proceedings, as his predecessors had at Little Rock. He thought it was the Federal Government's duty to protect Americans in the peaceful exercise of their constitutional rights to travel and speak, if state authorities would not. His brother, the President, authorized federal intervention.

On May 21, 1961, Attorney General Kennedy sent a force of five hundred federal marshals to Montgomery under the direction of the Deputy Attorney General, Byron R. White. The Governor of Alabama, John Patterson, objected. In a long telegram to the Attorney General he said Alabama did not need assistance from any federal marshals to maintain order. He did not mention the assaults on the freedom riders at Birmingham and Anniston.

"We do not need their help, we do not want their help, and in fact we do not want them here in Alabama," the Governor said.

"Federal marshals do not have a legal or constitutional right to be here. Their presence is unwarranted and will only further complicate and aggravate the situation. I consider the presence

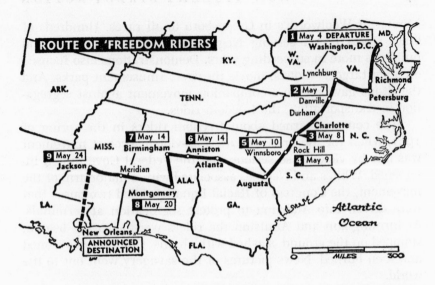

ROUTE OF 'FREEDOM RIDERS'

1 May 4 DEPARTURE Washington, D.C. MD.

W. VA.

KY.

Lynchburg VA.

Richmond

ARK.

TENN.

2 May 7 Danville

Petersburg

Durham

Charlotte

3 May 8 N.C.

MISS.

7 May 14 Birmingham

6 May 14 Anniston

5 May 10 Winnsboro

Rock Hill

9 May 24 Jackson

Meridian

Atlanta

4 May 9

S.C.

ALA.

Augusta

Montgomery

8 May 20

GA.

Atlantic Ocean

LA.

New Orleans

ANNOUNCED DESTINATION

FLA.

0   MILES   300

of these federal marshals a trampling upon and encroachment on the rights of the State of Alabama and our citizens as well."

The Attorney General sent back this curt reply: "The United States Government needs assurance by action—not words—that its citizens will be safe in the State of Alabama."

The Attorney General turned out to be right. Governor Patterson needed lots of help before calm was restored. Before the weekend was over, the Governor's deputy was to call on the Justice Department for additional manpower.

The students arrived at the Montgomery bus station before the marshals got to town, and they were assaulted. But the critical moment came on Sunday evening, May 21st, when Dr. King was in the Negro First Baptist Church preaching non-violence to fifteen hundred parishioners. White and his marshals were on hand now. The *Times* reported from Washington:

> Just after ten P.M. Mr. White reported by telephone to the Attorney General that a mob was gathering. Kennedy immediately called his brother, the President, who was at his country home in Middleburg, Virginia. With the approval of the President, the Attorney General telephoned Governor Patterson in Montgomery and told him more men were needed to control the gathering mob. The Governor assured Kennedy that everything was under control, but said he would do what he could.

At just about that moment, the Attorney General was telephoned by Dr. King. He told the Attorney General, "They're moving in on the church."

Kennedy told Dr. King, "The marshals will stop them."

He said Dr. King left the phone for a moment, then returned and said, "You're right."

Within the next few minutes the Alabama Director of Public Safety, Floyd Mann, telephoned the federal command post at Maxwell Air Force Base, near Montgomery. He asked Deputy Attorney General White to "commit any reserves."

"We've committed all we have," White replied. "They are at your disposal."

By early morning, the mob around the church was broken up and the Negroes inside were able to return to their homes. But the tension had not ended. The next day, Monday, Montgomery was an armed camp. A *Times* correspondent described it:

This city lay sleepily last night under a quarter moon, its graceful old homes shuttered and silent beneath spreading oaks and magnolias. But the Greyhound bus station echoed to the martial sounds of military rule. Olive-green jeeps and big trucks roared up to the station. Troops in combat dress, rifles at the ready, jumped to the pavement, formed quickly into squads and marched briskly to their assigned positions. Infantrymen with fixed bayonets forced civilians down a sidewalk away from the area, their faces set grimly beneath the steel helmets. These National Guardsmen, all Alabamians, obviously had little stomach for the task, but as one said, "orders are orders."

Outside the station's main entrance stood a sandy-haired, trim six-footer of one hundred and eighty pounds. The twin white stars of a major general were stitched into the collar of his blouse. Henry V. Graham, a Birmingham real estate executive when out of uniform, shares his men's dislike for the job at hand. But as Alabama's adjutant general he is charged with maintaining order in this city's racial crisis.

Turning to a taxi driver who had had too much to

drink, the General first sought to use reason. "I'm from Alabama and you're from Alabama, I assume," he said. "Now, why don't you cooperate with us?" The driver persisted in remaining, whereupon the officer ordered him sharply across the street.

"This is about as distasteful a duty as a soldier can take," General Graham remarked to newsmen. "You start putting a rifle butt in your own people's stomachs and it's rough.

"After all, we're dealing with our own people, who are emotionally upset about this thing. And I'm not going to pass judgment on their views."

When another group of freedom riders arrived, General Graham and his men protected them from violence—but not from arrest. The *Times* story said:

> The group was headed by the Reverend William S. Coffin, Jr., the chaplain of Yale University. He explained that the four whites and three Negroes had assembled for the ride through a spontaneous decision. Their reception at the bus terminal here was orderly. A mob of several hundred persons, described by an eye-witness as a "rough-looking group," watched in silence as the party descended from the bus and entered two waiting automobiles. Two hundred National Guardsmen and a score of local police stood by.
>
> The seven riders were charged with disorderly conduct when they sought service at a segregated lunch counter.
>
> "Now everyone is happy," General Graham commented. "This is what they wanted and we have accommodated them. They've been arrested quietly, like they wanted to be, and now I'm happy, too."
>
> A crowd of about one hundred and fifty, mostly white, cheered as the mixed group was removed to jail.
>
> "That's where they ought to be all the time!" a man shouted.

As a result of the Alabama disorders over the freedom rides, Attorney General Kennedy moved to wipe out racism in all aspects of interstate transportation. On his petition, the Interstate Commerce Commission outlawed segregation in all trains and buses and terminals, requiring even the removal of those coercive signs seen widely in the South: "Waiting room for colored intrastate passengers." The order was effective November 1, 1961—in theory. It was in fact obeyed in most of the South. But the story was different in some rural areas and, especially, in Mississippi.

When freedom riders moved into Mississippi, their objective was the same: to test desegregation orders by passive resistance. And once again, in such towns as Jackson and McComb, they were met by violence.

On November 29th, five Negro students—three young men and two girls—arrived in McComb, "the Camelia City of America," just after the town's Main Street had been decorated with glittering tinsel and papier-mâché Christmas bells. They were met at the bus station by a mob of cursing whites, shouting "Kill 'em! Kill 'em!"

Claude Sitton of the *Times* described the scene:

> The weather was sunny but brisk as small knots of whites and Negroes gathered along the sidewalks of Canal Street near the pink stucco terminal. Youths in duck-tail haircuts and blue jeans crossed and recrossed the street from the terminal to the "City Billiard Parlor and Dominoes."
>
> No policeman was in sight when the five freedom riders arrived in a taxi and walked up to the glass-jalousied entrance of the white waiting room. An elderly white man in a gray felt hat and work-stained clothes blocked the way and sought to persuade them not to enter. But he stepped aside and the five filed into the joint waiting room and café, past the brightly lighted pinball machines and back to the lunch counter in the rear.
>
> Jerome Smith, twenty-two, the leader of the group, walked over to the ticket window and the four other Negroes took seats at the lunch counter. George Raymond, eighteen, asked twice in a firm voice for service. He was ignored.
>
> A. P. McGehee, operator of the bus terminal, walked behind the counter. Tapping his finger on the counter for emphasis, he told each of the Negroes: "Greyhound does not own this building; Greyhound does not own this restaurant. You get out of here."

At this point, a youth grabbed a half-filled cup of coffee from a table and walked rapidly down the line of stools at the counter. When he reached Raymond, he struck him sharply at the base of the skull with the cup and saucer, spilling coffee over the Negro's head and back.

Smith then waved to the four others to join him in a row of seats at the front of the waiting room. As they got up to move, a short, wiry white man of about thirty-five jumped at the Negro leader and began beating him with his fists. The Negro doubled over and ducked his head under a rain of blows to the back of the neck, the shoulder and the stomach. "I'll kill him! I'll kill him! I'll kill him!" yelled the white.

A dozen white youths and men in the small but angry crowd joined in pummeling the Negroes. They chased them around and over counters and tables in the waiting room of the terminal before kicking them out the door. The mob tossed one youth into the air again and again in the street outside, kicking and beating him as he struck the pavement.

Although the three youths and two girls were mauled severely, none was seriously injured. They fled to safety at a Negro hotel after escaping from their assailants in two taxis and a truck.

Sitton and other northern newspapermen were not safe themselves in McComb. That first day the mob apparently thought they were F.B.I. men and let them alone, but a few days later several northern reporters were beaten up. And the editor of the McComb *Enterprise-Journal,* John Oliver Emmerich, who was sixty-two years old and a heart patient, was smashed in the head by a man who accused him of being responsible "for those out-of-town newspapermen being here."

Federal forces were not sent to McComb because, in time, local officials decided to prevent violence and fight out the issue of segregation in the courts. They obtained from the local federal judge an injunction against any further demonstrations by C.O.R.E. That was eventually set aside by the U.S. Court of Appeals for the Fifth Circuit—but not until May, 1963.

Southern officials were beginning to discover that "law" could be used most effectively to hamstring demonstrators. Thus, in

1961, three hundred and five freedom riders were charged with "breach of the peace" when they tried to desegregate the bus terminal in Jackson, Mississippi. Three years later their cases were still on appeal, and they were still bearing the burden of appeal bonds.

It was "law," not violence, that was the effective weapon against demonstrators on the next big battleground—Albany, Georgia, in the summer of 1962. On August 15th, Hedrick Smith of the *Times* caught the mood of the city:

> The Negro porter locked the barbershop door and pulled the shade for the evening. A fly buzzed lazily toward the television set. "Soviets launch another space man, Congress discusses tax cut, and more news from Albany, Georgia," said a voice from the television set.
>
> "More news from Albany, Georgia," snorted an elderly barber snapping his scissors with irritation. "This town's been in the headlines too long already. When's this 'nigger business' going to stop?"
>
> At another chair, a hand fended off a razor and a lathered face spoke a quiet damn for the Rev. Dr. Martin Luther King, Jr., who has led a month of continuous racial protests here.
>
> The white citizens of Albany (pronounced al-BENN-y) ache for relief from the national attention focused on the city's racial problems. Some accuse the national press of overemphasizing their troubles. They have nicknamed the three national networks the Negro Broadcasting Company, Colored Broadcasting System and the Afro Broadcasting Company.
>
> "I'll tell you what makes me sick," said a gray-haired woman in an air-conditioned office. "It's the way those reporters line up and take that man's [King's] picture and ask him questions. They write down everything he says. It makes me sick."
>
> White concern finds its readiest outlet in the "People's Forum" of the daily newspaper, the Albany *Herald*. There is a daily drumbeat of letters berating the civil-rights movement, attempting to link it with Communists, or upbraiding Negroes for not being satisfied with their lot. Other writers praise Chief of Police Laurie Pritchett

and the City Commission for standing firm on segregation. Still others advise whites to discharge their Negro
maids and handymen. Occasionally there is a semi-liter-
ate letter from a Negro who voices the themes of the
Negro cause. An editorial footnote explains that the letter
is reprinted verbatim.

The editor of the Albany *Herald* is James Gray, an
articulate and outspoken segregationist, whom Albany
Negroes consider their principal enemy.

Albany is a town well peopled with transplanted
northerners who can out-southern the native southerners.
Gray, a native of Westfield, Massachusetts, and a graduate of Dartmouth College in 1937 (he still wears white
bucks), is the most prominent of these.

Albany is a city of considerable wealth and sophisti-
cation for its size (population: 57,000). Its streets and
sidewalks are wide and clean. Its economy centers on
two military installations and expanding textile, candy,
farm-implement and furniture industries. It is embel-
lished by surrounding pecan and peanut farms and the
plantations of wealthy corporation executives. It is a
community accustomed to social pleasures that are enjoyed discreetly. The city's eighty churches live in peaceful coexistence with wide-open gambling at night spots
and the bars of the town's hotels and motels. Both
gambling and the sale of mixed drinks are prohibited
under state law, but night spots in Albany and surrounding Dougherty County have found a way to live with the
law.

The explanation offered by a knowledgeable Albanian
is this: "It's all done in a high-class way. You don't see
any drunks roaming the streets or causing trouble. We
wouldn't stand for that. Albany is a moral town."

Similar discretion has been the hallmark of the city's
handling of racial demonstrations. Demonstrators are
arrested not for violating segregation ordinances but for
disorderly conduct or creating disturbances.

"The city says it doesn't enforce segregation," one
Negro leader said. "Actually, what it means is that it
doesn't invoke segregation."

James Forman, executive secretary of the Student

Non-violent Coordinating Committee, one afternoon took four young Negroes to a sit-in protest in a motel. He objected to the police about their arrest and walked away. Forman, a Negro, was about to drive off in his automobile when a police car pulled up beside him and an officer shouted: "Hey, Forman, the chief wants to see you."

The Negro leader approached and the patrolman, smiling, told him: "You're under arrest for contributing to the delinquency of a minor."

When Dr. King at one point went to jail for "parading without a permit," he was asked by the *New York Times Magazine* for a report on what was happening in Albany. He wrote, in part:

> A few weeks ago, I was convicted in the City Court of Albany, Georgia, for participating in a peaceful march protesting segregated conditions in that community. I decided, on the basis of conscience, not to pay the fine of $178 but to serve the jail sentence of forty-five days. Just as I was about to get adjusted to my new home, Reverend Ralph D. Abernathy and I were notified that some unknown donor had paid our fines and that we had to leave the jail. As the Atlanta *Constitution* suggested shortly after, we have now reached a new landmark in race relations. We have witnessed persons ejected from lunch counters during the sit-ins and thrown into jails during the freedom rides. But for the first time we witnessed persons being kicked *out* of jail.
>
> Victor Hugo once said that there is nothing more powerful in all the world than an idea whose time has come. Anyone sensitive to the present moods, morals and trends in our nation must know that the time for racial justice has come. The issue is not *whether* segregation and discrimination will be eliminated but *how* they will pass from the scene.
>
> During the past decade, some intelligent leaders in the South have recognized inevitability. Others, however, have tried vainly to stop the wind from blowing and the tides from flowing. These recalcitrant forces authored concepts like nullification and interposition, along with such uglier evils as bombings, mob violence and eco-

nomic reprisals. But the idea whose time had come moved on. Over the rubble left by the violence of mobsters, many communities resumed their normal activities on a new basis of partial integration.

These changes have been unevenly distributed and in some communities may be barely perceptible, yet enough has been accomplished to make the pattern of the future sharply clear. The illusions of the diehards have been shattered and, in most instances, they have made a hurried retreat from the reckless notions of ending public education and closing parks, lunch counters and other public facilities.

But in the tradition of old guards, who would die rather than surrender, a new and hastily constructed roadblock has appeared in the form of planned and institutionalized tokenism. Many areas of the South are retreating to a position where they will permit a handful of Negroes to attend all-white schools or allow the employment in lily-white factories of one Negro to a thousand whites. Thus, we have advanced in some places from all-out, unrestrained resistance to a sophisticated form of delaying tactics, embodied in tokenism. In a sense, this is one of the most difficult problems that the integration movement confronts. But I am confident that this stratagem will prove as fruitless as the earlier attempt to mobilize massive resistance to even a scintilla of change.

What of the future? Will it be marked by the same actions as in the past? This is not easy to answer with precision. Certainly there will still be resistance—but I am convinced the old South has gone, never to return. Many of the problems today are due to a futile attempt by the white South to maintain a system of human values that came into being under a feudalistic plantation system and that cannot survive in a democratic age.

If the South is to grow economically, it must continue to industrialize. Day after day, the South is receiving new, multimillion-dollar industries, and with the growth of urban society the folkways of white supremacy will gradually pass away. The arrival of industry will increase the purchasing power of the Negro, and with that will come improved medical care, greater educational opportunities and more adequate housing. And every such development will result in a further weakening of segregation.

Probably the most powerful force, however, in breaking down the barriers of segregation is the new determination of the Negro himself. For many years the Negro tacitly accepted them. He was often the victim of stagnant passivity and deadening complacency. While there were always lone voices in the Negro community crying out against segregation, conditions of fear and apathy made it difficult for them to develop into a mass chorus. But through the forces of history something happened to the Negro.

He has come to feel that he *is* somebody. And with this new sense of "somebodiness" and self-respect, a new Negro has emerged with a new determination to achieve freedom and human dignity whatever the cost may be.

This is the true meaning of the struggle that is taking place in the South today. One cannot understand the Montgomery bus boycott, the sit-ins and the Albany, Georgia, movement without understanding that there is a new Negro on the scene with a new sense of dignity and destiny. Thousands of Negroes have come to see that it is ultimately more honorable to suffer indignity than accept segregation in humiliation.

Fortunately, the Negro has been willing to use a creative and powerful force in his struggle for racial justice—namely non-violent resistance. This is not meant as a substitute for litigation and legislation, which must continue. But those who adhere to the method of non-violent, direct action recognize that legislation and court orders tend only to declare rights—they can never thoroughly deliver them.

Only when the people themselves begin to act are rights on paper given life blood. Life is breathed into a judicial decision by the persistent exercise of legal rights until they become usual and ordinary in human experience.

The method of non-violent resistance is effective in that it has a way of disarming opponents. It exposes their moral defenses, weakens their morale and at the same time works on their conscience. It makes it possible for the individual to struggle for moral ends through moral means.

One of the most persistent philosophical debates throughout the centuries has been over the question of ends and means. There have been those, like Machiavelli, who have argued that the end justifies the means. This, I feel, is one of the greatest tragedies of communism. Read Lenin as he says, "Lying, deceit and violence are justifiable means to bring about the aim of a classless society."

This is where the principle of non-violence breaks with communism and any other method which holds to the same belief. In a real sense, the means represent the ideal in the making—the end in process. So, in the long run, destructive means cannot bring about constructive ends because the ends are pre-existent in the means.

Non-violent resistance also provides a creative force through which men can channelize their discontent. It does not require that they abandon it, for this kind of discontent is sound and healthy. Non-violence simply saves it from degenerating into morbid bitterness and hatred. Hate is always tragic. It is as injurious to the hater as it is to the hated. It distorts the personality and scars the soul. Psychiatrists, believing that many of man's inner conflicts are rooted in hate, are now saying: "Love or perish." And this is the beauty of non-violence. It says you can struggle without hating; you can fight war without violence.

It is my great hope that as the Negro plunges deeper into the quest for freedom he will plunge even deeper into the philosophy of non-violence. As a race, Negroes must work passionately and unrelentingly for first-class citizenship—but they must never use second-class methods to gain it. They must never succumb to the temptation of using violence in the struggle.

I feel that this way of non-violence is vital because it is the only way to re-establish the broken community. It is the method which seeks to implement just law by appealing to the conscience of the great decent majority who through blindness, fear, pride or irrationality have allowed their consciences to sleep.

The non-violent resisters can summarize their message in the following simple terms: We will take direct action against injustice without waiting for other agencies to act. We will not obey unjust laws or submit to unjust practices. We will do this peacefully, openly, cheerfully—because our aim is to persuade. We adopt the means of non-violence because our end is a community at peace with itself. We will try to persuade with our words—but if our words fail we will try to persuade with our acts. We will always be willing to talk and seek fair compromise, but we are ready to suffer when necessary and even risk our lives to become witnesses to the truth as we see it.

So far, I have discussed only the problem as it exists in the South. But this is not to suggest that the problem is merely southern. No section of the country can boast of clean hands. Segregation may exist in the South in overt and glaring forms, but it exists in the North in hidden and subtle ways. Discrimination in housing and employment is often as bad in the North as it is anywhere. The racial issue confronting America is not a sectional issue but a national problem.

Nor must anyone assume that the problem is almost solved and that people can therefore sit complacently by the wayside and await the coming of the inevitable. Human progress is neither automatic nor inevitable. The Darwinian theory of evolution is valid in biology, but when a Herbert Spencer seeks to apply it to the whole of society there is little evidence to support it.

The most superficial look at history shows that no social advance rolls in on the wheels of inevitability. It comes through the tireless efforts and persistent work of dedicated individuals. Without this hard work, time itself becomes an ally of primitive forces and social stagnation. Unnecessary delays have already been suffered in the civil-rights struggle through a lack of vigorous action.

To outline the problem is to chart the course of the Negro freedom movement. A piece of freedom is no longer enough for human beings nor for the nation of

which Negroes are part. They have been given pieces—
but unlike bread, a slice of liberty does not finish hunger.
Freedom is like life. It cannot be had in installments.
Freedom is indivisible—we have it all, or we are not
free.

For all of its power, the non-violent direct action so per-
suasively expounded by Dr. King was not enough in Albany,
Georgia. The marchers marched, the jails were filled, and still a
Negro could not get a cup of coffee at a downtown lunch counter. The Negroes turned to the traditional weapon, the law. But
when they sued to challenge segregation statutes, the city council
repealed the ordinances; the police went on arresting, saying
they were just enforcing the wishes of private-property owners.
It was now up to the Supreme Court to say whether the Constitution permitted arrests in such circumstances.

Like any movement, the racial protest demonstrations eventually lost some of their momentum. The most committed
segregationists, as in Albany, devised new strategies to combat
them. As Dr. King had predicted, tokenism proved a difficult target. Whites who had made Atlanta, and Chapel Hill, North
Carolina, models of progressive race relations for the South were
deeply resentful when Negroes demonstrated there against the
vestiges of racism. Northerners lost some of their sympathy
when demonstrators appeared in their own communities and
pressed close to the secret racial citadels of the northern heart—
the all-white suburb, the nearly all-white school.

It is also true that the movement did not stay always in the
noble path laid out by Dr. King. New civil-rights groups that
arose by the score were more abrasive and less responsible.
Ends were sometimes confused: How could Manhattan's public
schools, with seventy-five per cent of the children Negro or
Puerto Rican, be perfectly "integrated"? And means were sometimes not up to Dr. King's elevated standard.

Cambridge, Maryland, marked an early corruption of the
protest movement. There Negroes used shotguns as well as pick-
ets. And there they had the vote—the instrument whose value
Dr. King so clearly saw—and refused to use it.

Cambridge is a town of fourteen thousand persons, a fourth
of them Negroes, on Maryland's Eastern Shore. The shore is on
the other side of Chesapeake Bay from the rest of Maryland,

isolated geographically until the construction of the Bay Bridge in 1952 and historically parochial and southern in outlook.

The Negroes in Cambridge wanted desegregation of restaurants, lunch counters, the town's only movie theatre, the public schools and the volunteer fire department.

Their tactics—and the bitter white response—led to events described by Hedrick Smith in a dispatch from Cambridge, July 12, 1963:

> Governor J. Millard Tawes sent 425 rifle-carrying National Guard troops into this racially explosive Eastern Shore town today. He acted after six whites had been hit by gunfire during wild violence last night.
>
> Brigadier General George M. Gelston of Baltimore, assistant state adjutant general and commander of the troops, invoked Maryland's modified martial law after the shootings. He imposed strict evening curfews, banned further racial demonstrations, prohibited the carrying of firearms and the sale of liquor, and decreed other stiff security measures. He announced his security decrees to Mrs. Gloria H. Richardson, chairman of the Cambridge Non-violent Action Committee, and other Negro leaders.
>
> After dark, in defiance of the curfew, about one hundred and fifty Negroes and a few whites marched down the center of the street from Bethel A.M.E. Church toward the downtown area singing freedom songs.
>
> General Gelston, accompanied by one other officer, marched up the street to meet them. As the General confronted the marchers, he raised his hands and they stopped. One of their leaders told them to sit on the ground. They sat for about fifteen minutes in the middle of the street, singing freedom songs and listening to a prayer. When the General finally asked them to disperse, the Negro leaders turned around and led their group away singing.
>
> The Guard troops then moved out in squads to take positions at the border of the Negro section of town. It was in this no-man's land that whites and Negroes have clashed repeatedly.
>
> The shooting came after a "freedom walk" staged by about two hundred and fifty Negroes to the Dorchester

County Courthouse, at about eight P. M. They were jeered and pelted with eggs by a crowd of about seven hundred whites. The State Police kept the two groups at bay for a while, then drove them apart with eight police dogs. After an hour's lull, the first gunshots were heard; and then law and order went to pieces for nearly three hours. Two white men and a twelve-year-old boy were hit by shotgun fire shortly after ten-fifteen P.M.

Two carloads of whites drove through the Negro section, exchanging gunfire with Negroes. Three cars, punctured by bullet holes, pulled up to the Greystone National Guard Armory in the ensuing two hours. From one stepped an off-duty National Guardsman in green fatigue uniform, with blood streaming down his face.

"We're hurt," he said. "Take us to a hospital."

The three Guardsmen had been hit by a gun blast that punched a hole through their windshield.

At about two A.M., as the city regained quiet and order, Major George E. Davidson of the State Police told newsmen there was "shooting all over the city—almost on the scale of warfare."

The leader of the Cambridge movement was a forty-one-year-old woman, Mrs. Gloria Richardson, whose family had been in Cambridge for generations. Her face mirrored deep distrust and bitterness. A profile in the *Times* said that during the city's racial troubles, as she assumed the leadership, she had been "transformed from a timid, stage-frightened agonizer over the plight of the Negro to an intransigeant militant, willing to flout friendship and the Federal Government to protest in the streets."

Attorney General Kennedy, in an effort to settle the Cambridge issues peacefully, called Mrs. Richardson and other principals in the dispute to Washington. For seventy-two hours he pleaded with her and with white officials to put aside suspicions and animosities. At length an agreement was announced: In return for an end to demonstrations, the demands for desegregation would be met. But there would be a public referendum on a local ordinance to outlaw segregation in places of public accommodation.

"Now we have an agreement on paper," the Attorney General said. "Whether it will be implemented, whether it will mean something for that city, its citizens and the country, is going to depend on the effort, the good judgment, the confidence, the faith of the Negroes and whites alike."

Mrs. Richardson did not meet Mr. Kennedy's test. She had agreed to the referendum, but shortly before it was held, on October 1st, she changed her mind and urged Negroes to boycott it. She said it was "wrong to put our constitutional rights to the vote of a white majority." But she was in error legally, for the Supreme Court had not established that there was a constitutional right to non-discriminatory service in private business establishments—far from it. And even if there was hope that the legal rule she sought might someday be established, would it not have been preferable for the town of Cambridge to face the issue itself, locally, and arrive at a just answer?

Only forty per cent of the registered Negroes voted in the referendum. The anti-segregation ordinance lost, 1,720 to 1,994.

Direct action failed to break down racial barriers in Albany, because it was up against men whose hearts were not ready to be moved. It failed in Cambridge because it was not true to its own ideals.

But the movement that began in Greensboro on February 1, 1960, was mostly one of success, not failure. In the year 1963 alone, by the Justice Department's reckoning, lunch counters were desegregated in more than three hundred cities, and hotels and theatres in almost as many, and all before the new federal Civil Rights Act wrote the immediate objectives of the sit-in movement into law. Nor is success to be measured only by such statistics.

The real significance of the protest movement was psychological. Most of all it was the image of those students, Negro and white, risking their education and their careers and even their physical safety for an ideal. The courage of the students, as Dr. King said, transformed the Negro's image of himself and gave him a new will to struggle for equal rights. And it opened the eyes of all white men but those who would not see to the reality of racial discrimination.

Chapter 7

The Role of the Federal Government

$\mathcal{S}$peaking in Newark, New Jersey, during the 1952 campaign, General Eisenhower said that "State by state, without the impossible handicap of federal compulsion, we can and must provide equal job opportunities for our citizens, regardless of their color, their creed or their national origin. Here is one sound approach: If I am elected . . . , I will confer with the governors of the forty-eight states . . . ."

Such talk was in the oldest of American political traditions. Fear of power in the central government had been an original reason for the nature of the American political system, the federal scheme, with much power retained in the states. Not even the tremendous centralizing impulses of the Civil War, two World Wars and the Great Depression had wiped out the American habit of viewing Washington with suspicion. Not even the widespread evidence of ineptitude and corruption in state governments had wholly dispelled the notion that there was something safer and sounder about them.

As a practical matter, however, reliance on the states was misplaced in the area of civil rights. It was the very states in which action was most needed—the southern states, where the Negro was held in a subservient economic, social and political status—that would not act. President Eisenhower could have conferred endlessly with governors about fair-employment-practices legislation (in fact he never did hold such a meeting), and no southern governor would have gone home and proposed a state F.E.P.C.

Politicians do not operate in a vacuum. The reason they pushed no vigorous program of federal action against racial discrimination until recently was that the voters were not, as a whole, demanding such a program. A poll of the North in 1952 would doubtless have shown general sympathy with civil-rights objectives. But the deep commitment needed to overcome southern resistance to change did not then exist.

As President, Dwight Eisenhower made it clear that his reluctance to commit his own or the Federal Government's authority to battle against discrimination reflected no mere expediency but a philosophy of government. Asked about a federal fair-employment-practices bill at a 1954 press conference, he said: "I have made my position clear many dozens of times. I believe there are certain things that are not best handled by punitive or compulsory federal law."

The same year he was asked about proposed legislation to eliminate racial segregation in interstate transportation. "I will take a look," he said, "because I am not sure. I would have to consult the Attorney General and see what he says about our authority there." That was a comment about the one area of national life, interstate commerce, where history most clearly established plenary federal authority. Moreover, the Supreme Court had held eight years earlier, in 1946, that racial segregation in interstate commerce was unconstitutional. Three months after that comment, President Eisenhower was asked again at a press conference about the bills against segregation in interstate transportation. "The Attorney General hasn't given me any opinion on the bills," he said. "I haven't seen them; I know nothing about them. I think my general views on the whole subject are well known, and you also know that I believe in progress accomplished through the intelligence of people and through the cooperation of people more than law, if we can get it that way."

There were two themes in those statements. One was a preference for state as opposed to federal action. The other was a grave doubt about the efficacy of law of any kind to bring about genuine improvement in race relations: "I don't believe you can change the hearts of men with laws or decisions."

President Eisenhower urged sympathetic understanding of the adjustment the South had to make after the School Segregation decision of 1954. "Now let us remember this one thing," he said in 1956, "and it is very important: The people who have this deep emotional reaction on the other side were not acting over these past three generations in defiance of law. They were acting in compliance with the law as interpreted by the Supreme Court of the United States under the decision of 1896." He referred to *Plessy v. Ferguson*, upholding the constitutionality of separate-but-equal facilities for Negroes. But in fact the South had been notoriously non-compliant with the equal aspect of that rule. For decades Negro education in the South had been almost entirely neglected.

"Let's never forget this," the President repeated on a later occasion. "From 1896 to 1954 the school pattern of the South was built up in what they thought was absolute accordance with the law, the Constitution of the United States, because that's what the decision was, that equal-but-separate ruling. As I have always believed, we have got to make certain reforms by education. No matter how much law we have, we have a job in education, in getting people to understand what are the issues here involved."

One of the most persistent criticisms of Eisenhower as President was that he did not follow that advice himself. He made no effort, from his most influential position, to educate. He rarely talked about the real "issues here involved"—the cruelty of one human being to another, the handicap of being born with a black skin, the damage done to the white soul in the process of subjugating the Negro.

During the campaign to end segregation of the buses in Montgomery, Alabama, when the leaders were prosecuted, the President was asked at a press conference how he felt "about Negroes being brought to trial for refusing to ride the Montgomery buses."

"Well, you are asking me, I think," President Eisenhower said, "to be more of a lawyer than I certainly am. But, as I understand it, there is a state law about boycotts, and it is under that kind of thing that these people are being brought to trial."

Despite his disclaimer of legal knowledge, he had given an essentially legalistic answer. He had said nothing about the real issue—the indignity of separating bus passengers by their color.

His refusal ever to say whether he thought the Supreme Court had been right in the School decision brought the heaviest criticism on President Eisenhower among civil-rights supporters. He explained later, in his reminiscences, that he really had approved but thought it inappropriate to comment. It was his consistent position; as he said in 1956: "I think it makes no difference whether or not I endorse it. The Constitution is as the Supreme Court interprets it; and I must conform to that and do my very best to see that it is carried out in this country."

The first Eisenhower Administration did have some notable pages in its civil-rights record. The most impressive achievement was in the District of Columbia. In 1952 the capital was a segregated city. Negroes could not eat in a downtown restaurant or even at a drugstore lunch counter; they were excluded from the major movie theatres and hotels; the school system was segregated. President Eisenhower ordered immediate action to desegregate the schools after the 1954 decision so that the District could be a model, and the change was made swiftly. Another Supreme Court decision ended segregation in eating places. Members of the White House staff persuaded theatres to end their color bar and used their influence to open jobs in Washington to Negroes.

The President also set up committees to work against employment discrimination in the Government and on the part of companies with Government contracts. The latter especially was a promising conception, although the committee never had the support from the top needed to make a real breakthrough in skilled jobs for Negroes. On other problems within the Federal Government quiet administrative action by Eisenhower aides was effective. The navy yards in Charleston, South Carolina, and Norfolk, Virginia, were desegregated, for example, and so were forty-seven veterans' hospitals.

But these areas of achievement were within direct federal authority, uncomplicated by any issue of federal-state relations. Where there was federal-state conflict, particularly on the question of school segregation, Presidential leadership was not asserted. A compelling example was the case of Autherine Lucy.

Miss Lucy, a Negro, was admitted to the University of Alabama under federal court order in February, 1956, and then removed by the university when rioting flared. The President's comment was as follows: "While there has been an outbreak that all of us deplore, when there is a defiance of law, still the chancellor and the trustees, the local authorities, the student body and all the rest of them have not yet had an opportunity, I should think, to settle this thing as it ought to be settled. I would certainly hope that we could avoid any interference with anybody as long as that state, from its governor on down, will do its best to straighten it out." The Alabama authorities straightened it out by permanently expelling Miss Lucy for making "outrageous" charges against them in her suit for reinstatement in the university. The Federal Government did nothing, although university officials had appealed to Attorney General Brownell for help; Miss Lucy eventually dropped the case. The University of Alabama was not desegregated until seven years later —and even then, Negro leaders said they still remembered as with burned fingers the Federal Government's inaction in the Lucy case.

President Eisenhower was not alone, politically, in 1956 in taking a hands-off attitude toward the developing school-integration crisis. At the conventions in 1956 neither party exactly embraced the Supreme Court's decision. The Republican platform said the party "accepts the decision." The Democrats said only that it had brought "consequences of vast importance"; an attempt to amend the plank, adding a pledge to help carry the decision out, was overwhelmingly defeated on the floor. Adlai Stevenson was asked at a meeting with a Negro group in Los Angeles early in 1956 whether he would use the armed forces, if necessary, to enforce the decision. He said: "I think that would be a great mistake. That is exactly what brought on the Civil War. It can't be done by troops, or bayonets. We must proceed gradually, not upsetting habits or traditions that are older than the Republic." President Eisenhower's answer was not much different when he was asked at a press conference on July 17, 1957, whether he would ever use troops to enforce a court integration order.

"I can't imagine any set of circumstances," Mr. Eisenhower said, "that would ever induce me to send federal troops . . . into any area to enforce the orders of a federal court, because I believe that common sense of America will never require it."

Two months and one week later the President sent federal troops to Little Rock, Arkansas, to enforce the school-desegregation order of a federal court. He acted, he could fairly have said, because the common sense of America had failed. A situation that neither he nor Adlai Stevenson had been willing to imagine —defiance of the Constitution and the courts by the governor of a state—had come to pass.

Governor Faubus's posting of National Guardsmen to prevent the admission of nine Negro children to Central High School in Little Rock occurred on the morning of a Presidential press conference. Mr. Eisenhower's reaction that morning was hardly resolute. After expressing again his belief "that you cannot change people's hearts merely by laws," he said that "there seems to have been a roadblock thrown in the way" of the court-approved plan for desegregation in Little Rock, "and the next decision will have to be by the lawyers and jurists." In fact, the next decision had to be by the President. Would he allow federal authority to be publicly and contemptuously overthrown?

There was much justified criticism of President Eisenhower for his first reaction to the defiance of law in Little Rock. He could have telephoned Governor Faubus that very morning and made clear that defiance would not be tolerated. He could have made a strong appeal at his press conference for obedience to law. He could have begun immediately to rally the southern business leaders who had such respect for him. Indeed, the criticism goes back farther, for Mr. Eisenhower's failure to speak out for compliance with the Supreme Court decision between 1954 and 1957 had left the moderates without leadership at a crucial time—and encouraged the Faubuses to think they could defy the courts.

But in the end, in the Little Rock crisis, President Eisenhower did decide to fight for the vindication of federal law. As he said in 1964, it was an inescapable decision for a President. In many ways it was the vital decision of the decade, for it so greatly enlarged the Federal Government's commitment to the revolution in race relations.

It is surely one of the great ironies of our time that a President who so deeply believed in the independence of the states, who was so genuinely reluctant to use federal power and who took so cautious and gradual an approach to racial change should have been responsible for this great act of federal intervention. But of course it was much more than an irony. Orval Faubus and the mobs in Little Rock aroused the American people as they had not been aroused before on the racial issue. New forces were released that changed the whole current of history in a way that no President would have found easy to resist. General Eisenhower did not resist. His own philosophical views were unchanged, but he understood and exercised the responsibility of the Presidency. He told the country when he sent in the troops:

"The very basis of our individual rights and freedoms rests upon the certainty that the President and the Executive Branch of Government will support and insure the carrying out of the decisions of the federal courts, even, when necessary, with all the means at the President's command. Unless the President did so, anarchy would result."

The first significant effect of the Little Rock affair was on the legal powers of the Federal Government. In the American legal tradition, constitutional litigation has been brought by private parties—such as the Negro parents who sued in Little Rock and elsewhere to have their children admitted to white schools. The Federal Government, it was thought, had no general power to enter into such lawsuits. Little Rock changed the pattern. There the Government acted to vindicate its special concern by entering the private lawsuit as an *amicus curiae*, a friend of the court. The judge, Ronald N. Davies, invited the Justice Department to come in, and the Eisenhower Administration always took the position that it entered this and later cases only on such judicial invitations. But in fact, at Little Rock, the Department privately asked to be invited by Judge Davies. As an *amicus* the Department did just about everything the actual party to a lawsuit does; it moved for an injunction against Governor Faubus, for example, to bar his further interference with school desegregation. There were respectable lawyers who thought our system did not permit such Government activity as an *amicus*, and in truth there were no precise precedents. But the law responds to felt needs. The challenge posed by Orval Faubus led to a major enlargement of the role played by the Federal Government in racial litigation.

The year 1957 saw another event of outstanding symbolic and practical significance for the enlargement of the federal role in race relations. This was the passage of the first Civil Rights Act to get through Congress since 1875. Once more there were ambiguities and fumblings in the part played by President Eisenhower, although his Administration must receive credit for the eventual breakthrough—along with the Democratic Majority Leader of the Senate, Lyndon B. Johnson.

The central provision in the 1957 act allowed the Justice Department to bring suits on behalf of Negroes denied the right to vote. When the bill was first proposed in 1956, the President did not ask for this authority, limiting the measure instead to the creation of a Civil Rights Commission and a new Civil Rights Division in the Justice Department. But Attorney General Herbert Brownell, Jr., who had been unable to get the voting title past the President, tried another route. He got a friendly congressman to ask him, Brownell, for a draft of a bill enlarging Justice Department power to sue. Then the Administration's division on the issue was concealed from public view until, during the 1956 campaign, the President came around and endorsed the expanded legislative proposal. (The story of Brownell's remarkable performance is told in a book by J. W. Anderson, *Eisenhower, Brownell and the Congress: the Tangled Origin of the Civil Rights Bill of 1956–57.*) In addition to the voting title, a murkily worded section of the bill, Part Three, sought general power for the Justice Department to sue in behalf of any civil right—including, although the backers did not exactly emphasize this, desegregated schools.

The bill passed the House and arrived in the Senate on June 20, 1957. There the Republicans used a novel parliamentary move to save it from death in the southern-dominated Judiciary Committee: They proposed to by-pass committee consideration and put the measure directly on the calendar. All the Democratic regulars opposed the move—among them Lyndon B. Johnson and John F. Kennedy—but enough all-out Democratic liberals joined the Republicans to carry the day, forty-five to thirty-nine. Much credit for the success of this crucial maneuver must go to the Republican leader, Senator William F. Knowland of California.

On July 2nd the southern leader, Senator Richard B. Russell of Georgia, made a major speech. He denounced the bill as "cunningly devised," saying that the Administration talked only of voting rights but that schools were the real target in Part Three.

"I doubt very much if the full implications of this bill have ever been explained to President Eisenhower," Senator Russell said. The next day it appeared that he was right. At a press conference a reporter noted Senator Russell's speech and asked the President whether he would be willing to limit the bill to voting rights. "Well," Mr. Eisenhower said, "I would not want to answer this in detail, because I was reading part of the bill this morning and I —there were certain phrases I didn't completely understand." This was taken as a reference to Part Three, and the President's statement that he did not understand his own bill doomed that provision. The Senate struck it out on July 24th, by a vote of fifty-two to thirty-eight.

There was much talk of filibuster, but in the end the Senate debated the bill only a month. The reason was Lyndon Johnson. He persuaded Senator Russell that the times demanded civil-rights legislation and that standing against a moderate bill devoted largely to the least arguable right of citizenship, the right to vote, could only be self-defeating. The Senate passed the bill on August 7th by a vote of seventy-two to eighteen, with Lyndon Johnson and four other southerners in the majority. It was this legislative episode, more than any other, that made Senator Johnson a national political figure and made possible his nomination for the Vice Presidency three years later.

In the last years of the Eisenhower Administration there were no events so dramatic as Little Rock or the 1957 Civil Rights Act. The Justice Department became increasingly involved in the school struggle. Herbert Brownell's successor as Attorney General, William P. Rogers, had Department lawyers watching each of the developing crisis points. He told the South in a 1958 speech that desegregation was "inevitable." When Governor Jimmie H. Davis of Louisiana followed the Faubus path and tried to block the admission of Negro children to New Orleans white schools in 1960, Mr. Rogers warned the Governor that he would "use the full powers of my office," and the Justice Department participated actively as an *amicus curiae* to have a whole barrage of new Louisiana laws held unconstitutional.

President Eisenhower, on the other hand, continued to sound the same themes of aloofness from the battle against racial injustice. In August, 1958, when the decisive test of Virginia's Massive Resistance program was at hand, he was asked whether he had any plans for speeches, conferences or other action to head off racial tensions in the new school year that would start the next month. He said he had none.

"I have consistently tried . . . ," the President said, "to show my belief that mere law will never solve this problem. I believe we have got to look inside ourselves. . . . I just say all of us have to work; and if I could think of anything I thought would be effective in August or in the two or three weeks before the schools start—why, I certainly shouldn't hesitate to do it."

That same month the President was asked about a report that he thought school integration should proceed more slowly. "It might have been," he replied, "that I said something about 'slower,' because I do say, as I did last week, we have got to have reason and sense and education. . . ." It is perhaps not surprising that the progress of desegregation slowed almost to a stop by the end of the Eisenhower years. Judges do not articulate all their reasons for deciding to order a beginning now on school desegregation in a difficult district—or school boards their reasons for starting voluntarily—but they are not insensitive to the mood of Washington. There was no sense of urgency in 1958, 1959, 1960, and the number of districts embarking on integrated schools each year fell to a mere handful.

The Justice Department used the new authority conferred by the 1957 Civil Rights Act in the voting field spottily, to put it most kindly. The Administration had a fair point in its claim that it wanted to begin with airtight cases, and it is also true that the Senate held up for six months the confirmation of the first head of the new Civil Rights Division, W. Wilson White. But Mr. White turned out to be one of the most feeble initiators in history of what was advertised as a bold new program. It was not until the last days of the Eisenhower Administration, when Harold R. Tyler, Jr., headed the Civil Rights Division, that any zeal began to be shown. The most imaginative use of the new statute was the successful litigation by the Department to prevent economic retaliation against Negro tenant farmers who voted for the first time in Haywood and Fayette counties in Tennessee. The shortcomings of those first years of enforcement are summarized by the fact that not a single voting suit was brought in the state where the most notorious discrimination existed, Mississippi.

The Eisenhower record ended, in 1960, with the passage of a second Civil Rights Act, which served mainly to plug loopholes in the 1957 statute. The Civil Rights Commission that had been created by the 1957 law inspired a provision for federal voting referees to register Negroes when local officials would not; but this idea, promising as it seemed, bore little fruit when it was tried in subsequent years.

The 1960 election campaign brought home, if nothing else had, how the issue of racial discrimination had been transformed from the matter of tepid righteousness it had been to most of the country just a few years before to a vital concern.

The Democrats and Republicans, who in 1956 had done their best to avoid a stand on the Supreme Court's School decision, now vied in enthusiasm. Both platforms endorsed federal aid to school districts beginning desegregation and legislation to let the Justice Department bring school suits. Both endorsed an executive order to end discrimination in federally assisted housing, and both called for new steps in the voting field. The Democrats were brave enough to use those fighting words, Fair Employment Practices Commission.

As the campaign developed, it appeared that Senator Kennedy was aiming more for the votes of Negroes and others concerned with civil rights, and Vice President Nixon more for the votes of white southerners. The Democratic candidate talked a lot about the role of the President. "He must exert the great moral and educational force of his office," Senator Kennedy said on September 9th in Los Angeles, "to help bring about equal access to public facilities—from churches to lunch counters—and to support the right of every American to stand up for his rights— even if that means sitting down for them. For only the President, the representative of all interests and all sections, can create the understanding and the tolerance which is necessary if we are to make an orderly transition to a completely free society. If the President does not himself wage the struggle for equal rights— if he stands above the battle—then the battle will inevitably be lost."

Nixon got into difficulty because of some statements in the South. He made no segregationist comments, and no one suggested that he held racist views. The charge was, rather, that he soft-pedaled civil rights while purporting to be bold on the issue. Thus in Jackson, Mississippi, on September 24th he told an audience: "I know that all of you are aware . . . of my deep convictions on this issue. . . . It would not be appropriate for me to come before an audience like this and talk one way in the South and another way in the North." But he never went on to say what his convictions were. He said only that the civil-rights issue was "complex" and was a problem for the North as well as the South.

One of the crucial events of the campaign was the affair of Dr. Martin Luther King. At the height of the campaign, on October 25, 1960, Dr. King was jailed by a Georgia judge. The ostensible reason was that he had violated probation, imposed earlier on a flimsy traffic charge, by engaging in a sit-in. Georgia was the heart of southern Democratic country, and the jailing seemed to present obvious opportunities for Vice President Nixon to embarrass the Democrats.

Mr. Nixon said nothing. Why he said nothing is one of the mysteries of American politics, still unresolved. The Justice Department, whose top officials were close to the Vice President, prepared a statement for President Eisenhower to issue on the King case. It said: "It seems to me fundamentally unjust that a man who has peacefully attempted to establish his right to equal treatment free from racial discrimination should be imprisoned on an unrelated charge, in itself insignificant. I have asked the Attorney General to take all proper steps to join with Dr. Martin Luther King in an appropriate application for his release."

The statement was never issued. Nixon evidently did not learn about it in the heat of the campaign. Whether it was vetoed by his advisers or by President Eisenhower or his staff is not known.

Senator Kennedy had a team that had been working on civil rights for him since the convention. It included his brother-in-law Sargent Shriver and a young man who had been at the Civil Rights Commission and was personally close to Dr. King and other Negro leaders, Harris L. Wofford, Jr. Mrs. King, who was expecting a child shortly, called Wofford when her husband was jailed. He tried to reassure her about Dr. King's safety and then thought about what Senator Kennedy could do to help. The idea of a telephone call to Mrs. King occurred to him, and he tried all one day to reach the candidate's party to suggest the idea—but without success. The next morning Wofford telephoned Shriver, who was at the Merchandise Mart in Chicago, and told him the idea. Shriver, who had been trying to think of what could be done, liked it. He drove out to a motel at O'Hare International Airport, where Senator Kennedy happened to be at that point, and urged the call. Others in the entourage were skeptical, but Shriver got the candidate alone in a room, dialed the number in Atlanta and put Senator Kennedy on the phone. Mrs. King later described the conversation as follows: "Senator Kennedy said he was very much concerned about both of us. This must be hard on me. He wanted me to know he was thinking about us and he would do all he could to help. I told him I appreciated it and hoped he would help." The Senator's campaign manager, his brother Robert, called the judge in the case and asked whether there was any reason Dr. King could not be released on bail. There was none, and he was bailed.

The import of these events was lost at the time to, among others, the editors of the *New York Times*. The Washington bureau of the *Times* learned of Senator Kennedy's telephone call to Mrs. King and wrote a substantial story. It was cut to three paragraphs. But after the election President Eisenhower expressed the view that the calls by John and Robert Kennedy—"a couple of phone calls," as he put it unhappily—had swung the Negro vote to the Democratic column. There was some reason for his view. In the last week of the campaign supporters of Senator Kennedy printed two million copies of a pamphlet on the King affair, headed *"No Comment" Nixon Versus a Candidate with a Heart, Senator Kennedy*. In Chicago alone two hundred and fifty thousand copies of the pamphlet were handed out in the last few days before election. Senator Kennedy carried Illinois by some eight thousand votes.

Whether because of the King episode or for broader reasons, Mr. Kennedy got a far larger percentage of the Negro vote than Adlai Stevenson had in 1956. In Nashville, Tennessee, President Eisenhower carried three Negro wards in 1956 by 3,258 to 2,861. They went for Mr. Kennedy in 1960 by 5,710 to 2,529. In the largely Negro Sixth Assembly District of Brooklyn, New York, the vote was 13,754 Democratic to 8,973 in 1956 and 22,777 to 5,808 in 1960. There were many other examples of larger Democratic pluralities in traditionally Democratic areas of the North, and of Democratic gains in southern cities where the racist views of local Democrats had been turning Negroes to the G.O.P. The shift may have been as helpful to Senator Kennedy in the South as in the North. He had more Negro votes in Texas and North and South Carolina than his slim margins of victory in each of those states; the same was true in Illinois, New Jersey and Michigan.

With John Kennedy as President, the pace of federal activity on civil rights rose sharply. In a dozen new ways the Government took a hand in the race-relations revolution that was now openly exploding. The responsibility fell mainly upon the President's brother Robert, the Attorney General, and his extraordinary assistant for civil rights, Burke Marshall, a quiet man whose devotion to equal rights is to intense that even his taciturnity seems to cry out against injustice. Half a decade earlier the Justice Department did not even have a Civil Rights Division. Now the racial problem was the Attorney General's first concern, the burden that never left him. He and Burke Marshall were on the telephone with southern governors and mayors and police chiefs and lawyers. Marshall toured the South when there was no crisis, talking quietly to leaders of opinion about the changes that were coming irresistibly. When tensions exploded into crisis, he would send someone down to advise, to mediate. There was the unforgettable scene of Marshall's first assistant, John Doar, walking between massed police and a crowd of young Negro marchers after Medgar Evers' funeral in Jackson, Mississippi, calming the angry Negroes, persuading them to drop the rocks that had started to fly. It was a role that a few years before no Justice Department lawyer could have dreamed of playing.

In the thousand days of the Kennedy Administration there was accelerating change in every aspect of race relations, and always with federal involvement.

In voting, the Justice Department moved for the first time into Mississippi, bringing nineteen suits there in three years. Even Sunflower County, the home of the Senate Judiciary Committee's powerful chairman, James Eastland, was not exempt. The Department brought successful contempt actions against a Mississippi registrar who evaded court orders, and it used novel tactics to protect would-be Negro voters from intimidation. In two broad suits it called for an end to the constitutional-interpretation tests given to voting applicants in Mississippi and Alabama. In the first three years of the 1957 Civil Rights Act, under the Eisenhower Administration, ten voting cases were filed; in the next three there were forty-five.

Transportation was an area of swift developments. In May, 1961, soon after the new Administration took office, violence met freedom riders who were trying to desegregate bus terminals. The Attorney General then asked the Interstate Commerce Commission for a sweeping order against bus and rail segregation, and the usually centipedal I.C.C. issued the regulations four months later. Segregation ended at all these terminals in the South except a few where surreptitious police tactics were combated by lawsuits. The Justice Department scrutinized the country's airports and found fifteen with segregated facilities. Thirteen desegregated voluntarily after approaches by federal officials, the other two after lawsuits were filed. Attorney General Kennedy could say in 1963: "Systematic segregation of Negroes in interstate transportation has disappeared."

Employment discrimination was the subject of President Kennedy's first executive order on civil rights. It combined the functions of the two Eisenhower committees on jobs in Government and with Government contractors in a new Committee on Equal Employment Opportunity that was given much broader powers. Government agencies were told directly that they must hire substantial numbers of Negroes, and an aggressive policy opened many more jobs with the large Government contractors. There was less progress in opening up the channels of apprentice training in discriminatory unions, an area where the Government's power was limited without new legislation.

An executive order prohibiting racial discrimination in federally assisted housing had been a major Kennedy pledge in the campaign, but it turned out to present more difficulties than the stroke of the Presidential pen described in campaign oratory. Delay in issuing the order brought much public criticism. Mr. Kennedy finally issued it on November 24, 1962. The order covered all housing receiving direct federal subsidies and the huge share of the market with mortgages guaranteed by the Federal Housing Administration. It was a sign of the swift rise of expectations that this coverage, which seemed so far-reaching to the Eisenhower Administration that it considered but declined to issue any housing order at all, was now criticized as too narrow. The contention was that the order should have reached out to a share of the housing market with a tenuous federal connection, mortgages by banks whose deposits were federally insured. But the immediate problem was really not coverage but enforcement of the order. As experience with state fair-housing laws showed, it was a long way from the declaration of the right to the actual opening up of the white suburbs to even a few Negro families.

On the school front, the Kennedy Administration abandoned

its predecessor's position that would enter litigation only at a judge's invitation to protect the integrity of a court order. Two months after taking office Robert Kennedy brought the Government into two Louisiana school cases as an *amicus* without any invitation and without any immediate threat of violence, to attack some new state statutes. He sought also to enter the litigation over Prince Edward County, Virginia, where all public schools had been closed since 1959 to avoid integration. Though the judge there refused to admit the Justice Department to the case, the Department expressed its views strongly in the Supreme Court, and in 1963 led the way to establishment of a temporary free school in the county. Most important in the school field was the unpublicized work of the Attorney General and Burke Marshall in easing the way for desegregation. Marshall and his aides toured the South, reasoning with local officials, and Kennedy used his political connections in the South. In ways not easily categorized the whole climate for school desegregation was made more favorable. After a steady decline since 1955 in the number of districts starting desegregation each fall, the graph turned upward again in 1961.

The following table shows the number of school districts that desegregated each year after the 1954 decision. The first three figures include any desegregation during the calendar year; after that the figure is for the number of newly desegregated districts as the school year opened in the fall of that year.

YEAR	DESEGREGATED SCHOOL DISTRICTS
1954	*150*
1955	*362*
1956	*200*
1957	*38*
1958	*13*
1959	*19*
1960	*17*
1961	*31*
1962	*46*
1963	*166*

Georgia, South Carolina, Alabama and Mississippi all had their first touch of integration during the Kennedy years. The critical school test was, of course, the admission of James Meredith to the University of Mississippi in the fall of 1962. The Federal Government had come a long way in the five years since Little Rock. Instead of being taken by surprise, its lawyers watched the case from the earliest moment. Long before the climax, the Justice Department had taken over, as a friend of the court, the actual management of the lawsuit. The Attorney General and even the President were on the telephone with Governor Barnett. The Deputy Attorney General, Nicholas deB. Katzenbach, was in charge of operations at the university. It turned out, tragically, to be a military operation. The Kennedy Administration, seeking to avoid any charge of using too much force too soon, used marshals instead of troops to escort Meredith onto the campus. But Governor Barnett's promises to maintain order were broken, and two men were dead before soldiers arrived to reinforce the marshals and put down the campus riot.

Finally, in the midst of these mushrooming developments, the Government became involved in the sit-in campaign that opened so many lunch counters and other places of public accommodation to Negroes in the South. The Justice Department had no general legal authority in this area, but it was drawn into many incidents in a mediator's role. The notable example was the violent outbreak in Birmingham in May, 1963, when pictures of police dogs turned on Negroes shocked the world. Burke Marshall went down to Birmingham, somehow got the leaders of the white community at least to listen to the Negro complaints and arranged the truce that eased an extremely dangerous situation and opened the way for gradual desegregation.

President Kennedy had made clear from his campaign onward that he intended to rely primarily on expanded executive action, not new civil-rights legislation. In 1962 the Administration did propose a bill to declare six grades of schooling proof of literacy for voting purposes, but there was neither sufficient political leadership nor demonstrated public support for it, and the measure died in a Senate filibuster. In February, 1963, the President proposed a mild bill to speed up the processes of voting cases and authorize federal aid for school districts beginning desegregation. (His message, in a last riposte to the Eisenhower era, called the 1954 decision "both legally and morally right.") But the forces at work on the country's race relations were moving too fast to be met by that legislation. The crisis that spring in the streets of Birmingham changed the thinking of the Kennedy Administration—and of the country. The moral issue was starkly defined in the use of dogs to keep men from demonstrating for the right to drink a cup of coffee next to human beings of another color. And Americans looked to the Federal Government for an answer.

It had really been Robert Kennedy, not his older brother, who had the deep emotional commitment to equal rights for the Negro. The President seemed to many to convey an air of detachment even as he dealt with such crises as the fighting in Oxford, Mississippi; his words were of law and order and rights in the abstract, not of the pain suffered by individuals because of their race. But now, in June, 1963, that changed, and the commitment of the Federal Government was etched deeper than it had ever been.

On the night of June 11, 1963, after the confrontation with Governor George Wallace over the admission of Negroes to the University of Alabama, President Kennedy spoke to the nation. Much of his televised speech was extemporaneous. His words could not have been more personal.

"If an American, because his skin is dark," the President said, "cannot eat lunch in a restaurant open to the public; if he cannot send his children to the best public school available; if he cannot vote for the public officials who represent him; if, in short, he cannot enjoy the full and free life which all of us want, then who among us would be content to have the color of his skin changed and stand in his place? . . .

"Are we to say to the world—and much more importantly, to each other—that this is the land of the free, except for the Negroes; that we have no second-class citizens, except Negroes; that we have no class or caste system, no ghettos, no master race, except with respect to Negroes? . . .

"We face, therefore, a moral crisis as a country and a people."

Eight days later, on June 19th, President Kennedy sent to Congress the most sweeping civil-rights legislation in history. The proposals were to outlaw exclusion of Negroes from hotels, restaurants, theatres and other places of public accommodation; to let the Justice Department bring suits for desegregation of schools; to prohibit discrimination in any state program receiving federal aid; to outlaw racial barriers in employment and labor union membership. They were proposals that even a few months

THE CIVIL RIGHTS BILL — FOUR KEY PROVISIONS

PUBLIC ACCOMMODATIONS: Discrimination in hotels and places of entertainment is forbidden.

States without laws against discrimination in public accommodations

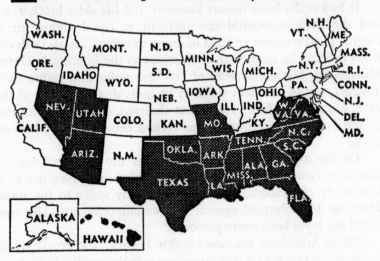

SCHOOL INTEGRATION: Attorney General is authorized to initiate suits on behalf of individuals.

Counties having both white and Negro school children but none attending the same schools

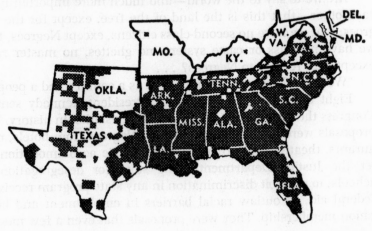

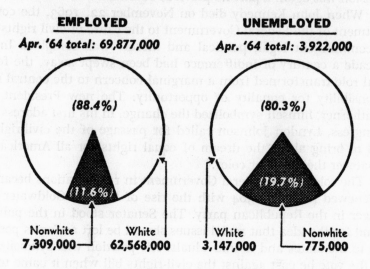

FAIR EMPLOYMENT: A Federal commission is to be set up to investigate discrimination in hiring.

EMPLOYED

Apr. '64 total: 69,877,000

(88.4%)

(11.6%)

Nonwhite
7,309,000 — White
62,568,000

UNEMPLOYED

Apr. '64 total: 3,922,000

(80.3%)

(19.7%)

White
3,147,000 — Nonwhite
775,000

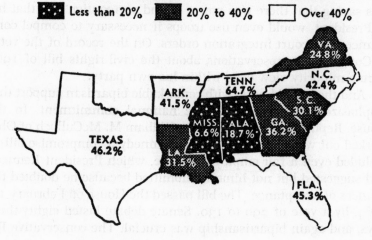

VOTER REGISTRATION: Tactics used by some in South to keep Negroes from voting are barred.

Percentage of Negroes of voting age who are registered

Less than 20%   20% to 40%   Over 40%

VA.
24.8%

TENN.
64.7%

N.C.
42.4%

ARK.
41.5%

S.C.
30.1%

MISS.
6.6%   ALA.
18.7%   GA.
36.2%

TEXAS
46.2%

LA.
31.5%

FLA.
45.3%

earlier would have seemed fantastic. There followed a series of White House meetings with leaders of business, labor and the professions, to encourage support of the legislation and of local efforts against racial discrimination. This personal effort at moral suasion was again a part no previous President had essayed.

When John Kennedy died on November 22, 1963, the commitment of the Federal Government to the cause of civil rights— a commitment legal, political and moral—was complete. In a decade a century of indifference had been swept away, the federal role transformed from a marginal concern to the central responsibility for equality of opportunity. The new President, a southerner, himself symbolized the change. In his first address to Congress, Lyndon Johnson called for passage of the civil-rights bill to bring alive "the dream of equal rights for all Americans whatever their race or color."

The role of the Federal Government in race relations became a renewed issue in 1964 with the rise of Senator Goldwater to power in the Republican party. The Senator stood in the public mind for the idea that racial issues should be left as far as possible to the states and to individuals. His position was symbolized by the vote he cast against the civil-rights bill when it came to a test in the Senate. But even Senator Goldwater, with his states' rights orientation, had moved a long way in his views. In 1960, in his book *Conscience of a Conservative*, he had said, with the southerners, that the Constitution gave the Supreme Court and the Federal Government no power at all to deal with racial discrimination in schools. But he changed that view and by 1964 was saying that there was power to end segregation and that he, as President, would even use troops if necessary to compel compliance with court integration orders. On the record of the votes in Congress, his reservations about the civil-rights bill of 1964 were a minority view even within his own party.

And the bill did pass, with remarkable bipartisan support that emphasized the breadth of the national commitment. In the House, Republican Representative William M. McCulloch of Ohio worked out with Attorney General Kennedy a compromise bill; it included even a fair-employment title, which President Kennedy had suggested but not himself submitted because he doubted the chances of acceptance. The bill passed the House on February 10, 1964, by a vote of 290 to 130. Senate debate lasted eighty-three days, and again bipartisanship was crucial. The conservative Republican votes needed for the required two-thirds margin to close debate were provided by the efforts of the minority leader, Senator Everett McKinley Dirksen of Illinois. On June 10th the Senate invoked cloture for the first time in its history in a civil-rights debate; the vote was seventy-one to twenty-nine. The bill passed the Senate, seventy-three to twenty-seven, on June 19th. That was exactly a year from the day President Kennedy had proposed the legislation, saying it should be enacted "not merely for reasons of economic efficiency, world diplomacy and domestic tranquillity— but above all because it is right."

President Lyndon B. Johnson signed the bill into law on July 2, 1964.

Chapter 8

The Right to Vote

In July, 1961, John Hardy, a Negro college student in Nashville, Tennessee, went down to Walthall County in southern Mississippi to help Negroes there register as voters. Walthall County had 4,400 white and 2,500 Negro residents of voting age. Virtually every white was on the voting rolls, but not a single Negro. Hardy set up a voters' school, instructing Negroes how to fill out the application form and how to interpret the long and complicated constitution of Mississippi to the satisfaction of the Walthall County regisrar, John Q. Wood.

On September 7, 1961, Hardy accompanied two Negro residents of the county, Mrs. Edith S. Peters and Lucius Wilson, down to Wood's office in Tylertown. Hardy waited outside while the two applicants went in. Wood flatly refused to let them apply, saying only: "You all have got me in court." Hearing this, Hardy walked in and introduced himself politely. But he was not able to say much more than his name.

Registrar Wood pulled a gun out of a desk drawer and ordered Hardy to leave. As Hardy turned around and started to walk out, Wood hit him on the back of the head with the gun, swore at him and told him never to come back. Mrs. Peters and Wilson, who had watched the whole episode, helped Hardy out of the courthouse. His head was bleeding profusely, and he was staggering. After resting for a few minutes, Hardy found the county sheriff, Edd Craft, and told him what had happened. Craft arrested Hardy for breach of the peace. When Hardy tried to talk some more about it, Craft threatened to beat him within an inch of his life and locked him up in jail.

Hardy was scheduled for trial on the breach-of-the-peace charge September 22nd. Two days before then, the Federal Government brought an independent suit in the Federal District Court to enjoin the prosecution. This was an extraordinary proceeding, but the Government said the circumstances were extraordinary. The false charge against Hardy, it said, was designed to frighten Negroes out of trying to register; the suit sought an injunction against this and any other tactics of intimidation.

In court the next day neither Wood nor other Walthall County officials disputed the facts presented by Justice Department lawyers. But District Judge William Harold Cox declined to issue a temporary restraining order against the prosecution of Hardy. He relied on the traditional doctrine that federal courts will not interfere with state criminal proceedings, that defendants must go on up through the state courts and seek review eventually in the United States Supreme Court.

Judge Cox also refused to certify the case for an immediate appeal, and he would not stay the prosecution of Hardy temporarily to allow time for an appeal. But the Government lawyers did not give up. They went to Judge Richard T. Rives of the United States Court of Appeals for the Fifth Circuit and asked for a stay pending appeal, and at this point the county officials agreed to put off Hardy's trial until the issue was settled. On October 27, 1961, after hearing the appeal, the Fifth Circuit reversed Judge Cox and ordered him to issue a restraining order against the prosecution. The opinion, by Judge Rives, said: "It can really not be expected that Negroes who have lived all their lives under the white-supremacy conditions which exist in that area of Mississippi will continue their efforts to register and otherwise to exercise their rights and privileges of citizenship if, in addition to being threatened and beaten, they will also be prosecuted in state court with all that such a prosecution entails."

The story of John Hardy and Walthall County, Mississippi, indicates the terrible obstacles that must be overcome to win the franchise for the Negro in the deepest South: intransigeant registrars unashamed of the least subtle tactics to keep Negroes from voting, a corrupt and brutal local law-enforcement process, federal trial judges who themselves reflect local prejudice, or at least are unwilling to break with traditions of deference to the states. But the story does not reflect only these difficulties of the voting struggle. It also points up the encouraging factors—the determination of the Negro to vote in the face of a resistance that would terrify most men, and the commitment of the United States Government to help him.

To a foreigner studying American history the most surprising thing about the struggle for the right to vote must be the fact that it is still going on. The question would seem to have been settled in 1870 by the Fifteenth Amendment, in language that could hardly have been simpler or more comprehensive: "The right of citizens of the United States to vote shall not be denied or abridged by the United States or by any State on account of race, color, or previous condition of servitude."

But the southern counter-revolution that deprived the freed Negroes of their rights in the last years of the nineteenth century found ways to escape that seemingly all-embracing amendment. First came the requirement that voters pay a poll tax, a major barrier to the impoverished Negroes. Over the years the racial impact of the poll tax waned, and in the five states that retained it—Alabama, Arkansas, Mississippi, Texas and Virginia—its effect was as great on poor whites. On January 23, 1964, the Twenty-fourth Amendment to the Constitution outlawed the poll tax in elections where federal officials are chosen.

Mississippi, which pioneered the poll tax, also invented another device—the requirement that a would-be voter be able to understand and interpret the state constitution. The effect was to give a registrar just about unlimited discretion to pass or fail any applicant. Negroes failed. Then there was the "grandfather clause," which allowed anyone to vote without tests if he or a forebear had voted in 1866 or earlier, but subjected everyone else —which meant all Negroes—to rigorous educational tests.

The purpose of these measures was not only to prevent Negroes from voting in the future; it was to purge from the rolls Negroes who had been playing an active part in the political process since the Civil War. It was, in short, a cold-blooded effort to restore white supremacy, to keep the Negro from all influence in society. The fact that Negroes did freely vote in the South for decades after the Civil War is too often forgotten. As late as the turn of the century, after years of white efforts to purge the rolls, nine per cent of Mississippi's voting-age Negroes could still vote. Today, after years of effort by the Federal Government to restore the rights suppressed then, only five per cent of Mississippi's Negroes are registered.

It was not long before the Supreme Court pierced the veil of "qualifications" in the various southern registration schemes and found racism. In 1915 it struck down as a violation of the Fifteenth Amendment Oklahoma's grandfather clause. Oklahoma then passed a law declaring that all who had voted in 1914 would remain eligible for the ballot in the future, while all others would have to register in a special twelve-day period, between April 30 and May 11, 1916. It took until 1939 for this statute to come before the Supreme Court, which found it invalid as an attempt to perpetuate the grandfather clause by other means. Justice Frankfurter, writing for the Court, said the Fifteenth Amendment "nullifies sophisticated as well as simple-minded modes of discrimination."

There was one more legal string to the southern bow, the white primary. On the theory that primaries were private party affairs, not official elections covered by the Constitution, Negroes were forbidden by state statutes to vote in primaries—which in the South are the meaningful elections. In 1927 the Supreme Court, in an opinion by Justice Holmes, held the Texas white-primary statute unconstitutional. In 1932 the Texas Democratic Convention, without benefit of any state law, voted to exclude Negroes from all party affairs, and the Supreme Court for the moment found this approach sufficiently ingenious; a 1935 decision said Negroes were now excluded from the Texas Democratic primary by a purely private action, not by the state, and so the Constitution did not apply. But nine years later, in 1944, the Supreme Court took another and more realistic look at the Texas primary. It found that in Texas the Democratic primary was a vital part of the whole official election process and that the state hence could not escape responsibility for racial discrimination in the primary's conduct. The Court overruled its 1935 decision. The white primary was now, finally, unlawful.

But law and fact are often strangers in southern race relations. The fact was that many years after the Supreme Court held the white primary unlawful, Negroes still could not vote in large areas of the South. In dozens of counties where Negroes were in the majority, none or at most only a handful were registered.

The white supremacists who kept Negroes from voting did so by methods so crude, so inhuman, so patently unlawful that they can only be called cynical. Hitting John Hardy on the head with a gun is one example. The Government's suit to end voting discrimination in Walthall County brought out others. One technique was simply not to let Negroes apply. Some who went to the Walthall registrar's office were told to "go home and study the constitution." Once three were informed that the registration books were "closed" for four months before the election; when they came back after the election, they were told they could not register then because no election was coming up.

When Negroes were allowed to apply in Walthall County, the applications were found incorrect for one reason or another—most often for "failure" on the constitutional-interpretation test. Negroes were all given difficult, lengthy sections of the Mississippi constitution to explain—sections on eminent domain, suspension of habeas corpus, disqualification of judges for consanguinity. In any case, it was entirely within the registrar's discretion to say whether an applicant had explained satisfactorily, and he always decided that the Negroes had not. This included Negro applicants with college degrees. But at the same time whites were registered who could not write their own names. The registrars gave white applicants simple sections of the constitution to interpret, and wrote the answers for them if help was needed. Every white applicant "passed" the test.

In George County, Mississippi, a white voter named John Cecil McMillan was given a simple section of the state constitution to interpret, one usually given to white applicants: "There shall be no imprisonment for debt." He wrote: "I thank that a Neorger should have 2 years in collage before voting because he don't under stand."

McMillan passed and was registered. His case is reminiscent of the Louisiana white voter who challenged a Negro registration form for what he called "error in spilling."

Southern registrars did not have to resort to constitutional-interpretation tests. Very often they rejected Negro applicants for some trivial error, such as giving their age in years instead of the exact number of years, months and days, or filling in the blank for "race" with the word "Negro" instead of "black"—or vice versa. Or Negroes would be told that they had failed but not why —it was "against the rules" to disclose the "error." In Alabama some counties used a voucher system, in which no one could register unless someone already registered "vouched" for him; since there were no or almost no Negroes on the books, that took care of that. If all else failed, there were threats. A Negro army sergeant, who got his discharge, went home to LeFlore County, Mississippi, and went down to the courthourse to register, was told by the clerk that he would have to leave his name and address because she was too busy; half an hour later two white men came by his house and told him to stop stirring up trouble. Elsewhere Negroes who tried to register lost their jobs or their credit or could not get their cotton ginned.

By the mid-1950's, a decade after the white primary became theoretically illegal, it was evident that the Negro would never win the ballot in parts of the South unless he got some help from outside. The combination of existing white supremacy, political and social, and of utter ruthlessness in denying the most basic rights, made the Negro helpless in the backward rural areas of many states and in the resistant cities and towns of Mississippi, Alabama and northern Louisiana. As on other issues, effective help could come only from the Federal Government. The way was opened for federal intervention by the Civil Rights Act of 1957, which for the first time authorized the Justice Department to bring suits against voting discrimination.

By 1957 there were no southern senators who stood up and said right out that citizens should be denied the right to vote because of their color. The filibusters instead made pro forma arguments about states' rights, and in the end they allowed the voting bill to pass without a real fight. That might have suggested that the new law would be easy to enforce, that the South as a whole was now ready to comply with the Fifteenth Amendment. But anyone who had such an expectation was disappointed, for the years since 1957 have seen dogged, resourceful resistance to the law by perhaps one hundred southern counties.

Macon County, Alabama, provides a case history of intransigeance. The county is in south central Alabama, just east of Montgomery, and it is one where fear of letting Negroes exercise the rights of citizenship is not unexpected. The reason is the population ratio—4,405 white persons, according to the 1960 census, and 22,287 Negroes.

In modern times the white minority of less than twenty per cent had held absolute dominion by the simple tactic of not letting Negroes vote. In 1958, when the Federal Government first began concerning itself with conditions in Macon County, virtually every white man and woman of voting age in the county was registered. Only about one thousand of the twelve thousand potentially eligible Negroes were on the rolls, and their registration had come to a stop.

Negroes had not failed for lack of qualifications. Macon County is the seat of the renowned Tuskegee Institute and thus has an unusual number of highly educated Negro professionals. Through the Tuskegee Civil Association they made unrelenting efforts to win voting rights. The whites stood them off by using what Judge John R. Brown of the Fifth Circuit Court of Appeals called "an unsophisticated, patent double standard."

Everything was made easy for white persons applying to register. They were assisted with their forms, given no literacy tests, approved despite glaring errors. Negroes, on the other hand, were made to take lengthy written tests and then flunked because of trivial errors, or for no stated reason at all. Each new registrant had to have a registered voter vouch for him, and the registrars adopted an alleged rule that no one could vouch for more than two new voters a year—alleged, because the board allowed white persons to vouch for three applicants in a single day. The board of registrars met most of the time in rural areas where Negroes were afraid to appear and did not try to register. It engaged in a slowdown, taking hours or days to handle a single application. It put Negroes on a "waiting list" and then put new white applicants at the head of the list.

In October, 1958, the Civil Rights Commission began looking into the Macon County voting picture. Its request for a look at registration records was rejected. The Commission then went to Federal District Judge Frank M. Johnson, Jr., and he ordered the records produced. Rather than comply, the registrars resigned. When the Commission held a hearing in Alabama, the registrars of Macon and other counties refused to testify.

On February 9, 1959, the Justice Department filed suit to end what it termed systematic denial of the vote to Macon County Negroes over "many years." It was only the second case brought under the 1957 act. On March 6th Judge Johnson dismissed the case, on the ground that the registrars' resignation left no one to sue. He rejected the Department's contention that it could bring the case directly against the State of Alabama. That decision was upheld by the Fifth Circuit. The Justice Department pressed on to the Supreme Court, but before a decision was reached Congress solved the problem of the resigning registrars in the Civil Rights Act of 1960.

The 1960 statute was designed in part to prevent southern officials from destroying voting records, as some Alabama registrars had attempted to do; the act required preservation of records and assured the Justice Department access to them. It did two other things directly relevant to the Macon County situation: It explicitly allowed the Department to bring voting suits against a state; and in the absence or non-feasance of registrars it permitted the appointment of federal referees who could register voters.

On May 6, 1960, the very day the new statute became law, Governor John Patterson of Alabama appointed a registration board for Macon County, its first in eighteen months. The object was to forestall the appointment of federal referees. The new board steadfastly maintained the bars against Negroes.

But the law finally did work in Macon County. On March 17, 1961, Judge Johnson entered a sweeping decree requiring the registrars to end their discriminatory tests, meet regularly and handle Negro applications expeditiously. He ordered the immediate registration of fifty-four named Negroes; and he saw to it that his orders were obeyed. The following September the registrars resigned again. Judge Johnson said he would name referees if the state did not replace them at once. It did. In succeeding years Judge Johnson continued to demand, and to scrutinize, regular reports from the registrars, and to warn them whenever any sign of dilatory tactics appeared.

The Macon County episode demonstrated that a determined Federal Government could prevail, finally, with the help of a dedicated federal judge, against the maneuvers of resourceful white officials. But what if the federal judge in a locality is governed not by his oath of office but by local attitudes? What if he joins in the game of evading the law?

On August 11, 1960, the Justice Department made a demand under the 1960 act to inspect the voting records of Bolivar

County, Mississippi. The local registrar, Mrs. Walter Lewis, declined to make the records available. On January 11, 1961, the Government sued to see them. The case was brought before Federal District Judge Claude F. Clayton. For six months nothing happened. On July 26, 1961, Mrs. Lewis filed several motions, some of them attacking the constitutionality of the 1960 law and one demanding more definite statements from the Justice Department. On November 28, 1961, Judge Clayton granted the latter in part, requiring the Department to furnish full details of any racial discrimination by Mrs. Lewis on which the demand for the voting records was based. Since the Justice Department was merely investigating—seeking the records to find out whether there had been any discrimination—it felt it could not comply with this order and petitioned for reconsideration.

Judge Clayton did nothing. The Government then decided to go to the Fifth Circuit Court of Appeals for an order directing Judge Clayton to act on the case. At this point he set a hearing, and after it ended, on July 19, 1962, the judge set aside his order for a more definite statement. Mrs. Lewis now renewed her constitutional claims. On November 16, 1962, Judge Clayton rejected those and ordered her to produce her records—but only those relating to the eligibility of anyone eligible to vote in 1960. Since this limitation obstructed the whole point of the inquiry— to find out why Negroes had been found ineligible—the Government went to the Fifth Circuit again. On December 6, 1963, the appeal was decided in the Government's favor; Judge Clayton was ordered to make Mrs. Lewis produce all relevant records. She sought a rehearing and then petitioned the Supreme Court for review. On May 18, 1964, it declined to hear the case.

Thus nearly four years were consumed in the Bolivar County case over what should have been a simple, preliminary step— inspecting the voting records. If the Justice Department found in the records the discrimination it suspected, it would have to bring a new suit to make Mrs. Lewis comply with the Constitution and laws. And the case would again be before Judge Clayton.

The experience under the 1957 act has shown that the most persevering Federal Government effort, even though it finally overcomes legal booby traps, cannot actually add large numbers of Negroes to the voting rolls unless another ingredient is present. That is a will in the local Negro community to obtain the franchise.

"Apathy" among southern Negroes was much discussed in the years just after 1957 as a reason for the low rate of Negro registration. Certainly Negroes in many rural areas were afraid. Certainly others had been so degraded by decades of virtual serfdom that the ballot was a far-off, abstract concept. Certainly the schools provided for Negroes were so inferior in many places that ignorance abounded. But despite these legacies of white supremacy, Negroes did want to vote. Given some hope, they displayed the most amazing determination and courage. Claude Sitton of the *Times* gave an example in a story filed from Canton, Mississippi, on February 29, 1964:

> A drama symbolic of the Negro's fight for voting rights is unfolding here beneath the magnolias on the lawn of the Madison County Courthouse. Yesterday and again today long lines of Negroes, some wrinkled and bent with age, waited patiently before the white-columned entrance of the century-old brick building for their turn to apply for registration. Some were afraid that this challenge to white political supremacy might cost them their jobs, or worse. All knew it would likely prove futile.
>
> Only one Negro applicant at a time is permitted in the registrar's office. Of the more than two hundred and sixty who waited outside Friday and the more than fifty there Saturday, only seven finally got inside to take the test. Those seven must have sensed the futility anew as they passed through the office door of L. F. Campbell, the circuit clerk and voter registrar. On its glass window is a red, blue and gray sticker bearing a Confederate battle flag and the message, "Support Your Citizens Council," a militantly segregationist organization.
>
> Outside in a chill wind, the waiting Negroes stood stiffly on the concrete walkways or along the black, wrought-iron fence that was set in place one hundred and six years ago when the courthouse was built. A sheriff's deputy in a black leather jacket, black slacks and black western boots paced up and down the lines, an automatic carbine swinging in his left hand and a wooden club dangling from his belt. A bone-handled revolver rode loosely in a holster on his left hip.
>
> Now and then the Negroes were joined by others who had walked there by two's, seven and a half blocks from

pleasant green Holiness Church, staging area for this Freedom Day sponsored by the Congress of Racial Equality in cooperation with the National Association for the Advancement of Colored People and the Student Non-violent Coordinating Committee.

Police auxiliaries in blue helmets and makeshift uniforms mounted a shotgun guard along the route. Sheriffs and deputies from Madison and surrounding counties, wearing ten-gallon hats and driving white cars with as many as three radio antennae, patrolled the streets. City policemen armed with nightsticks, revolvers, and a variety of shotguns and rifles snapped orders at the Negroes as they shepherded them through a crosswalk to the court-house grounds. Occasionally, law-enforcement officers clustered in the entrance spoke derisively to prospective applicants whom they knew.

State and local officials in plain clothes photographed Negroes, newsmen, agents of the Federal Bureau of Investigation, observers from the National Council of Churches and, sometimes, other plainclothesmen. Spotters with field glasses watched over the activity from second-floor windows. The State Highway Patrol manned a police radio network set up in a command post in the court-house.

At one time, Madison's Negro residents—now seventy-two per cent of its population of 32,904 persons—were among its most prized assets. But industrialization and agricultural mechanization have all but eliminated the need for their labor. Most whites say they would like to see the Negroes leave.

In keeping with the custom of most rural Deep South counties in which Negroes outnumber whites, politics here is viewed as "white folks' business" by most. A leading white citizen of Canton said that despite the proposed voting legislation there would be no marked increase in Negro participation "until Bobby [Robert F.] Kennedy comes down here with some federal marshals." As many as four hundred and seventy-five Negroes were once on the voting rolls. But this high point was followed quickly by the defeat of the registrar who put them there.

Because of the refusal of county officials to release

information, the latest statistics available are those filed by the Justice Department in a voting suit against the state and six other counties. These show that one hundred and twenty-one Negroes, or 1.1 per cent of those in Madison County of voting age, were registered in 1962. The corresponding figure and percentage for whites that year was 5,458 and 97 per cent.

What can happen when the Negro demand for political rights makes a breakthrough was described by Wilma Dykeman and James Stokely in the *Times Magazine* on September 24, 1961. Their focus was on Memphis and two adjoining rural counties in western Tennessee—Haywood and Fayette. Memphis, a fast-growing city, had some tradition of Negro voting despite the Deep South atmosphere. But the neighboring counties were characteristic Black Belt areas, geographically near Mississippi and reminiscent, the authors said, "of the hot, brooding, rural landscape of Faulkner."

The population of Fayette County is 68.9 per cent Negro, and that of Haywood County 61.3 per cent Negro. In Haywood County, until August, 1960, no Negro had ever voted since Reconstruction days. In Fayette, the Justice Department says, only seventeen Negroes voted between 1952 and 1959. This is consistent with many other southern counties where Negroes have been almost totally barred from voting.

The attitude fostering this situation was expressed by one white man in Fayette County who said: "Sure I reckon it's all right for a nigger to vote if he wants to and it don't harm nothing, but what if they all begun to vote here! We'd be swamped. You put *yourself* in *our* place and you'll see why we got to keep *them* in *their* place."

His statement is quite typical and—in sharp contrast to many of the arguments about school desegregation—reflects less moral conviction about Negro disenfranchisement than the practical consideration of being outnumbered at the polls.

The Rev. June Dowdy, pastor of two churches in Fayette County, told a reporter that when he went to register in Somerville he was sent from one place to another and in general given the run-around. "Finally, I asked one white man where the registration office was and he directed me to go down to Hatchie Bottom. That's the swamp along the Hatchie River, where a Negro was lynched back about 1940 after he tried to vote."

In the spring of 1959, the Fayette County Civic and Welfare League was formed under the leadership of a Memphis lawyer, J. F. Estes, who organized a similar group in Haywood later that summer.

"Before that, fear hung over the Negroes there," Estes, a large, smiling, oratorical man, said, "and farming and religion was their life. To think of politics—or even buy a new car or dress too well—was to cross the Hindenburg line. But we began to preach that fear was un-Christian. 'Fear prevents you from becoming a good citizen of this country, and it will prevent you from becoming a citizen of God's country,' we said.

"Then I took a murder case in Fayette County, and for the first time folks there heard a Negro lawyer asking prospective white jurors if they believed Negroes should vote—and some of them answering yes. This helped ease some of their fear. After the trial, we formed our Civic Leagues—we knew better than to use the word "vote" in our titles, of course—and Negroes began to register.

"After a little while, whites began to sit up and take notice and then they began their tactics of registering one Negro every hour or so, while the others waited out in the hot sun; or the election commission would resign, and it might take months to set up a whole new commission.

"By the winter of 1959-60, Negro landowners who had registered to vote began to be refused crop loans for the coming season. Now, down here, that advance is the difference between life and death as a farmer. With outside help, we managed to tide them over, but then, in the spring and summer of 1960, Negro tenants began to register, too, and as soon as the cotton and corn and other crops were harvested that fall, white landlords began throwing them off their farms.

"Some of the landlords said it was because they were mechanizing and didn't need tenant help any more. But we know their purpose was to depopulate the counties."

He smiled, but resumed quickly: "Of course, mechanization on the farms is a big problem here and in many other rural counties, but it's not common sense that all at once these landlords could do without all those very tenants who showed any intention of voting."

Small Negro merchants, like John McFerren and Scott Franklin, were hit early and hard, when local wholesalers refused to deliver them goods, especially gasoline, or to extend credit.

There were more farm evictions and "Tent City" sprang up—thirteen tents in an open field, housing, at the peak of use, some one hundred people. Some families have been living there since last December.

The tents became a symbol, in the nation's eyes, of Deep South resistance to Negro voting, and Negro persistence in the art of economic and political survival. Aid from a wide variety of sources poured into the area. "Negroes there shed some of their hopelessness," one Negro leader says, "and the Government in Washington backed them up in their determination to be free and full participants in democracy." A federal injunction forbade local officials to block Negro registrations. And, as a result of federal intervention, Fayette and Haywood landlords were instructed that they could not evict tenants without proving in court that the eviction was not an attempt to interfere with the Negroes' voting rights.

The results of the campaign are already noticeable. In last November's election, an estimated eight hundred Negroes voted in Haywood County. Between 1959 and the end of 1960, some nine hundred to one thousand registered and voted in Fayette.

The pattern of events in Memphis was forecast in a 1959 report by the Southern Regional Council, which stated: "The next big breakthrough in the field of suffrage may well be revitalization of the existing Negro vote in the South." This revitalization is an important part of what Negro leaders in Memphis are at present seeking to accomplish. They have approximately seven hundred volunteers under ninety-four ward and precinct captains shepherding new voters through the registration process. But, in addition, they are searching out ways to demonstrate and keep flexible the potential of power already in their grasp.

"Those boys are smart and plenty tough," one white

politician admits. "They're not taking any more white palaver about fair principles. They're strictly on a quid pro quo basis. They don't have the votes to elect a candidate yet, but they sure can defeat one. And they know it—and we've learned it!"

"Recent contests here in Memphis have created some 'election return liberals,'" Dr. Hollis Price, Negro president of LeMoyne College, says quietly. And Frank Kilpatrick, checking over workers' kits in the hustling downtown headquarters of the registration drive, points out, "Since our last election, forty-three Negroes have been appointed to political jobs in Memphis—mostly by men who ran as segregationists before they counted up the precinct returns."

The outstanding Negro figure in the city's politics today is a young lawyer, Russell Sugarmon. A slim, bespectacled Harvard graduate, he might be dubbed an Ivy League frontiersman in the new South.

Two years ago, he ran for the important office of Commissioner of Public Works and made such an excellent showing that, as he later explained, "We won everything but the election." Recent appointments of Negroes to the Memphis Transit Authority, the Traffic Advisory Commission, the office of tax collection, as deputy sheriffs, and in other political posts, have given him—and Negro voters—some of the spoils of victory. When asked what the Negro vote in Memphis needs today, Sugarmon confidently replies, "A few more elections." Then he refers to the carefully indexed, impressive ward-and-precinct organization being built up in the city. The mood is one of deep, hard-hitting excitement and commitment to victory.

"That music you hear on Beale Street ain't the blues any longer," the proprietor of a small Negro business says. "It's the ring of cash registers and voting machines growing louder."

Dykeman and Stokely concluded that effective Negro leadership at the local level made all the difference in the effort to obtain leverage in the political system. But there are areas where white supremacy is so total that local Negroes cannot put together a real registration campaign. In such counties—and they are the heart of the voting problem in the South—federal officials soon recognized the need for Negro leadership from outside. There had to be an organized effort throughout the South, with some central headquarters supplying manpower and funds for the areas gripped by fear.

To interest the national Negro organizations in such a campaign was more difficult than might be expected. The Attorney General at the end of the Eisenhower Administration, William P. Rogers, could not persuade the various groups to tackle the voting problem on a broad new scale. The Kennedy Administration ran into the same problem. Its civil-rights chief, Assistant Attorney General Burke Marshall, said later that when the President and Attorney General "urged Negro leaders to concentrate on voting, they were at first met with suspicion. It was as if they were asking Negro leaders to divert their energies, and those of their organizations, into channels which would require as little change and movement as possible."

But eventually even the most militant civil-rights groups began to understand that a registration campaign, though less dramatic than sit-ins, might be more important in the long run. Members of the organizations, many of them students, began to set up registration schools in remote, medieval counties of Mississippi and Louisiana and Alabama and Georgia. They often were met by a white reaction that would have frightened older persons away, but still they persisted. And the local Negroes took courage from them.

Claude Sitton of the *Times* painted a typical scene in a classic story filed from Sasser, Georgia, on July 26, 1962:

> "We want our colored people to go on living like they have for the last hundred years," said Sheriff Z. T. Mathews of Terrell County. Then he turned and glanced disapprovingly at the thirty-eight Negroes and two whites gathered in the Mount Olive Baptist Church for a voter-registration rally. "I tell you, cap'n, we're a little fed up with this registration business," he went on.
>
> As the seventy-year-old peace officer spoke, his nephew and chief deputy, M. E. Mathews, swaggered back and forth fingering a hand-tooled black leather cartridge belt and a .38-caliber revolver. Another deputy, R. M. Dunaway, slapped a five-cell flashlight against his left palm again and again. The three officers took turns badgering

the participants and warning of what "disturbed white citizens" might do if this and other rallies continued.

Sheriff Fred D. Chappell of adjacent Sumter County, other law-enforcement officials and a number of the disturbed white citizens clustered at the back of the sanctuary. Outside in the black night, angry voices drowned out the singing of the crickets as men milled around the cars parked in front of the little church on the eastern edge of this hamlet in southwestern Georgia.

On the wall was an "All-American Calendar" advertising a local funeral home. It displayed pictures of President Kennedy and past Presidents.

The concern of Sheriff Zeke Mathews, "twenty years in office without opposition," is perhaps understandable. Terrell County has 8,209 Negro residents and only 4,533 whites. While 2,894 of the whites are registered to vote, only fifty-one Negroes are on the rolls, according to the Secretary of State's office.

On September 13, 1960, Federal District Judge William A. Bootle handed down the first decision under the Civil Rights Acts of 1957 and 1960. The judge enjoined the Terrell County Board of Voter Registrars from making distinctions on the basis of race or color, illegally denying Negroes their rights under state and federal laws, and administering different qualification tests for the two races. Judge Bootle refused a request from the Justice Department that he appoint a voter referee to oversee the registration; but he retained jurisdiction in case further court directives might become necessary.

Nevertheless, Negroes contended that because of fear and intimidation, subtle and not so subtle harassment and delaying tactics, they still found it difficult to register.

Field secretaries for the Student Non-violent Coordinating Committee, an Atlanta-based civil-rights organization, began a voter-registration drive in the county last October. Two workers of the student committee active in Terrell County were present as the meeting opened with a hymn, "Pass Me Not, Oh Gentle Saviour." They are Charles Sherrod, twenty-five, from Petersburg, Virginia, a Negro, who took part in the sit-in demonstrations in 1960 against lunch-counter segregation, and Ralph

Allen, twenty-two, a white student at Trinity College, from Melrose, Massachusetts. Some of the participants said they had driven here from adjoining Lee and Daugherty counties to encourage others by their presence. Among them were two other workers in the student committee, Miss Penelope Patch, eighteen, of Englewood, New Jersey, a white student at Swarthmore College, and Joseph Charles Jones, twenty-four, a Negro from Charlotte, North Carolina.

After the hymn, Mr. Sherrod, standing at the pine pulpit on the rostrum, led the Lord's Prayer. The audience repeated each line after him. Overhead, swarms of gnats circled the three light globes and now and then one of the audience would look up from the pine floor to steal a fearful glance at the door.

Mr. Sherrod then read from the Scriptures, pausing after completing a passage to say: "I'm going to read it again, for they're standing on the outside."

The sound of voices around the automobiles parked beside the church could be heard as license numbers were called out. And the faces of the audience stiffened with fear. A group of thirteen law officers and roughly dressed whites clumped through the door at this point. One pointed his arm at three newspaper reporters sitting at the front and said: "There they are."

"If God be for us, who can be against us," read Mr. Sherrod. "We are counted as sheep for the slaughter."

With the exception of Deputy Dunaway, who stood smoking a cigarette at the rear, the whites withdrew to confer among themselves.

Mr. Sherrod began another prayer. "Give us the wisdom to try to understand this world. Oh, Lord God, we've been abused so long; we've been down so long; oh, Lord, all we want is for our white brothers to understand that in Thy sight we are all equal. We're praying for the courage to withstand the brutality of our brethren."

And, in this county where Negroes have frequently fallen under the club, the blackjack and the bullet, no one appeared to doubt that the brutality of which he spoke would be long in coming.

Nevertheless, the audience swung into a hymn with

gusto, singing "We Are Climbing Jacob's Ladder." The
deputy in the doorway swung his flashlight against his
palm and looked on through narrowed eyes. Lucius Holloway, Terrell County chairman of the voter-registration
drive stood up. "Everybody is welcome," he said. "This is
a voter-registration meeting."

Sheriff Mathews, trailed by Deputy Dunaway, burst
into the sanctuary and strode to the front. Standing before
the reporters, but looking away from them, he began
to address the audience. "I have the greatest respect for
any religious organization but my people is getting disturbed about these secret meetings," he said. "I don't
think there is any colored people down here who are
afraid. After last night the people are disturbed. They
had a lot of violence in Albany last night."

The sheriff and chief deputy introduced themselves
to the reporters and shook hands. Negroes had said they
had been warned that the rally would be broken up, but
the law officers seemed taken aback by the presence of the
newsmen.

Sheriff Mathews then turned to the Negroes, saying
that none of them was dissatisfied with life in the county.
He asked all from Terrell to stand.

"Are any of you disturbed?"

The reply was a muffled "Yes."

"Can you vote if you are qualified?"

"No."

"Do you need people to come down and tell you what
to do?"

"Yes."

"Haven't you been getting along well for a hundred
years?"

"No."

The sheriff then said he could not control the local
whites and that he wanted to prevent violence. "Terrell
County has had too much publicity," he said. "We're not
looking for violence."

Chief Deputy Mathews then expressed his viewpoint.
"There's not a nigger in Terrell County who wants to
make application to vote who has to have someone from

Massachusetts or Ohio or New York to come down here and carry them up there to vote," he said.

The sheriff turned to Ralph Allen. "Ralph," he said, "I'm going to have to ask you to stay out of this county until this thing quiets off. I don't appreciate outside agitators coming in here and stirring up trouble and it's causing us a lot of trouble. I've helped more colored people than any man in the South, I reckon. Would you mind telling me who pays you?" he asked Mr. Allen.

The student replied that he received a subsistence allowance from the committee.

"They give you your orders?"

"They place me."

The chief deputy took over the questioning.

"Then you got Terrell County—that's your project, huh?"

A long exchange of forceful questions followed. After that, Deputy Mathews turned to the others and told them: "There is a prohibit to register between now and December."

Under Georgia law, registration goes on throughout the year, although only those registered at various specified times prior to the primaries and elections may vote in them.

Sheriff Mathews then pointed to the crowd of whites at the back of the sanctuary.

"Gentlemen," he said to the reporters, "those are all of them. The people have lost faith and respect in the coordinating bunch. They don't have to have it, cap'n. They don't have to have it."

Deputy Mathews informed the Negroes that it would not be "to your interest" to continue the meeting.

"You don't have to have nobody from Massachusetts to come down here and help you find the way to the courthouse," he said.

In another reference to Mr. Allen, he commented: "I don't think he's got any business down here, to tell you the damn truth."

Deputy Mathews turned to Deputy Dunaway and ordered him to take the names of all those present.

"I just want to find out how many here in Terrell

County are dissatisfied," explained Sheriff Matthews.

Turning to a local Negro and pointing at Mr. Allen, the chief deputy then said: "He's going to be gone in two weeks, but you'll still be here."

As the names were collected, Deputy Mathews began pressing questions on Mr. Sherrod and interrupting him sarcastically as the Negro tried to reply.

He turned to Mr. Allen again. Shaking a finger in his face, he said: "You couldn't get a white person to walk down the street with you."

When Deputy Dunaway asked the names of five Negro youths sitting on a bench with Miss Patch, they refused to give them.

"I wouldn't either," said Deputy Mathews.

As the sheriff walked away, he said to reporters: "Some of these niggers down here would just as soon vote for Castro and Khrushchev."

The Negroes began humming a song of protest popularized during the sit-in demonstrations, "We Shall Overcome." And as the law officers withdrew to the outside, the song swelled to a crescendo.

The business meeting then got under way. Miss Patch reported on her work in Lee County. Mr. Allen told of having been knocked down twice last Saturday, beaten and threatened with death by white men in Dawson, the county seat. Charles Jones asked Mr. Holloway if anything had been heard from the Justice Department regarding an investigation into the dismissal of a Negro teacher.

"No," replied the chairman.

Shortly after ten o'clock, the Negroes rose and joined hands in a circle. Swaying in rhythm, they again sang, "We Shall Overcome." Their voices had a strident note as though they were building up their courage to go out into the night, where the whites waited.

Lucius Holloway prayed. "Our concern is not to destroy," he said. "Our concern is not to displace or to fight, but to build a community in which all our children can live and grow up in dignity."

The Negroes then filed out the front door past the group of law officers. "I know you," said one officer to a Negro. "We're going to get some of you."

Flashlight beams slashed through the darkness to spotlight the face of Miss Patch as the white student climbed into an automobile with some Negroes from Lee County. The whites standing by cursed but made no move toward the car. Miss Patch and her companion pulled out behind the station wagon in which the newsmen were riding. But the air had been let out of the right front tire of the wagon, forcing it to stop close to the church. The other car stopped, too.

Carloads of whites roared past again and again while the tire was being changed. A deputy stopped and said with mock solicitude, "Help you, cap'n?" He drove away grinning.

Sitton, after his years of covering the southern racial situation, was not an optimist. He doubted that the slow judicial process relied on by the Civil Rights Acts of 1957 and 1960—and 1964—could register significant numbers of Negroes in the resistant areas. Burke Marshall conceded, in a lecture at Columbia University in 1964, that the Government had apparently not succeeded in seven years "in making the right to vote real for Negroes in Mississippi, large parts of Alabama and Louisiana, and some counties in Georgia, South Carolina and Tennessee." Certainly the figures from Mississippi were discouraging. The Justice Department since the Kennedy Administration took office had filed more than a dozen voting suits there, and still fewer than five per cent of the voting-age Negroes were registered.

And yet history was not without hope in the voting field. In Macon County, Alabama, the determination of the Justice Department and of Judge Johnson had made a difference in the real world. In 1964 the number of Negroes registered passed the number of whites. In the Democratic primary on May 5th, four Negroes ran for county offices—and all were elected. John Herbers of the *Times*, reporting from Tuskegee on May 20th, said the Negroes were refraining from trying to seize political control. "Instead," he wrote, "they appear to be attempting to use their new power for the general welfare of the county's twenty-six thousand citizens and thus to dispel the fear that has haunted whites since Reconstruction. Moreover, there are indications that, in the long run, the large Negro vote may improve race relations by eliminating extremists from office and establishing communication between whites and Negroes."

Nor is litigation necessary in every case. Sometimes officials will recognize the Constitution and federal law when their duty is pressed home to them. Something like that seems to have happened in Baker County, Georgia, not far from Terrell County and its Sheriff Mathews. After a visit to Baker County in 1960, Claude Sitton concluded that substantial Negro voting could not happen there. Three years later he returned. In the *Times* of July 10, 1963, he wrote:

> One of the most significant advances in voting rights for the southern Negroes is taking place in this Black Belt community of southwest Georgia. Not one Negro was registered two years ago in Baker County, although Negroes made up two-thirds of its 4,543 residents. Today, 300 are among the 1,860 persons on the voting roll.
>
> Negro leaders interviewed here this week predict confidently that one thousand others will be registered by the end of this year. This, coupled with planned action to purge the lists of five hundred whites who have died or moved away, could give the Negroes a majority. These leaders and white officials attributed the change to the Kennedy Administration policy of pressure and persuasion carried out here by Jerome Heilbron, a Justice Department lawyer from Washington, and to a registration campaign conducted by local Negroes.
>
> There were some tense moments during the registration of the Negroes and their participation in a nonsegregated local election. On one occasion a white official found it necessary to eject another from the courthouse. But in a county where politics, even on a uni-racial basis, has sometimes been of the cut-and-shoot variety, the results are considered astonishing by local observers.
>
> This gently rolling stretch of piney woods, swamps of moss-draped gum and cypress, pastureland and fields for corn and peanuts lies twenty-five miles from both the Alabama and Florida state lines. Its residents are rich or poor, with few in between. Much of the county is divided among large plantations, some owned by wealthy northerners. It is famous for its quail hunting, and former President Dwight D. Eisenhower occasionally sampled the shooting here. Some small farmers prosper but others find it difficult to scratch a livelihood from the

sandy clay. Although a number of Negroes own farms, most work as hands on the plantations.

Negroes told a visitor here three years ago that no matter what the Federal Government did to give them the franchise they would still be hesitant to vote because of the economic and physical retaliation that might follow.

"I don't want my throat cut," one man explained.

"It doesn't make any difference what Congress and the Supreme Court say the law is," a white overseer asserted. "It won't make a damn in Baker County, not during this generation."

Paul Phipps, a Negro carpenter whose wife teaches school here, said then that they both wanted to register but would not make the attempt. "I don't want my job cut off and my wife's job cut off," he explained.

Despite these obstacles, some Negroes continued to press for the ballot. Among them was J. A. (Josh) Williams, an eighty-three-year-old farmer who was virtually blind. "I believe somebody is going to have to die to get my rights," he said. "We're not going to get anywhere by being afraid. These white folks wouldn't treat us like they do if we had the right to vote."

Mr. Williams died without seeing his wish fulfilled. Lee Hilson Hall, a fifty-two-year-old farmer, took his place as leader of the county's Negroes. But Mr. Hall met with no more success than had Mr. Williams until Mr. Heilbron arrived at the courthouse in September, 1961, to confront the three voter registrars who had taken office three months before. The Justice Department aide, who was born in Fort Smith, Arkansas, brought with him a complaint setting forth the Government's case against the county's registration practices.

W. E. Rooks, the chief registrar, recalled this week that the legal document was signed and ready for filing in the Federal District Court. Mr. Heilbron discussed the situation with Mr. Rooks and the other registrars, Luther Timmons and Byron Tabb. He told them that he had seen Negroes paying taxes; and that, under the American system, those who pay taxes and were otherwise qualified, were entitled to vote. The registrars agreed.

"We really had no choice," said one.

"They're sincere, honest men, who wanted to do the right thing," Mr. Heilbron said.

"He didn't have to show us that suit, but he did," commented Mr. Tabb. "He didn't tell us what to do; he showed us."

The other registrars also praised the Justice Department official. "We were well pleased with his cooperation," Mr. Rooks said.

The first Negroes registered were accepted by the registrars December 1, 1961. Among them were Mr. and Mrs. Phipps and a son and daughter of the late Josh Williams.

Mr. Hall, with the assistance of his brother, W. M. Hall, Jr., began encouraging others to apply for registration. The whites showed some hostility initially, he said. "I started out and they 'looked' a little," he recalled. "But Mr. Heilbron gave us that good strength and they backed up just as nice as you please."

The Hall family, which owns a five-hundred-acre farm and a country store, encountered no serious trouble. Its members and some of their kinsmen are among the county's most respected citizens.

Neither of the brothers favors participation in the registration drive by any civil-rights organization. "I don't think it would be a proper idea to interfere as long as you're doing well, because Baker County has been lifted up," Lee Hilson Hall said.

Race relations in the county have already improved generally as the result of the Negroes registration and participation in a recent County Commissioners' election, according to him. They accounted for almost one-third of the ballots cast. However, he said other changes were needed. "We're going to put some colored commissioners in after this term," he asserted. Although three Negroes are listed on the current trial jury venire, "they get the dumbest ones they can find," the leader contended, and then challenge them and thus prevent them from serving.

Mr. Hall implied that Washington's interest in the Baker County situation had been the chief factor in the

Percent Negro population by states: ☐ Less than 20%   ▨ 30% to 39%
▥ 20% to 29%   ▓ 40% and over

Percentage of Negroes of voting age who are registered [00%]
Where Negroes have staged protests since Feb.1 ●

VA. [19%]
Greensboro
High Point
Winston-Salem
Richmond
Hampton
Newport News
Suffolk
Norfolk
Portsmouth
Elizabeth City
Nashville ●
TENN. [59%]
Chattanooga
Concord
Charlotte
Raleigh
Henderson
N. C. [25%]
ARK. [30%]
Rockhill
Columbia
Durham
Fayetteville
ALA. [14%]
Orangeburg
Birmingham
Tuskegee
GA. [22%]
Denmark
S. C. [11%]
TEXAS [32%]
MISS. [4%]
Montgomery
LA. [22%]
Tallahassee
Daytona Beach
Deland
Tampa
St. Petersburg
Sarasota
FLA. [26%]

The figures are for 1960, just before the intensive registration efforts of
Negro organizations and of the Kennedy Administration began. For figures
four years later see the map at the end of Chapter 7.

progress made here. "When our Government says it's time,
then it must be time," he declared.

Perhaps most significant was that the Negro groups did
finally agree to make the franchise a top objective and to work
together on the problem. In 1963 all of the leading organizations
joined in the Voter Education Project. There was substantial
financing from private philanthropic sources. The Justice Department followed the work closely, and the momentum carried
on through the 1964 registration period. The result was no revolution, especially not in Mississippi. There were irresponsible
students in some places, and in others the white resistance proved
too strong. But over-all the figures undeniably showed progress.

There are about five million Negroes of voting age in the
South. As late as 1961 only about twenty-five per cent, 1,250,000,
were registered. By the middle of 1964 the leaders of the Voter
Education Project were able to say that two million could now
vote—forty per cent of the potential. Statistically, it was even
more important that Negro voters in the South amounted to nearly

fifteen per cent of total registration. Negroes are not a majority in any southern state, but it does not take a majority for a group to have influence—if it can vote. Attorney General Kennedy has said that when any group gets up to a figure of twenty per cent of total registration, "politicians listen."

Only a foolish optimist would believe that the vote will answer all problems of racial discrimination in the South. Racial inequities go on in areas where there have been no voting barriers for years. But at least officials are likely to listen. In Georgia, where the most dramatic increases in Negro registration have come, they are listening hard. When twenty per cent of the voters who elect the county sheriff are Negroes, old-fashioned brutality tends to disappear. And though it is no panacea, the right to vote is crucial for one reason above all: It gives the Negro the sense of being part of American society; it offers people who are increasingly less content with unequal treatment the hope for change within the system. Burke Marshall warned that what happened in any Mississippi county mattered to all of us: "The domestic tranquillity is at stake, for the Negro cause against discrimination is indivisible. When Negroes are excluded from participation in their government in even one county and state authority is twisted to make it happen while federal authority appears powerless to take effective steps, the gulf between Negroes and whites everywhere is widened, and the chances of racial conflict increased. At the least, the generation of students that sees this take place are to some extent losing faith in their government, with consequences for the future that cannot be foreseen."

Chapter 9

Two Cities: New Orleans and Atlanta

The setting was familiar—a Senate committee hearing room in Washington. And the testimony was familiar—a plea for national legislation to eliminate segregation. "A hundred years ago," the witness said, "we made every American free in theory. Now the challenge is to make every American free in fact."

What was out of the ordinary was that the witness was not a northerner, not a Negro, not a leader of a civil-rights organization. He was the Mayor of Atlanta, capital city of Georgia, "Empire State of the South." He had journeyed to Washington in July, 1963, to plead for immediate passage of a public-accommodations law. Without it, he warned, "cities like Atlanta might slip backwards. Hotels and restaurants that have already taken this issue upon themselves and opened their doors might find it convenient to go back to the old status." And if that were to happen, he predicted, one result might well be "the old turmoil of riots, strife, demonstrations and picketing."

The speaker was Ivan Allen, Jr., elected to office in 1961. One might point out—indeed, he did so himself—that integration in

Atlanta was less than complete. "For example," said Mayor Allen
in his statement before the Senate Commerce Committee, "one of
Atlanta's top-flight restaurants served only sixteen out of Atlanta's two hundred thousand Negro citizens during the first
week of freedom from discrimination." Only six months after the
Mayor's testimony Negroes were picketing in Atlanta against
token desegregation, and hooded Ku Klux Klansmen brawled in
the streets with Negro students staging sit-ins.

But Mayor Allen's testimony was no less remarkable for all
that. His hearers were impressed by his courage and saw in his
words a hope of ultimate racial peace. "I am humbled in your
presence," Senator John Pastore of Rhode Island said to the
witness.

Atlanta, the city that Sherman set in flames in 1864 when he
began his march to the sea, became the largest city of the Southeast after World War II, a center of commerce, a gleaming and
thriving industrial community that for a variety of social and
pocketbook reasons wanted to be known as a "city too busy to
hate." The reason that Atlanta came to symbolize enlightened
southern adjustment to racial change can be summed up in one
word: leadership. Atlanta had responsible newspapers, the *Journal* and *Constitution*, with a sensitive editor who was so often the
South's conscience, Ralph McGill. For a generation, from 1937 to
1961, the city had a progressive Mayor—William B. Hartsfield—
who was not afraid to fight the reactionary powers of rural
Georgia. Atlanta had a responsible Negro community, economically the best off in the South. None of these elements made
change come easily or overnight to Atlanta. But Negroes and
whites could and did talk. There was a process for adjustment of
differences.

Part of Atlanta's wisdom may have come from seeing what
had happened in other places where there was no moderate leadership, no courage, no dialogue between white and black, no
process to encourage change without violence. An especially
painful example was provided by New Orleans, a cosmopolitan
and international city that might have seemed as likely as Atlanta to accept the demands of the mid-twentieth century in race
relations. The difference was leadership: In New Orleans the
great white middle group, the moderates, stood silent. There was
no effective political resistance to the backward, racist forces of
rural Louisiana. Even within New Orleans the segregationist Citi-

zens Councils and other strident voices of white supremacy were allowed to dominate. The city's newspapers, the *Times-Picayune* and *States-Item*, were, like Atlanta's, under a single ownership; but instead of leading their readers into the modern world, as Ralph McGill did in Atlanta, the New Orleans papers were the kind to banner a story on the capture of a Negro purse-snatcher and repeatedly refer to him not by name but as "the Negro."

The moment of reckoning for New Orleans came in 1960, when desegregation of public schools began. It began only after years of indecision, maneuver, and evasion, involving not only the public but the parochial schools in the heavily Roman Catholic city. In February of 1956 Archbishop Joseph Francis Rummel had prepared a pastoral letter to be read at all masses in the New Orleans archdiocese. "Racial segregation," the letter said, "is morally wrong and sinful." It announced that integration would begin in the elementary schools of the archdiocese on a gradual basis, a grade at a time. The student body of the New Orleans parochial school system was then made up of sixty thousand white and twelve thousand Negro youngsters.

While the state's segregationists were reacting to this declaration of intent (one hastily proposed piece of legislation, backed by four Roman Catholic legislators, would have put the Catholic schools under state segregation laws), they suffered another blow. Federal District Judge J. Skelly Wright ordered the public schools of New Orleans to eliminate racial barriers with "all deliberate speed." This did not mean, Judge Wright added, that the schools would be "completely desegregated overnight, or even in a year or more." He said: "The problem of changing a people's mores, particularly those with an emotional overlay, is not to be taken lightly. It is a problem which will require the utmost patience, understanding, generosity and forbearance, and from all of us of whatever race. But the magnitude of the problem may not nullify the principle. And that principle is that we are, all of us, free-born Americans with a right to make our way unfettered by sanctions imposed by man because of the work of God."

While Judge Wright spoke of "deliberate speed" and Archbishop Rummel had pointed to an immediate beginning, neither speed nor desegregation ensued. Instead, a powerful opposition to these two spokesmen thrust forth its own leaders, and in New Orleans and in Baton Rouge, capital of the state, a long campaign of vilification, harassment and legislative hindrance began

Men of money and power joined poor whites in the movement to preserve segregation. Their strategy paired the threat of
popular anger with legislative sparring, and it proved immediately effective. Bowing to "certain difficulties that still remain,"
Archbishop Rummel delivered a second pastoral letter, just six
months after his first, declaring that "we are not now prepared to
introduce integration generally." Instead, he said, desegregation
of parochial schools would begin in September, 1957. But that
date, too, came and went without any breaking of the color line
in classrooms, and as the months went by it became evident that
Catholic schools would not be desegregated until the process had
become effective in the public schools of New Orleans.

Louisiana is separated into three divisions—the largely
French-Catholic bayou area in the southern part of the state;
New Orleans, a melting pot that is basically Catholic and highly
cosmopolitan; and north Louisiana, the Protestant hill country,
where life is rigorous and where prejudice against Negroes, Catholics and the easygoing Mardi Gras city has long been a way of
life. Huey Long had built his kingdom on the envy, fear and distrust felt by north Louisiana's hillbillies and "rednecks" for New
Orleans, and his obedient legislators had systematically stripped
the carnival city of many of its powers to govern itself. After
Long's assassination, and particularly after the end of World
War II, New Orleans nevertheless surged forward as a major sea-
port, as an industrial center, as a tourist mecca, and as a city that
seemed ready to act with moderation on racial issues. More than
symbolism was involved when the liberal Roman Catholic mayor,
deLesseps Morrison, gave the keys of the city to Dr. Ralph J.
Bunche, then Under Secretary of the United Nations. Between
1955 and 1960, there was token desegregation of the professional
schools of Louisiana State University in New Orleans, and New
Orleans obeyed orders by Judge Wright to admit Negroes on
equal terms to buses, parks and sports events. North Louisiana
saw what was happening, as did the extremists within New
Orleans, and were determined that it would not extend to the
public schools.

Judge Wright had ordered the New Orleans School Board in
1956 to prepare a plan for gradual integration. When none had
been offered by July, 1959, he set a deadline of March 1, 1960,
and when that passed with no sign of action—it was deliberate
inaction, members of the School Board acknowledged—Judge

Wright on May 16th decreed his own plan. It provided that integration be started in first-grade classes with the beginning of the school term in September, 1960, and that it be continued on the basis of a grade a year. For this decision, a *Times* biographer said, Judge Wright was called a traitor to his class by some of his former friends. The report continued:

> He no longer is invited to their homes. They avoid him when they meet in the Boston Club on Canal Street. The "class" to which Judge Wright belongs is southern and white. He was born into it in New Orleans in 1911. He has lived all his life there.
>
> Friends say that his many anti-segregation decisions between 1955 and 1960 did not necessarily reflect Judge Wright's private convictions. But they were the law of the land as he construed them in his capacity as a judge of the United States Court of the Eastern District of Louisiana. He has experienced threats against himself, his wife and their thirteen-year-old son as well as ostracism and the burning of crosses in the yard of his New Orleans home.

Responsible New Orleanians accepted the inevitability of Judge Wright's edict, and the question seemed to them to be not if or when, but how many Negro children would have to be admitted to the all-white public schools. At the state capital, however, the legislature went into practically continuous session, using up an estimated $700,000 to adopt anti-integration measures.

Three men were the directors of this effort to interpose state law between the Government of the United States and the citizens of New Orleans. First in official rank among them was Governor Jimmie H. Davis, composer of such songs as "You Are My Sunshine," "Baby's Lullaby" and "Bed Bug Blues," who had crooned his way to juke-box popularity and political office, accompanying himself on his guitar. Davis had served as governor from 1944 to 1948, and had then been elected again in 1960 in a heated, racist campaign. During the fight for primary victory (tantamount to election in Louisiana) he had sworn that he would go to jail if necessary to keep the schools segregated.

William ("Call Me Willie") Rainach of north Louisiana had contended with Davis and Mayor Morrison of New Orleans in a

1959 primary for the gubernatorial post. Rainach, the most ardent white supremacist, had placed third. To prevent the moderate and Roman Catholic Morrison from winning in the run-off ballot, Rainach swung his support to Davis—and in so doing forced Davis into taking a tough stand on civil rights.

The third man in the group held no high state office but was in real terms the most powerful—Leander H. Perez, then District Attorney of Plaquemines and St. Bernard parishes (counties), considered by many to have been the man who set the fuse for the explosions that shook New Orleans in mid-November, 1960. A millionaire oil man, Perez was a force in racist activities throughout the South.

As the fall of 1960 approached, the state legislature, inspired by this triumvirate of segregationists, executed every possible evasive or delaying tactic that could be put into statute form. One act empowered Governor Davis to assume personal control of the New Orleans public schools, thereby superseding the School Board of New Orleans, a group that had reluctantly decided it had to carry out token desegregation. While Davis's ploy was swept aside by a three-member panel of federal judges—one of whom was Judge Wright—it did bring about a two-month delay in integration. The School Board requested the delay on the ground that it had not been able, because of state actions, to prepare for an orderly transition. Judge Wright granted their request, stating his belief that the group was acting "in good faith." And so November 14th became the date set on which public-school integration in the Deep South was finally to take place. Four little Negro girls were selected to be enrolled as first-grade pupils in two previously all-white schools.

Events moved with the confusing quickness and jerkiness of an old-time movie chase. The indefatigable legislature was called in again; and Citizens Council meetings were held to demonstrate the depth of white fury. Harnett T. Kane, writing for the *Times Magazine*, told of one at which a "group of children, half of them blackface, the others unpainted, were called on stage and instructed to kiss and neck with abandon, demonstrating the 'perils of the future.'"

To no avail. On the morning of November 14, 1960, federal deputy marshals escorted four Negro girls into two white elementary schools while angry crowds hurled frustrated jeers and insults. Claude Sitton reported:

Many white parents withdrew their children from school. Marching youths sang "Glory, glory segregation" to the tune of the "Battle Hymn of the Republic," and legislators filled the capitol at Baton Rouge with threats and a flood of oratory.

Orleans Parish (county) school officials ignored a special legislative session's action in asserting control of the education system last night and proclaiming a school holiday. The legislators defied restraining orders issued against them by Federal District Judge Wright. They dispatched state policemen, unarmed and in plain clothes, to the city's forty-eight elementary schools. But school principals politely refused to obey the written demands delivered by the troopers, who had been sworn as sergeants-at-arms. Instead, they carried out instructions from the president of the Orleans Parish School Board to conduct classes as usual.

The legislators then voted to remove four of the School Board's members. A fifth member, Emile F. Wagner, Jr., opposed the decision to comply with the desegregation ruling. He was not mentioned by the lawmakers in the ouster resolution. Several hours later Judge Wright issued an order restraining the legislature from carrying out the dismissals. He also transferred from state to federal jurisdiction a suit designed to force a return to segregated classes. The judge then nullified it.

There were no crowds at first outside McDonogh No. 19 School on busy St. Claud Street or at the William Frantz School in a quieter neighborhood on North Galves Street, several miles away. The identities of the schools and those of the pupils had been withheld by the Board. But the police guard soon drew several hundred spectators to both schools. William Frantz has a normal enrollment of five hundred and seventy-five pupils. Only one hundred and five appeared today and less than fifty were left when the closing bell sounded this afternoon. Of the usual complement of four hundred and sixty at McDonogh a total of ninety-four showed up and a few more than thirty remained until the end of classes.

On the following day, November 15th, only twenty pupils attended classes at McDonogh and only forty-five at Frantz. Sitton said that a procession of mothers "moved in and out of the schools removing books and other belongings of their children. Many vowed that their children would not return to classes so long as the Negroes were there."

Meanwhile, tension increased in the city. Shouting demonstrators crowded around the schools, teenagers raced through the streets in cars draped with Confederate flags, and nine whites were arrested on charges ranging from disturbing the peace to insulting patrolmen. A mass rally of segregationists was called for November 16th so that further "peaceful demonstrations" could be planned. Some five thousand foot-stomping, whooping Citizens Council members and sympathizers attended the meeting, and heard a call for a march on the offices of the School Board. "This is total war in many respects," they were told. "We must use every weapon at our command."

They did. The first major eruption followed. Sitton reported:

Marauding youths surged through New Orleans streets today in demonstrations against school integration that were marked by sporadic rioting, assaults and vandalism. An undetermined number of Negroes were attacked by whites and four were taken to hospitals. The police arrested more than fifty persons. Estimates of the number who participated in the demonstrations ranged upward from two thousand. There was some property damage, mostly to automobiles, windows and neon signs. The police used motorcycles and mounted patrolmen to clear the streets. When these measures proved ineffective, they brought up two fire trucks and turned hoses on the jeering demonstrators.

The violence continued tonight, erupting in scattered areas of the city in attacks on one race by another. The police reported numerous incidents of Negroes throwing rocks, bricks and bottles at passing automobiles and buses. Joseph I. Giarrusso, the Superintendent of Police, called it a tragedy. "I never remember anything like this in New Orleans before," he said. "It's sad to think that people would create chaos in the city, with nothing to accomplish."

The demonstrations today began when hundreds of

high school students gathered on the City Hall steps. They chanted "two, four, six, eight, we don't want to integrate." They soon were joined by a group of mothers, some accompanied by small children, and a sprinkling of adult men. After a foot-stamping, shouting parade through City Hall they swept back across the green lawn of the mall. Leaderless at this point, they then raced across a parkway, blocking traffic. Apparently someone told them the location of the School Board offices and they moved in that direction.

Six policemen met the head of the column in the middle of Carondelet Street, only half a block from the School Board building. Reinforcements were rushed to the scene. Motorcycle patrolmen roared back and forth through the demonstrators, forcing them onto the sidewalks. Shortly after eleven A.M. the crowd began falling back to the City Hall, breaking up into knots of thirty to forty youths.

Spotting a Negro painter on a scaffold, a group sought to shake him off. Others hurled rocks at the painter and several neon signs. Demonstrators stopped a car driven by a Negro and began to rock it back and forth, then pounded on the automobile top with the boards and the bricks and kicked it. A wad of flaming newsprint was tossed into another car with Negro occupants, along with two soft-drink bottles. One group, which had been joined by men ranging in age from eighteen to twenty-five, obtained a large bag of ice cubes. As a bus passed, they threw the ice at its Negro occupants. One woman was knocked unconscious and taken to a hospital.

On November 19th, the schools closed for a week for Thanksgiving. During this period, it was hoped that some solutions might be found to the pressing problems occasioned by the enrollment of the four Negro six-year-olds. A legal response had to be made to the state legislature's latest device—it had again declared the School Board to be out of office, and had placed an economic stranglehold on the group by threatening that any checks the Board issued would be worthless.

In New Orleans the intense pressure on white parents to keep their children away from the boycotted schools edged on may-

hem, and reprisals were taken on the parents of the Negro youngsters who had entered the two grade schools. The father of a
six-year-old girl who was transferred from a Negro school to
William Frantz had been discharged as a filling-station helper.
The man's employer, W. E. Smith, said: "I wouldn't have a nigger
working for me with a child in a white school. Would you?" He
conceded that the Negro had been employed by him for four
years and that he was a good worker. He said whites in the area
had telephoned him, warning they would boycott the station if he
continued to employ the man.

At one Citizens Council meeting Leander Perez told his listeners that desegregation was part of a Communist conspiracy to
overthrow the United States, and for their alleged part in this
"plot" he denounced the National Association for the Advancement of Colored People and "Zionist Jews." He said: "Don't wait
for your daughter to be raped by these Congolese. Don't wait until the burr-heads are forced into your schools. Do something
about it now."

When school sessions resumed, the campaign of harassment
against the handful of white parents who continued to send their
children to the two boycotted, desegregated schools grew uglier.
Screaming, spitting women clawed at the Reverend Lloyd A.
Foreman, a white Methodist minister, who walked past them, his
daughter's hand clasped in his. On December 4th, Claude Sitton
wrote about another victim of this anger:

> Some white parents have withheld their children from
> school because of the small but rowdy group of extremists
> who swarmed around Frantz throughout the week. The
> police have stepped in to break up incidents of violence,
> but they have avoided any action that might indicate they
> were enforcing the integration ruling.
>
> One person who braved the gangs was Mrs. Orlando
> Gabrielle, who knew moments of terror as she made the
> eight-block round trip from her apartment to the school
> with her six-year-old daughter, Yolanda. On Tuesday and
> again on Wednesday, roughly dressed women tagged at
> the heels of the forty-two-year-old mother and screamed
> insults into her ears. Burly policemen broke up attempts
> to drag her down on two occasions. Before emerging to
> face her hecklers one sunny afternoon, Daisy Gabrielle

told why she had chosen to defy the militant segregationists. She sat smiling on a sofa in her four-bedroom apartment beneath a paper plaque that said: "If we walk with
Christ in the sunshine, He will walk with us in the
shadows."

A former WAC whose husband fought the Japanese
through New Guinea's jungles, she is the mother of six
children ranging in age from fourteen months to fourteen
years. Her husband, whom she calls Jerry, is a meter
reader with the City Water and Sanitation Board. Mrs.
Gabrielle was born in San José, Costa Rica, the daughter
of a custom shoemaker. She came to Louisiana with her
family when she was seven. She described herself as "almost a problem child," who only completed elementary
school. Nevertheless, in slightly accented English, she
spoke of her love for reading and demonstrated more than
a passing knowledge of the works of Shakespeare and
Emerson, from whom she learned "the law of compensation."

"It isn't the fault of these colored people that they
were brought here," she said. "If you uproot a people,
there is a penalty for it. This is the penalty the South has
to pay. This is the law of compensation I spoke of."

Mrs. Gabrielle conceded that at first she feared for the
safety of her daughter and herself, "but I decided I could
never give in to mob violence." To steel herself in the face
of the jeering women, she said she had closed her mind
and repeated a part of the Twenty-third Psalm—"Yea,
though I walk through the valley of the shadow of death,
I will fear no evil." She bears no hatred for her tor-
mentors.

"I have compassion for them," she said. "They are
going through the deepest hell. They have been presented
with a new idea and they are expected to accept it just
like that. They have to grow into it."

Her neighbors, Mrs. Gabrielle said, "think I'm a fool.
One lady told me I was making a spectacle of myself,"
she said. "She said I was sacrificing my neighbors. I told
her when it comes to sacrificing my neighbors for my
principles, I'd sacrifice my neighbors. Neighbors change;
principles never do."

Others in New Orleans who believed in the necessity for orderly compliance began to make their views known. A group of forty-six ministers, representing the three major faiths, placed an advertisement in the city's daily newspapers pleading for an end to the disturbances. Perhaps most significant, however, was the determination shown by the teachers and principals of the two integrated schools. Their salaries had been stopped by the action in Baton Rouge; yet they reported for work. The state legislature threatened them with arrest if they did not walk out of the schools, and also promised to resume paying them as soon as they did leave Frantz and McDonogh. Yet they stayed on. Some months later, in a message to the Civil Rights Commission's third annual conference on schools in transition, President Kennedy spoke of these forty men and women as "loyal citizens" who were meeting their responsibilities and the challenge of desegregation "with quiet intelligence and true courage. The whole country is in their debt," he said, "for our public-school system must be preserved and improved."

Although few realized it at the time, the battle in New Orleans had now been won by the Government of the United States. There would still be skirmishes, and in Baton Rouge the ritual of defiance would go on; but integration had come, and Governor Jimmie Davis had not gone to jail to prevent it. Nor had any of the laws frantically produced by the legislature in special session been able to achieve more than delays. The southern dream known as "interposition" had been shattered on November 30th by a three-judge federal court in New Orleans. On December 12th the Supreme Court made it clear that an appeal of this decision would be a waste of time. As the months went on it became evident that state officials would back down rather than go to jail for contempt of court. President Kennedy, Attorney General Kennedy and the federal courts moved with increasing speed and determination to set aside each of Baton Rouge's forays into evasion.

When a law was passed permitting citizens of school districts to vote to abandon public schools faced with desegregation orders, it was struck down by three federal judges from New Orleans. "This is not the moment in history for a state to experiment with ignorance," their opinion said. "When it does, it must expect close scrutiny of the experiment." The court ruled that the local option law, Act II of a special session of the Louisiana legislature in 1961, violated the equal-protection clause of the Fourteenth Amendment to the Constitution on two counts. First, the court said, "it is a transparent artifice to deprive the [Negro] plaintiffs of their constitutional right to attend desegregated public schools." Secondly, it said, the state provided public schools in other parishes (counties) and that closing the schools in this one, St. Helena, would thus discriminate against the children in that parish, regardless of race. The court also ruled out the idea of state-aided "private" schools as substitutes for the public school system. It said that such a plan involved "such extensive state control, financial aid, and active participation that, in operating the program, the state would still be providing public education." It went on: "The state might not be doing business at the old stand, but the state would be participating as the senior, and not silent, partner in the same sort of business. Continuance of segregation at the state's public-private schools, therefore, would be a violation of the equal-protection clause."

On September 7, 1961, when the city's public schools opened for the second year of integration, New Orleans was peaceful. Eight more Negro pupils joined the four who were already enrolled and four more schools were added to the two that were no longer segregated. Uniformed members of the three-hundred-sixty-man police detail assigned to the six schools had little to do but twirl their nightsticks; the sixty deputy federal marshals ordered to the city by the Justice Department were not called out. And during recess at one of the integrated schools, the Negro pupils were seen playing with white children in the schoolyard. At another school, a first-grade Negro girl held hands with a white girl as they emerged from the building.

Now Archbishop Rummel decided to attempt integration of the parochial schools of the New Orleans archdiocese. Aware that this time his effort to desegregate the schools had to be carried through successfully—for if it failed, not only would the Church suffer, but whatever integration gains that had been made in two painful years in New Orleans might then be lost—the Archbishop moved carefully. The priests of the archdiocese supported his position. On March 27, 1962, he announced it to the public. Then, on March 31st, he sent letters of "paternal admonition" to a group of Catholics who had been among the most vitriolic foes of desegregation. Leander Perez was one of the group to receive the prelate's warning against continuation of his segregationist activities. So were Jackson G. Ricau, director of the South Louisiana Citizens Council, and Mrs. B. J. Gaillot, Jr., head of Save Our Nation, Inc.

On April 16th it was solemnly announced that these three segregationists had not ceased their attempts to "provoke" opposition to the desegregation of the church schools and that in consequence they had been excommunicated from the Roman Catholic Church. Perez asserted that the "purported excommunications" were a "move to frighten or terrorize the parents of parochial students," but that they would not achieve this goal. He added that he was "a lifelong Catholic," and would continue to be so, "regardless of communistic infiltration and the influence of the National Council of Christians and Jews upon our church leaders." Mr. Ricau declared that he would "continue to fight for racial segregation . . . serving God and begging His help and protection." Mrs. Gaillot said she would appeal to Rome, adding: "I don't know the mind of the Pope, but I do know what God has written in the Bible."

Despite the white supremacists, New Orleans was comparatively calm on September 4, 1962, when, for the first time in sixty-seven years, some one hundred and fifty Negro pupils entered previously all-white parochial-school classrooms. On the following day, however, in Weswego—a suburb of New Orleans— there were disturbances, as reported by Hedrick Smith:

> A segregationist crowd collected outside the school before it opened this morning, and there were mutterings when a nun bent over to hug one of the two Negro children as they arrived at school. There were cheers as several white parents went inside to remove their children, and boos from the crowd when a white woman arrived late and took her child inside. The police blocked off the street next to the school to prevent trouble.
>
> The disturbances reached their peak when the young Negro mother returned to school about 10:50 A.M. to pick up her two children.
>
> "Nigger, go home," one white woman shouted. "Go back across the canal. Go home."
>
> The crowd chanted a chorus of boos as the Negro mother walked slowly across the asphalt playground to the school with a small child in her arms. While the crowd awaited her return, its members urged policemen

Georgia railroad station, 1954.

Leonard Kamsler

John Kasper, the fanatic segregationist who stirred trouble in Clinton, Tennessee, picketed the White House in 1957 when President Eisenhower met on the Little Rock crisis with four moderate southern governors: Frank Clement of Tennessee, Luther Hodges of North Carolina, LeRoy Collins of Florida and Theodore McKeldin of Maryland. *Associated Press*

Mrs. Rosa Parks, the seamstress whose refusal to move to the back of a bus started the Montgomery bus boycott, was finger-printed by Deputy Sheriff D. H. Lackey. *Associated Press*

LITTLE ROCK CENTRAL HIGH SCHOOL

Federal troops had the job of escorting children into school for the first time in 1957. *Associated Press*

In North Little Rock, Negro students Richard Richardson and Harold Smith had to walk through jeering white boys when they attempted to enter a white school in 1957. *Arkansas Gazette*

The students who conducted the sit-ins were prepared for every kind of indignity. John R. Salter was sprayed with ketchup and mustard and finally beaten in Jackson, Mississippi. *United Press International*

The freedom rides in 1961 were met by violence, including the burning of this bus in Anniston, Alabama. *Associated Press*

In New Orleans in 1960 Mrs. Orlando Gabrielle braved crowds of hostile women to bring her six-year-old daughter Yolanda to a school that one Negro child had entered. *Associated Press*

"You cannot change people's hearts merely by laws." Dwight D. Eisenhower. *Associated Press*

Men used electrified cattle prods against other men—here in Plaquemine, Louisiana, in 1963. *United Press International*

Dogs in Birmingham, 1963. *Associated Press*

Also in Birmingham: A policeman kneels on a Negro woman. *Associated Press*

Governor George Wallace of Alabama, in his "charade," stops Deputy Attorney General Nicholas deB. Katzenbach at the door of the University of Alabama in 1963. Two Negro students were admitted later in the day. *Associated Press*

The widow of Medgar Evers, murdered Mississippi civil-rights leader, at his funeral in Arlington Cemetery. *George Tames, New York Times*

Negro youths in Jackson, Mississippi, marched to protest the Evers murder, and a riot was prevented only when John Doar of the United States Justice Department persuaded the marchers to disperse. *Associated Press*

The vote and how to get it are explained by a young civil-rights worker to a farmer in West Feliciana Parish, Louisiana. A Justice Department drive succeeded in 1963 in getting a Negro on the registration books there for the first time since 1902. *Bob Adelman*

The North came to learn about demonstrations, too. Police intervened in Harlem in June, 1963. *United Press International*

The March on Washington: 200,000 Americans between the Lincoln Memorial and the Washington Monument on August 28, 1963. *Paris Match*

The late John F. Kennedy with leaders of the March on Washington, August 28, 1963. Left to right, Whitney Young, National Urban League; Dr. Martin Luther King, Christian Leadership Conference; John Lewis, Student Non-violent Coordinating Committee; Rabbi Joachim Prinz, American Jewish Congress; Dr. Eugene P. Blake, National Council of Churches; A. Philip Randolph, AFL-CIO Vice-President; President Kennedy; Walter Reuther, United Auto Workers; Vice-President Lyndon B. Johnson; and Roy Wilkins, NAACP. *United Press International*

Two Government officials who carried the burden of the civil-rights effort were Attorney General Robert F. Kennedy, left, and his assistant for civil rights, Burke Marshall. They are shown in Kennedy's office, with his children's drawings on the wall. *George Tames, New York Times*

to ticket her car, which was parked in the road beside the school. And when the woman returned to the car, its windshield had been smashed.

The crowd formed a large semicircle around the car as the Negro mother put her little boy and girl into the car. A wiry white woman wearing black slacks, a white sleeveless blouse and a red bandana in her hair, shouted, "I'll get you, nigger. I guarantee I'll get you. They can get these goddam niggers out of here if we have to shoot 'em one by one."

As the Negro woman pulled her car away under the protection of both uniformed and plainclothes police, the white crowd closed in. The car was pounded and spat upon and someone threw a rock, about the size of a tangerine, at it. When the priests came out of the school with white children, they were booed and jeered, too.

About fifteen men, mostly in work clothes, stood across the street and shouted "nigger school" at three priests who did not respond. One man called at the priests, who were wearing full-length black cassocks, "we ought to paint them all black."

Protests against parochial-school desegregation in New Orleans eventually died down, as in the case of the public schools. But the Church did not prevail in the fief of Leander Perez, Plaquemines Parish. There, in the town of Buras, five Negro children were entered in a white parochial school on August 30, 1962. Within two weeks all the white students had been withdrawn, and they did not return even when the Negro children gave up the attempt at integration. That year the school was closed. On August 27, 1963, just before the start of a new school year, it was destroyed by a bomb.

Atlanta had her first taste of token school desegregation a year after New Orleans, in the fall of 1961, and the scene could hardly have been more different. In a city with a white population of nearly three hundred thousand, only two hundred and fifty persons turned out for a Ku Klux Klan rally. No marauding gangs raced through the streets of Atlanta, no shrieking women clawed at parents taking their children to school, no white boycott took place.

Peaceful desegregation did not just happen in Atlanta. Years of preparation and of determined political effort permitted it to happen. Atlanta, just like New Orleans, was at odds with a deeply conservative, deeply segregationist rural population. In Georgia the cities faced even steeper odds, for the state's political system was rigged against them. Georgia had the unit system for electing governors, senators and members of Congress. In the Democratic primary, equivalent to election, the counting was not by popular votes but by units—so many to each county, and many fewer to the big cities than their population indicated. As in other states, rural areas of Georgia already had disproportionate weight in a gerrymandered legislature; the unit system gave them the same unfair advantage in the choice of the governor, who naturally tended to defer to rural interests.

In 1956, in response to the Supreme Court decision, the Georgia legislature directed that state funds be withheld from any school or other educational institution desegregated by court order. The successful candidate for governor in 1958, Ernest Vandiver, pledged in his campaign that while he was governor not a single Negro would attend school in Georgia with a single white child. Many other politicians from the rural strongholds of power said they would rather close the schools than permit even a little integration.

This policy of all-out resistance on the part of Georgia's dominant political forces was vigorously opposed by Atlanta—by the newspapers of the metropolis, by Mayor Hartsfield, by community organizations working to save the public schools. To many outside observers their chances of changing the state policy would have seemed slim. Then, in January, 1961, there came a dramatic test that overturned the official attitude of the State of Georgia and had profound effects on the South generally. Two Negro students applied for admission to the University of Georgia in the term beginning that January. They were Charlayne Hunter, eighteen years old, honor graduate of an Atlanta Negro high school, and Hamilton Holmes, nineteen, an honor student and football star. On January 6, 1961, Federal District Judge William A. Bootle ordered them admitted.

On January 9th Governor Vandiver made his annual address at the opening of the legislature. Segregationists demanded and expected total resistance, but they were disappointed. The Governor said: "We cannot abandon public education. No one wants this. No one has ever proposed that this be done." He did not explain, but he was evidently reluctant to invoke the fund-cutoff statute and force the closing of the university when Miss Hunter and Mr. Holmes entered. And in that reluctance he had support not only in Atlanta. The University of Georgia, one hundred and seventy-five years old, had a special place in the hearts of Georgia citizens; many of the state's leading political figures were graduates. The idea of closing down Georgia's leading educational institution to frustrate the admission of two Negroes seemed to bring home to many, for the first time, the futility and self-destructiveness of the course on which the state had been fixed.

The next day, January 10th, Miss Hunter and Mr. Holmes enrolled at the University and attended their first classes. There were a few demonstrations on the campus in Athens, fifty miles east of Atlanta, but things went relatively peacefully. That was a Tuesday.

Wednesday was different. That night a howling mob of six hundred outsiders and students laid siege to the dormitory where Miss Hunter was living. For nearly an hour the mob raged out of control, hurling bricks and stones at the windows, and tossing firecrackers at a handful of city policemen trying to restore order. Ku Klux Klan members appeared (in mufti) and began to distribute racist pamphlets. The Mayor of Athens put in a call for help to the state police; he was told, he said, that such help could not be provided without the permission of Governor Vandiver.

However, police finally disbanded the rioters and at twelve-twenty Thursday morning Dean William Tate and highway patrolmen led Miss Hunter, weeping, from the dormitory. A police car took her and Mr. Holmes to their homes at Atlanta. In a statement the Dean said, "I am withdrawing Charlayne Hunter and Hamilton Holmes from the University of Georgia in the interest of their personal safety and for the safety and welfare of more than seven thousand other students . . . until such time as . . . it is safe and practical for them to return to school."

One of the students involved in the riot had shouted exultantly: "We're going to run the niggers off. It's going to be just like Alabama." Just five years earlier violence had forced Autherine Lucy out of the University of Alabama; state authorities had contrived to keep her out, and the Federal Government had done nothing about this defiance of federal law. But the student who thought that pattern would be repeated in Athens, Georgia, was mistaken. In another week President Eisenhower would be out of office, and it was quite clear that John F. Kennedy would not permit racism to override the Constitution; indeed, the experience at Little Rock doubtless indicated that Mr. Eisenhower would have intervened in the Georgia case if he had had to. But there never needed to be any formal intervention from Washington.

On January 13th Judge Bootle ordered the two Negro students readmitted. Governor Vandiver pledged all necessary state assistance in maintaining order. Miss Hunter and Mr. Holmes went back to their classes on Tuesday, January 17th. The next day Governor Vandiver addressed the legislature.

"I reject, as I know you do," he said, "any thought, suggestion, hint or encouragement of defiance of lawful processes or the subjecting of the children of Georgia to the bodily hazard of violence and mob rule. I must tell you quite frankly that a failure to resolve [the school crisis] will blight our state. Like a cancerous growth, it will devour progress—consuming all in its path, pitting friend against friend, demoralizing all that is good, stifling the economic growth of the state and denying the youth of Georgia their proper educational opportunity."

It sounded like what the leaders of Atlanta had been saying for years, but now it won applause from even the rural-dominated legislature. Governor Vandiver called successfully for repeal of the fund-cutoff law. He made clear that he was not only resolving the University of Georgia crisis; he was paving the way for the beginning of desegregation in public schools. That came the following fall in Atlanta. Charlayne Hunter and Hamilton Holmes went on to graduate from the university without further incidents of note. It made only a small splash in 1963 when Miss Hunter disclosed that she had married a white boy she met on campus, Walter Stovall.

Writing in the *Times Magazine* in May, 1962—half a year after Atlanta started school desegregation—Claude Sitton sought to explain the "good sense and dignity" that had prevailed there:

> The millennium has by no means arrived for the Negroes, who account for two out of five of the central city's 496,000 residents, or one out of five of the more than one million people in the metropolitan area. Their gains in such fields as public-school desegregation and equal job opportunities have been token at best. Only eight Negro

students, for example, now attend four previously all-white high schools. No important advance has come without pressure. Sometimes it has been exerted by the Negroes, who wield considerable political and economic power. Sometimes it has stemmed from the Federal Government. On other occasions, it has come from the city's white liberals or from a combination of these three forces.

The result is the virtual end of segregation by law—but not by custom. Few Negroes have exercised their newly won rights. Some have been discouraged by the actions and attitudes of whites. The reluctance of many others can be attributed to the apathy bred by a substandard cultural and economic status, the fear rooted in past experience and the inability to overcome the subtle inhibitions built into the social system through the years.

Nevertheless, the advances made by Atlanta are far greater than the most optimistic observer would have predicted ten years ago. There has been no defiance of the federal courts. In fact, Atlanta waged one of the most determined fights yet seen in the region against a rurally dominated state government over the issue of local option in public-school desegregation. Nor has there been any attempt to prolong resistance to demands for change made outside the courts once it became clear that to do so would be futile, dangerous or both.

Once a concession has been agreed upon, a majority of the city's professional, civic and business men have sought to persuade the white community that it should be made gracefully. Officials have asserted time and again that they would brook no disorder. And the threats of mob rule evoked by desegregation elsewhere in the South have never arisen here.

As a result, civic leaders from more than a dozen other southern cities have come here in recent months to learn whether Atlanta's experience might be helpful in resolving racial difficulties in their communities. One leading Atlantan—by no means a liberal—recalls that he told one such visitor that it often proved helpful to invite Negroes to lunch to discuss interracial problems.

"You mean to say you actually sit down and eat with them?" came the startled reply.

"Oh, sure. You don't even notice the difference after just a few minutes."

For the city's Negroes, the years from 1906—when a four-day race riot brought death to ten Negroes and two whites—to 1946 might well be called "the lean forty" from the standpoint of civil rights. Their goals were no more ambitious than to obtain streets, sidewalks and sewers, schools and funds with which to operate them, and police and fire protection. Moreover, there was the sporadic reign of terror carried on by the Ku Klux Klan. The hooded knights never controlled the city. But their floggings, cross-burnings and parades struck fear into the hearts of Negroes and the few nonconformist whites.

Barred from the countinghouses and law offices of Peachtree Street, Negroes established their own business and commercial colony along Auburn Avenue. There was the Citizens Trust Company, which weathered the Great Depression while banks throughout the nation were failing. Next door was the Atlanta *Daily World*, for a time the only Negro daily newspaper in America. Fortunes were made and the city's Negro community became, and remains today, one of the wealthiest in the nation.

Because of Auburn Avenue's economic weight, good race relations became good business for some influential whites. After the federal courts struck down Georgia's white-primary law in 1946, they became good politics as well. There was little opposition, then or now, to Negro registration in Atlanta. And because the Democratic nomination was tantamount to election, participation by Negroes in the primary brought a realignment of the political balance of power. "The lean forty" was coming to an end.

A year after the primary breakthrough, the city's aldermen approved the hiring of Negro policemen for Negro neighborhoods. A more sizable share of expenditures for public facilities began flowing into those neighborhoods. Other changes followed. But none involved a major breach in the wall of segregation.

Then came the 1954 Supreme Court decision against public-school segregation. Negroes' grudging acceptance of the status quo here and throughout the South dissipated almost overnight. The pressure on white Atlanta grew in depth and intensity.

Slowly, then with increasing rapidity, racial barriers began to fall, though not equally in every field. Public golf courses were desegregated under a federal court order. The city library's main branch began admitting Negroes after it became apparent that legal action was inevitable otherwise. A test case, described as "more or less friendly," ended Jim Crow seating in public transportation. The freedom riders rolled through Atlanta without incident en route to a riotous greeting in Alabama. A federal court order opened a restaurant in the old municipal air terminal to Negroes, and when its jet-age replacement went into operation not a vestige of discrimination could be found in its waiting rooms, cocktail lounges, rest rooms or restaurants. Restrictions have been removed in the legitimate theatre and desegregated groups attend functions in the municipal auditorium. When the city's new A.A.A. baseball team, the Atlanta Crackers, opened the season at Ponce de Leon Park, there was no segregation on the playing field or in the stands.

Throughout this period of difficult change, most white Atlantans have shown calmness, common sense and respect for the law. Possibly typical of their attitude were the remarks Chief of Police Herbert T. Jenkins addressed to his men as they began special training in preparation for school desegregation. "I am prepared to yield to the judgment of the Supreme Court," he said. "Why? As law-enforcement officers, there is no other position we can honestly take."

A significant factor in Atlanta's success has been the willingness of many whites—city officials and private citizens—to risk public displeasure while working to assure a peaceful change-over. The city's two white daily newspapers, the Atlanta *Journal* and the Atlanta *Constitution*, its clergymen and a group of housewives—the last organized under the name of HOPE (Help Our Public Education)—pioneered in a drive to keep the schools open even if doing so meant the end of segregation.

Cities—even southern cities—have such varied social, political and economic structures that few valid parallels can be drawn between them in the field of race relations. However, Atlanta's neighbors might find something of value in its pattern of change. The significance does not lie so much in the extent of the progress made here as in the fact that Atlanta has achieved this change with relatively little disruption or lasting bitterness. It has demonstrated an ability to learn from its own mistakes and those of others; it has produced leadership capable of applying those lessons. And its whites and Negroes have created a working relationship which promises to serve them well in dealing with the demands for more substantial adjustments likely to come in the future.

In a small law office in the heart of the business district sits the man who played perhaps the key role in this social drama, former Mayor Hartsfield. He believes Atlanta's booming economic growth, if nothing else, should convince other southern cities that it provides a stimulating example.

"We've accepted what is world opinion," he says. "We're not consumed with hatred of each other. We are free to use our talents and energies to grow and to attract industry. The leaders in these other cities can see the difference in the approaches of Atlanta and New Orleans to the problem, but they're afraid to speak out. They've got to assume leadership. Hate never built anything. There's nothing to be gained from hate but stagnation. Let's forget about fighting and go to work."

Chapter 10

Alabama: 1960-1963

In the spring of 1960, the *New York Times* sent Harrison Salisbury to Birmingham to report on race relations in the sprawling industrial city. He began his account, which was published on April 12th:

> No New Yorker can readily measure the climate of Birmingham today. Whites and blacks still walk the same streets. But the streets, the water supply and the sewer system are about the only public facilities they share. Ball parks and taxicabs are segregated. So are libraries. A book featuring black rabbits and white rabbits was banned. A drive is on to forbid "Negro music" on "white" radio stations. Every channel of communication, every medium of mutual interest, every reasoned approach, every inch of middle ground has been fragmented by the emotional dynamite of racism, reinforced by the whip, the razor, the gun, the bomb, the torch, the club, the knife, the mob, the police and many branches of the state's apparatus.
>
> In Birmingham neither blacks nor whites talk freely. A pastor carefully closes the door before he speaks. A

Negro keeps an eye on the sidewalk outside his house. A lawyer talks in the language of conspiracy. Telephones are tapped, or there is fear of tapping. Mail has been intercepted and opened. Sometimes it does not reach its destination. The eavesdropper, the informer, the spy have become a fact of life.

Volunteer watchmen stand guard twenty-four hours a day over some Negro churches. Jewish synagogues have floodlights for the night, and caretakers. Dynamite attempts have been made against the two principal Jewish temples in the last eighteen months. In eleven years there have been twenty-two reported bombings of Negro churches and homes. A number were never reported officially.

Birmingham's whites and blacks share a community of fear. "I have lived in Alabama all my life," said a newspaperman. "Birmingham is going to blow one of these days. And when that happens that's one story I don't want to be around to cover."

"Remember," a businessman said, "Birmingham is no place for irresponsible reporting. Be careful of what you say and who you mention. Lives are at stake."

"I'm ashamed to have to talk to you off the record," said an educator. "It is not for myself. But these are not ordinary times. The dangers are very real and people up North must realize that."

"Excuse me," an educated Negro woman said. "But I just don't understand the white people around here. They seem to act so crazy. It doesn't make any sense. Don't they know there is a limit to what people will stand?"

"If you sow hate, you reap hate," said a Negro pastor.

Three years later, in the spring of 1963, the Negro leadership decided that the time had come to make a massive effort to change the pattern of life in Birmingham. They had one hopeful omen. The well-known Police Commissioner, Eugene "Bull" Connor, Mayor Arthur G. Hanes and others in the city's furiously segregationist administration had been voted out of office in a November, 1962, special election that changed the city's form of government. Connor and Hanes refused to relinquish their positions, arguing that they should fill out their terms, but the very fact that more moderate candidates had attracted more votes seemed to be evidence that white Birmingham was ready to consider some changes in racial policy.

And so, on April 3, 1963, Negro leaders in the city of Birmingham launched a campaign to achieve at least the following goals: removal of racial restrictions in downtown snack bars, rest rooms and stores; adoption of non-racial hiring practices for such posts as salesgirls and secretaries; and formation of a bi-racial committee to carry on continuing negotiations for further desegregation. The Negro community in Birmingham—it numbered one hundred and fifty thousand, forty per cent of the city's population—was not then united in this effort. Some fearfully opposed any form of direct action. Some, strongly influenced by such militant northern groups as the Black Muslims, held these limited demands to be insufficient and therefore humiliating, and believed that only revolutionary mob action could succeed. But the dominant spokesmen felt that progress could be made "peacefully and prayerfully." The Reverend Fred Lee Shuttlesworth was the leader of this faction, and associated with him were the Reverend Dr. Martin Luther King, Jr., president of the Southern Christian Leadership Conference, and the Reverend Ralph D. Abernathy.

The protest movement began with attempted sit-ins at segregated lunch counters in downtown department stores and drugstores; these efforts were quickly halted by Connor's police force, and by the end of the first week more than one hundred and fifty demonstrators had been arrested. Twenty-four were tried, found guilty of breaking city ordinances, fined a hundred dollars each and sentenced to terms of one hundred and eighty days each—the men to labor on a prison farm, the women to work in a jail laundry.

The most certain route to jail—and the form of demonstration that became the chief tactical tool of the movement—was the "protest march." Birmingham held these to be in violation of a city regulation prohibiting parading without a license, and moved successfully in the city courts to obtain an injunction against such demonstrations. Martin Luther King and his associates refused to abide by the injunction. It was announced that on Easter Sunday there would be mass attempts to worship at white churches—kneel-ins. The practice had been for Negroes, when refused entry, to kneel on the church steps and pray.

Such a march began on Friday, April 12th. It was Good Friday, and at the head of the Negro column were Dr. King, the Reverend Abernathy, and the Reverend Shuttlesworth. Bull Connor and his police force were ready. They had with them, in addition to the usual paraphernalia of law-enforcement groups, a squad of snapping, snarling police dogs. While the demonstrators sang hymns and the dogs strained at their leashes, Connor's men arrested the leaders of the protest march. The three ministers were taken to Southside Jail and imprisoned.

For Dr. King, this arrest marked his thirteenth in the South since his assumption of a key role in the anti-segregation effort. And it achieved one of the desired objectives: It focused the attention of the nation—and of the White House in particular—on the sputtering fuse in Birmingham. On April 13th, Jack Raymond reported from Washington:

> President Kennedy, concerned over developments in Birmingham, called the Justice Department from his Easter vacation spot in Palm Beach this morning. Assistant Attorney General Burke Marshall said the President wanted to be informed about the jailing yesterday of the Reverend Dr. Martin Luther King, Jr., and other Negro demonstrators against segregation. An official explained President Kennedy's interest as a natural one in view of the "national concern" over incidents involving desegregation and the "prominence of the personalities concerned."
>
> The situation in Birmingham in certain respects resembles that in Albany, Georgia, officials explained, in that the Federal Government's grounds for intervention are limited to non-legal action. It appeared here that, as in the Albany situation, federal officials were seeking to mediate.

Within Birmingham, too, there were people seeking a racial truce. A group of eight white church leaders, representing the three major faiths, issued a statement calling the street demonstrations "unwise and untimely," indicating that they should cease in anticipation of the "days of new hope" that would presumably follow upon the swearing in of the new city administration.

The new Mayor—Albert Boutwell—and his City Council were indeed sworn in on the day after Easter, April 15th, and

Boutwell's acceptance speech did hint at future efforts to resolve the Negro-white crisis. "We are blessed by good conscience among all our people," he said, "and we have the intelligence and will to live and prosper in peace and, in good time, mutual respect and understanding." But Boutwell and his aides did not immediately take over the reins of government from Mayor Hanes and Commissioner Connor; the "lame duck" administration had moved the dispute to the courts of Alabama, and would not in the meanwhile step down. Declaring that "the time for compromise had passed," the Negro leadership therefore pressed forward a campaign aimed at forcing federal intervention.

Each day brought a few more minor demonstrations and additional arrests. The plan of the men who headed the direct-action campaign against segregation appeared to be to withhold major demonstrations until the new administration had taken office; while that matter moved toward a decision, sporadic efforts would go on—sufficient to preserve the unity of Birmingham's Negroes, sufficient to keep the eyes of the country turned toward Birmingham, sufficient to intensify the Government's will to work toward compromise, perhaps even sufficient to "get the Justice Department in." But not so intensive as to loose the explosive forces that had been building in this city of 341,000 and in the state of Alabama itself.

So far as Birmingham's Negroes were concerned, these tactics welded both their unity and their determination. They gathered by the thousands each day at what had become the staging area for the demonstrations—the Sixteenth Street Baptist Church, which overlooked a park in the Negro section near downtown Birmingham.

Large numbers of them were school children, some younger than ten. To criticism of the exposure of the children to possible danger, Dr. King replied, "Children face the stinging darts of segregation as well as adults." A Negro mother said, "These younger people are not going to take what we took."

Singing "We Shall Overcome" and chanting slogans, the demonstrators filed out of the church in groups, taking different routes toward City Hall. Most were quickly arrested, and they piled into paddy wagons or school buses in an almost festive mood.

On the afternoon of May 2nd, for example, about five hundred demonstrators—most of them in their teens or even younger —were arrested. Foster Hailey reported:

There was no resistance to arrest by the laughing, singing groups of youngsters, although some of the smaller participants dropped their signs and ran when the police approached. Most of the marchers fell to their knees and prayed as the police stopped them.

Half a dozen fire engines were deployed at strategic corners after the first hour of demonstrations. Hoses were strung at one point, but the water was not turned on. The city's squad of police dogs was not used. Every available police vehicle was pressed into service to haul the young demonstrators to jail or juvenile court. When even those, and some Jefferson County sheriff's cars, proved inadequate, school buses were used by the police.

The mood changed, however, on the following day. In the course of another mass demonstration a news photographer and two firemen were injured by bricks and hurtling broken bottles; students were bitten by police dogs; and youthful integrationists were sent sprawling by powerful streams of water gushing from fire hoses. "There was an ugly overtone to the events today that was not present yesterday," Hailey reported on May 3rd, continuing:

The students were less submissive today. Two or three groups walked around single patrolmen who ordered them to halt. But they did not attack the policemen or join in the missile-throwing. The barrage of bricks and bottles came from adult onlookers. Yesterday the adults also appeared to be in a happy mood, but today their mood turned ugly and bitter when the hoses were used against the students, and the squad of six dogs was brought up.

With the dogs and fire hoses, the police were largely successful in dispersing the student marchers before they left the Negro section. Fewer than five hundred were able to leave the Sixteenth Street Baptist Church before the police sealed its doors. Only two groups won their way through the police lines. One group of twenty reached City Hall, where they were arrested. Another group of ten got as far as the bus depot on 19th Street, where they also were taken into custody. In all, more than two hundred and fifty were reported arrested today.

All the demonstrations were held between one and three P.M. They followed by less than three hours a declaration by the two principal leaders of the month-old direct-action campaign against segregation here. The leaders said that the demonstrations would continue with increasing intensity until there were both "promise and action" from the city authorities and white merchants to start to end segregation.

"We are ready to negotiate," Dr. King said. "But we intend to negotiate from strength. If the white power structure of this city will meet some of our minimum demands, then we will consider calling off the demonstrations, but we want promises, plus action."

Impelled by the mounting emotions of the crisis, the Justice Department sent its top civil-rights expert to Birmingham in an attempt to bring about a truce. He was Burke Marshall, Assistant Attorney General in charge of the Department's Civil Rights Division, accompanied by Joseph F. Dolan, Assistant Deputy Attorney General. They arrived on Saturday, May 4th, while the demonstrations were continuing with fierce intensity, with the number of arrests in three days having exceeded eleven hundred.

Demonstrations were halted that afternoon for the remainder of the weekend at the request of the Reverend James Bevel, Mississippi field secretary of the Southern Christian Leadership Conference, who was on the scene as one of Dr. King's aides. Mr. Bevel said that he had seen several pistols and knives carried by spectators at the last demonstration, and was fearful of violence. While the brief truce was apparently not tied to the arrival of the Justice Department mediators, it did afford the two men an opportunity to meet spokesmen for the opposing factions.

When Monday came, the protest demonstrations resumed. Claude Sitton's account from Birmingham on May 6th said that "about a thousand Negroes—forty per cent of them juveniles— were arrested today as wave after wave of marchers chanted challenges to segregation." The Negro leadership had begun to draw increasingly on elementary-school pupils, he reported, and his story continued with quotations from a flyer distributed to youngsters by supporters of the movement:

"Fight for freedom first then go to school. Join the thousand in jail who are making their witness for freedom. Come to the Sixteenth Street Baptist Church now . . . and we'll soon be free. It's up to you to free our teachers, our parents, yourself and our country."

The Birmingham *News* reported that one Negro educator said his school had 1,339 students absent and only eighty-seven present. The juveniles are being held either at the Boys Home or in the 4-H Club building at the fair grounds. With those arrested today, the total number of both adults and juveniles in custody is estimated at 2,425. Authorities say they are unable to provide an accurate count.

There is no lack of space for more, according to Eugene Connor, Commissioner of Fire, Police and Education in one of Birmingham's two city governments. The dispute over which government is legal is in the courts. "All right," Mr. Connor said as the police loaded demonstrators into patrol wagons and school buses, "you-all send them on over there. I got plenty of room in the jail."

Connor, in shirt sleeves and with a straw hat cocked over one eye, watched the eager young marchers, some of whom ran to the waiting patrol wagons.

"Boy, if that's religion, I don't want any," he said.

"Freedom! Freedom! Freedom!" chanted the Negro girls and boys as the school buses swept by the commissioner on the way to jail.

"If you'd ask half of them what freedom means, they couldn't tell you," asserted Connor.

A sullen crowd of more than two thousand Negroes was held back at the staging area—the Sixteenth Street Baptist Church—by approximately one hundred policemen on that angry Monday afternoon. One woman who resisted a policeman's attempt to force her off a sidewalk was wrestled to the pavement by five patrolmen, one of whom pinned her down with a knee in her neck. A Negro man ripped a policeman's shirt and sought to wrest his revolver from him.

In this atmosphere of growing fury, Burke Marshall talked and talked and tried to find a way out. The first problem that had to be overcome, he found, was the utter lack of communication between the white and Negro communities. They had been estranged for so long that they had no idea what was in the other's mind—or how to find out.

The financial and other leaders of the Birmingham white community did not know what the Negro demonstrators wanted. When Marshall started meeting with them privately, they took the position that the whole campaign was the work of an "outside agitator," Dr. King. But gradually, with the quiet voice of Burke Marshall simply repeating facts, the white leaders came to realize that the Negroes of Birmingham felt themselves the victims of injustice and wanted change.

"There was a growing recognition," one white man said later, "by a lot of people, when they thought about it, that the Negroes were demanding something that wasn't so unreasonable—to have a cup of coffee at a lunch counter, to get a decent job."

Financial leaders also began to fear the economic effects on Birmingham of a real outbreak of violence. The county sheriff, Melvin Bailey, warned them on May 7th that unless a settlement were reached quickly, local law-enforcement forces could no longer handle the situation and martial law would have to be imposed. That might mean control of the city by the state's far-out segregationist governor, George Wallace.

Marshall told the white group that if they did not meet the present Negro leaders halfway, it would soon have to face more militant men—"hawks instead of doves," he put it. But he did not talk bluntly to the white group only. Meeting separately with Dr. King and the other Negro leaders, he warned them against the strategy of hoping to provoke intervention by federal troops. That would not really solve anything, he said. No outside force could impose a true settlement on Birmingham; its troubles had to be worked out from within.

Marshall's efforts with the white power structure of Birmingham were helped by telephone calls to businessmen there and to some who controlled Birmingham business from a distance, such as Roger Blough of United States Steel. President Kennedy made some of the calls himself, and others in his Cabinet joined in, among them Secretary of Defense Robert S. McNamara and Secretary of the Treasury Douglas Dillon.

On May 10th it was announced that the mediation efforts had succeeded. "The city of Birmingham has reached an accord with its conscience," declared three leaders of the protest movement, Dr. King and the Reverends Shuttlesworth and Abernathy. "The acceptance of responsibility by local white and Negro leadership offers an example of a free people uniting to meet and solve their problems. Birmingham may well offer for twentieth-century America an example of progressive racial relations, and for all mankind a dawn of a new day, a promise for all men, a day of opportunity, and a new sense of freedom for all America."

The accord committed white business and civic leaders, but not city officials, to pledges of action. The Negroes had settled for less than their original demands. The agreement provided for desegregation, within ninety days, of lunch counters, rest rooms and the like in large downtown stores (the Negroes had sought immediate desegregation); non-discriminatory hiring and promotion, including specifically the hiring of Negroes as clerks and salesmen in the stores within sixty days, and the appointment of a fair employment committee; release of all arrested Negroes on bond or personal recognizance (the Negroes had demanded dismissal of all charges); creation of a bi-racial committee to maintain a "channel of communications" between the races.

Observers wondered if the optimism and spirit of compromise implicit in these statements were justified. Mayor Hanes greeted the news of a pact by calling the white negotiators "a bunch of quisling, gutless traitors," while Governor George C. Wallace had dismissed the agreement even before its announcement. "I, as governor," he had said, "will not be a party to any such meeting to compromise on the issues of segregation."

In any event, the calm lasted but two days.

"Dawn broke in Birmingham today to the sound of crackling flames eating through buildings, the gush of high-powered hoses and the shouts of state troopers," reported Hedrick Smith on May 12th. His article continued:

> Much of a nine-block area looked as if a vicious storm had struck. Smashed and disabled police cruisers were abandoned in the streets. Seven stores and homes lay charred by fire. There was a hole in the brick wall of the A. G. Gaston Motel, caused by an explosion. Plate-glass windows were shattered in store after store in the Negro area.
>
> Heaps of rocks and bricks littered the streets. Glass

smithereens crackled under the feet of officers moving
along sidewalks. In front of the Sixteenth Street Baptist
Church, site of many Negro mass meetings during the
civil-rights drive here, smoke drifted upward from an
overturned taxi. Less than a block away the tire of a
motorcycle smoldered in the early light.

Troopers moved through the area in squads of a
dozen to twenty men, ordering residents into their homes
and outsiders away. By seven A.M., about three hundred
troopers and civilians were enforcing an uneasy peace
in a twenty-eight-block area. They sealed off the section
around the motel to everyone but officials and residents.

The blue-helmeted troopers, with night sticks, car-
bines, small arms and shotguns, later blocked every
street and alleyway leading to the area.

Riots had raged out of control for more than three hours
earlier on the morning of May 12th, after two bombings had
shaken the Negro section. Claude Sitton, writing later in the
day, reported that about fifty people were injured. "About twenty-
five hundred people joined the crowds that attacked the police
and firemen," he said. "The crowds wrecked scores of police and
private automobiles and burned six small stores and a two-story
apartment house." His article continued:

The first bombing demolished the front half of the
home of Reverend A. D. King. He is the younger brother
of the Reverend Dr. Martin Luther King, Jr. Mr. King
and his wife and five children escaped injury.

The second bombing rocked the A. G. Gaston Motel,
which has served as headquarters for the Negroes' integration campaign. Four persons were injured by the
blast, but none seriously enough to require hospitaliza-
tion.

The younger King arrived at the motel from his
bombed home at about 1:30 A.M. and joined other ministers in attempts to disperse the rioters. He succeeded
in attracting about three hundred Negroes into a parking
lot. "We're not mad at anyone," King told them. "We're
saying, 'Father, forgive them for they know not what they
do.' Violence," he said, "has always been the tactic of the
white man," and he urged Negroes not to adopt it.

Another minister called on the crowd to go home and to refrain from violence no matter what happened.

One block to the west, Negro civilian defense workers with the word "Police" stenciled on their hard hats helped the white policemen by holding back bands of angry rioters. A squad of irregulars wearing sports shirts, slacks and G.I. helmets swung down the street, some with double-barreled shotguns over their arms. A Negro emerged from the entrance of the motel and shouted across the street to the irregulars: "We don't have any guns. Why do you have guns?" The irregulars, accompanied by a squad of state troopers, charged across the street minutes later and into the motel enclosure. Negroes fled in terror as they were clubbed with gun butts and night sticks. The "thonk" of clubs striking heads could be heard across the street.

Dr. Martin Luther King flew here from Atlanta and announced tonight in a news conference that Negroes planned no protest demonstrations over the bombings. He indicated that Negroes would not renounce the desegregation agreement. "I do not feel the events of last night nullified the agreement at all," Dr. King said. "I do not think the bombings were perpetrated or even sanctioned by the majority of the white people in Birmingham."

Mayor Arthur J. Hanes, head of the City Commission voted out in a recent election but still holding office during litigation over control of the city government, said: "Martin Luther King is a revolutionary. The nigger King ought to be investigated by the Attorney General.

"This nigger has got the blessing of the Attorney General and the White House."

Then the Mayor said of Attorney General Robert F. Kennedy: "I hope that every drop of blood that's spilled he tastes in his throat, and I hope he chokes on it."

President Kennedy dispatched troops to ready positions near Birmingham on May 12th and took steps toward federalizing the state's National Guard if such action became necessary. It was emphasized, however, that direct intervention in Birmingham would take place only if state and local law enforcement failed.

On May 19th a Washington dispatch to the *Times* summarized the situation and asked a question:

One urgent question raised by the Birmingham
episode is what form the inevitably growing Negro protest is going to take. Will it be the peaceful route of
the Reverend Dr. Martin Luther King, Jr.? Or will it be
the road of black nationalism preached by the Black
Muslims?

During this week in Birmingham, after the bombings
and riots of last weekend, Dr. King was touring the houses
and the pool halls to counsel peace and non-violence. No
matter how much provocation there is from state
troopers, he said, the Negroes should not react emotionally.

But in Washington, Malcolm X, the Muslim leader,
was denouncing Dr. King and his stategy of non-violent
demonstrations. He told a Negro audience: "You need
somebody who is going to fight. You don't need any
kneeling in or crawling in."

The message that the Kennedy Administration has
been trying to get through to the people of Birmingham,
and of the South, is that if they do not accept Dr. King's
way they will get the Muslims' way. Burke Marshall
said that again and again to white businessmen as he
mediated in Birmingham. President Kennedy and his
brother, the Attorney General, told it to Alabama editors
visiting here this week.

There is a question on the white side, too, of what
forces will shape the future. Will it be the new moderates,
symbolized by the Birmingham businessmen who nego-
tiated with Dr. King? Or will it be the extreme segregationists, men like Governor George C. Wallace of
Alabama and Birmingham Comissioner Eugene (Bull)
Connor?

A person who has watched the Birmingham developments intimately said this week that the respected business leaders of that community "now know Dr. King
and his people are doing their best to prevent a God-
awful revolution." But Governor Wallace and Bull Connor do not see it that way. They are calling for sabotage
of the agreement promising a few mild concessions to
Negroes. The Governor's troopers are heightening resent-

ment in the Negro community by patrolling the streets with rifles and acting tough.

Any fair reading of the Birmingham experience and other recent events in the South would have to show the moderate forces gaining. The businessmen were hardly brave in Birmingham; it took days even to bring out the names of those who supported the racial agreement. But this was Birmingham, with a long history of racial intolerance, and it was progress to go that far.

The irresistible argument of the pocketbook is making moderate leaders out of businessmen in many parts of the South. Birmingham's reputation for racial tension has cut new plant investment there by more than three-quarters in the last few years. Other cities do not want that kind of record. And businessmen in Birmingham are finally taking the risk of leadership because they do not want economic decay.

Attorney General Kennedy said the most important lesson of the Negro-white negotiations in Birmingham was the value of reviving a "dialogue" in the South. In fact, talks between Negro and white groups are taking place in many cities of the South now.

What is unsettled is whether the mass of white public opinion will follow the new moderates and accept the inevitable changes peacefully. That is certainly far from settled in Birmingham—or in rural Alabama or Mississippi.

The political situation in Alabama makes trouble almost certain, regardless of how courageously and effectively the businessmen try to work things out with the Negroes. In this volatile picture the Federal Government's role is difficult. Its aim is to create reform from within, not to impose it from without—in short, to persuade the people of the South to accept the Negro's right to be equal.

The President's dispatch of troops to alert positions near Birmingham last Sunday made clear what everyone should have understood all along: He will not permit the racial struggle to run to bloodshed or brutal repression.

But Mr. Kennedy has made it just as clear that he does not want an armed occupation of the South. What,

then, can he do to help the Negroes in the face of resistance from men like Governor Wallace?

The question was soon to be answered by fast-moving events
in Alabama. Although Birmingham had been the primary scene
of conflict in the state in April and May, violence had also
erupted elsewhere. On April 23rd a white, thirty-five-year-old
Baltimore letter carrier had been murdered soon after crossing
into Alabama on a one-man freedom walk. William L. Moore had
hoped to deliver a plea for racial tolerance to the Governor of
Mississippi, and had been carrying sandwich-board signs on
his march. One placard read, "Eat at Joe's, Both Black and
White." The other said, "Equal rights for all—Mississippi or
bust." He had been shot at close range and left on U. S. Route 11.
On May 3rd, a group of ten members of C.O.R.E. and of the
Student Non-violent Co-ordinating Committee had attempted to
"complete" Moore's trek to Mississippi. Alabama highway patrolmen wielding electrical prod poles arrested the marchers while
white onlookers shouted approvingly, "Kill them!" and "Stick
them again!" and "Throw them niggers in the river!"

Perhaps the strongest segregationist voice in Alabama was
that of the newly elected Governor George C. Wallace, who had
campaigned on a bitterly racist platform, vowing to thwart personally any attempts at school or college integration in the state.
Wallace's emotional promises of resistance to federal authority
gave strong encouragement to the voicing of ugly threats by
ruffian segregationists.

"Little George," as the Governor is often called, frequently
stated that racial problems in Alabama were quite simply the
fault of "lawless Negroes." Trained in the ring—he had been a
Golden Gloves bantamweight champion in 1936 and 1937, and
had later fought a few professional bouts—he carried pugnacity
into politics after receiving his law degree at the University of
Alabama. As a state judge he denounced the United States Civil
Rights Commission and briefly evaded a federal court order to
produce voter registration records, threatening to jail any federal agent caught "trying to interfere" with his court. After his
election in 1962, with the greatest popular vote received in
Alabama, he defiantly proclaimed: "I say segregation now, segregation tomorrow, segregation forever!"

On May 21st, little more than a week after the Birmingham

riots, Federal District Court Judge Hobart H. Grooms—sitting in Birmingham—told the University of Alabama that it must admit two Negro applicants to its summer session, beginning on June 10th. The University applied for permission to postpone their admission, in view of "the present state of unrest in Alabama." The court refused.

Governor Wallace's reaction was prompt. At a news conference he read a statement saying: "I am the embodiment of the sovereignty of this state and I will be present to bar the entrance of any Negro who attempts to enroll at the University of Alabama."

The Justice Department moved to prevent the Governor from obstructing admission of the Negro students. Judge Seymour H. Lynne of the federal district court agreed with the Government request and specifically forbade Governor Wallace from "physically interposing his persons to block the Negroes," extending this prohibition to "all persons in active concert" with the Governor. A native of Decatur, Alabama, and a graduate of the University of Alabama Law School, Judge Lynne added two unusual paragraphs to his order. They read:

> May it be forgiven if this court makes use of the personal pronoun for the first time in a written opinion. I love the people of Alabama. I know that many of both races are troubled and like Jonah of old, are "angry even unto death" as the result of distortions of affairs within this state, practiced in the name of segregationalism.
>
> My prayer is that all of our people, in keeping with our finest traditions, will join in the resolution that law and order will be maintained, both in Tuscaloosa and in Huntsville.

Speaking over statewide television, Governor Wallace indicated that he might defy the court order. He coupled this threat, however, with a plea to the people of the state to "maintain law and order next week," and to stay away from the university campuses. "I will not let you down," he promised, "in this matter of standing up for you."

To many Americans it seemed that violence was inevitable—perhaps the sort of rioting that had taken place on the Tuscaloosa campus in 1956, when Autherine Lucy was briefly enrolled as a student, or perhaps the kind of battlefield mayhem that had occurred in 1962 at the University of Mississippi.

More than three thousand army troops were being held in readiness by the Government at military installations within Alabama. And out of what he called "an abundance of caution," Governor Wallace ordered a five-hundred-man military police unit to prepare to move into the area on Sunday, June 9th, to assist law-enforcement groups there. Already maintaining a watch on the campus and patrolling the area for miles around were some four-hundred and twenty-five state troopers and about four-hundred revenue agents, game wardens, and others deputized for the occasion.

The week began on a suspenseful note, with the nation's eyes turned toward Tuscaloosa. On Monday, June 10th, President Kennedy sent a wire to Governor Wallace sternly admonishing him not to carry out his campaign pledge to "stand in the schoolhouse door" to prevent the university's integration the next day. Wallace, already on the scene of the confrontation, retorted that his presence "guaranteed peace."

> Tuesday in Tuscaloosa Governor Wallace duly took his stand in the doorway of the building where students were to register for the summer session. There followed a kind of charade. Mr. Wallace went through the motions of carrying out his promise and federal officials evidently were willing to play along with him so long as he did not really resort to defiance.
>
> As they approached the doorway the Governor gave them a "stop" signal with outstretched hand. He refused to step aside and the federal party retreated and took the two Negro students involved—Vivian Malone and James A. Hood, both twenty—to their dormitories. When word of the Governor's stand reached Washington, the President signed a prepared order for federalization of part of the Alabama National Guard.
>
> About four hours later federalized Guardsmen arrived on the campus. With that the Governor walked off stage and Miss Malone and Mr. Hood walked in, to go through the registration routine. On the whole the white students seemed to take their presence in stride.
>
> In the White House that evening, June 11th, President Kennedy used the occasion to make a nationwide television broadcast.

He related briefly the events of the day in Tuscaloosa. Then he went on to talk about the larger issue of racial justice facing this country. It was one of the great speeches in the history of the American Presidency.

I hope that every American, regardless of where he lives, will stop and examine his conscience about this and other related incidents. This nation was founded by men of many nations and backgrounds. It was founded on the principle that all men are created equal, and that the rights of every man are diminished when the rights of one man are threatened.

Today we are committed to a worldwide struggle to promote and protect the rights of all who wish to be free. And when Americans are sent to Vietnam or West Berlin we do not ask for whites only.

It ought to be possible, therefore, for American students of any color to attend any public institution they select without having to be backed up by troops. It ought to be possible for American consumers of any color to receive equal service in places of public accommodation, such as hotels and restaurants, and theatres and retail stores, without being forced to resort to demonstrations in the street.

And it ought to be possible for American citizens of any color to register and to vote in a free election without interference or fear of reprisal. It ought to be possible, in short, for every American to enjoy the privileges of being American without regard to his race or his color.

In short, every American ought to have the right to be treated as he would wish to be treated, as one would wish his children to be treated. But this is not the case.

The Negro baby born in America today, regardless of the section or the state in which he is born, has about one-half as much chance of completing a high school as a white baby, born in the same place, on the same day; one-third as much chance of completing college; one-third as much chance of becoming a professional man; twice as much chance of becoming unemployed; about one-seventh as much chance of earning ten thousand dollars a year; a life expectancy which is seven years shorter and the prospects of earning only half as much.

This is not a sectional issue. Difficulties over segregation and discrimination exist in every city, in every state of the Union, producing in many cities a rising tide of discontent that threatens the public safety. Nor is this a partisan issue. In a time of domestic crisis, men of good will and generosity should be able to unite regardless of party or politics. This is not a legal or legislative issue alone. It is better to settle these matters in the courts than on the streets, and new laws are needed at every level. But law alone cannot make men see right.

We are confronted primarily with a moral issue. It is as old as the Scriptures and is as clear as the American Constitution. The heart of the question is whether all Americans are to be afforded equal rights and equal opportunities; whether we are going to treat our fellow Americans as we want to be treated.

If an American, because his skin is dark, cannot eat lunch in a restaurant open to the public; if he cannot send his children to the best public school available; if he cannot vote for the public officials who represent him; if, in short, he cannot enjoy the full and free life which all of us want, then who among us would be content to have the color of his skin changed and stand in his place?

Who among us would then be content with the counsels of patience and delay? One hundred years of delay have passed since President Lincoln freed the slaves, yet their heirs, their grandsons, are not fully free. They are not yet freed from the bonds of injustice; they are not yet freed from social and economic oppression. And this nation, for all its hopes and all its boasts, will not be fully free until all its citizens are free.

We preach freedom around the world, and we mean it. And we cherish our freedom here at home. But are we to say to the world—and much more importantly to each other—that this is the land of the free, except for the Negroes; that we have no second-class citizens, except Negroes; that we have no class or caste system, no ghettos, no master race, except with respect to Negroes.

Now the time has come for this nation to fulfill its promise. The events in Birmingham and elsewhere have so increased the cries for equality that no city or state or legislative body can prudently choose to ignore them. The fires of frustration and discord are burning in every city,

North and South. Where legal remedies are not at hand, redress is sought in the streets in demonstrations, parades and protests, which create tensions and threaten violence —and threaten lives.

We face, therefore, a moral crisis as a country and a people. It cannot be met by repressive police action. It cannot be left to increased demonstrations in the streets. It cannot be quieted by token moves or talk. It is a time to act in the Congress, in your state and local legislative body, and, above all, in all of our daily lives.

It is not enough to pin the blame on others, to say this is a problem of one section of the country or another, or deplore the facts that we face. A great change is at hand, and our task, our obligation, is to make that revolution, that change peaceful and constructive for all. Those who do nothing are inviting shame as well as violence. Those who act boldly are recognizing right as well as reality. . . .

In this respect, I want to pay tribute to those citizens, North and South, who've been working in their communities to make life better for all. They are acting not out of a sense of legal duty but out of a sense of human decency. Like our soldiers and sailors in all parts of the world, they are meeting freedom's challenge on the firing line and I salute them for their honor—their courage.

My fellow Americans, this is a problem which faces us all, in every city of the North as well as the South. Today there are Negroes unemployed—two or three times as many as whites; there is inadequate education; Negroes are moving into the large cities, unable to find work, young people particularly are out of work; they are without hope, denied equal rights, denied the opportunity to eat at a restaurant or a lunch counter or go to a movie theatre, denied the right to a decent education, denied almost today the right to attend a state university even though qualified.

It seems to me that these are matters which concern us all—not merely Presidents, or congressmen, or governors, but every citizen of the United States. This is one country. It has become one country because all of us and all the people who came here had an equal chance to develop their talents.

We cannot say to ten per cent of the population that "you can't have that right. Your children can't have the chance to develop whatever talents they have; the only way that they're going to get their rights is to go in the street and demonstrate."

I think we owe them and we owe ourselves a better country than that. Therefore, I'm asking for your help in making it easier for us to move ahead and provide the kind of equality of treatment which we would want ourselves—to give a chance for every child to be educated to the limit of his talent.

As I've said before, not every child has an equal talent or an equal ability or equal motivation. But they should have the equal right to develop their talent and their ability and their motivation to make something of themselves. We have a right to expect that the Negro community will be responsible, will uphold the law. But they have a right to expect the law will be fair, that the Constitution will be color blind, as Justice Harlan said at the turn of the century.

This is what we're talking about. This is a matter which concerns this country and what it stands for, and in meeting it I ask the support of all our citizens.

Thank you very much.

The events in Tuscaloosa had made it clear that a turning point had been reached. There was no longer even a shred of pretense that state resistance could prevail over the Federal Government. Everything the Governor had done in Alabama indicated that he knew he could not prevent the admission of the Negro students. He had been going through the motions of keeping a campaign promise.

Now the charade continued, for in compliance with the national law, elementary and high schools in three cities of Alabama were to be integrated next, when the fall term began. As September approached, the state grew tense. Trouble was feared in Tuskegee, Mobile and Birmingham. On May 16, 1963, the new administration in Birmingham had finally succeeded the Hanes-Connor group, and the unofficial desegregation pact had to some extent been implemented by the new Mayor and City Council. Yet violence had nevertheless occasionally erupted. Tear-gas bombs were detonated at one of the desegregated

department stores in mid-August. On August 21st, the home of
Arthur D. Shores, a Negro lawyer who represented plaintiffs in
the School Segregation case, was bombed, and this act had
touched off angry riots. And Mayor Albert Boutwell and other
whites active in the campaign to assure peaceful school desegregation had been receiving threatening letters and telephone
calls.

Governor Wallace, explaining that he did so "to preserve the
peace," moved suddenly on September 2nd to seal off the schools
with blue-helmeted state troopers or to otherwise delay their
openings. But those who had supported his efforts in the past
now conceded them to be futile, and one scathing comment after
another was expressed by officials and the press. The Montgomery *Advertiser*, previously a strong supporter of the Governor, now said that it had to "sorrowfully conclude that, in this
instance, its friend has gone wild. Alabama is not a banana
republic. It is in no need of an adventurer to ride down upon
local authority."

When Wallace placed National Guardsmen at the doors of
schools in the three cities to keep the Negro children out, President Kennedy federalized the Guardsmen and had them whisked
back to their armories, where they stayed to await further orders.
Thus twenty Negroes were able to enter previously all-white
schools in Alabama on September 10th. And thus Governor Wallace, this time without the applause of supporters, had again
acted out a meaningless ritual of defiance.

In Birmingham, where twenty-four Negro children were now
enrolled in public schools, things seemed at last to be quiet. The
Sixteenth Street Baptist Church, for so long the staging point
for protest demonstrations, was now once again fulfilling its
function as a house of worship and as a Sunday School for
youngsters.

On a quiet Sunday morning, September 15th, a children's
Bible class was in session at the church. Mrs. Ella C. Demand, a
Sunday School teacher, had just completed a lesson titled, "The
Love That Forgives." Now the Negro boys and girls in her class
waited in a lounge before attending an assembly in the main
auditorium. It was ten twenty-five A.M. Suddenly a thundering
blast shattered the peace, smashing gaping holes in the walls of
the church basement. Floors of offices in the rear of the sanctuary
were twisted and torn. Stairways were blocked by splintered

window frames, glass and timbers. Huddled together beneath a pile of masonry debris were the bodies of four girls from Mrs. Demand's class—Cynthia Wesely, fourteen; Denise McNair, eleven; Carol Robertson, fourteen; and Addie Mae Collins, fourteen. Fourteen other Negroes were injured in the explosion.

"This is the most distressing day in the history of Birmingham," said Sheriff Melvin Bailey. As the *Times* reported it:

> Hundreds of Negroes poured into the streets after the explosion. Some attacked the police with stones. The police dispersed them by firing shotguns over their heads. Johnny Robinson, a sixteen year-old Negro, was shot in the back and killed by a policeman with a shotgun. Officers said the victim was among a group that had hurled stones at white youths driving through the area in cars flying Confederate battle flags. When the police arrived, the youths fled, and one policeman said he had fired low but that some of the shot had struck the Robinson youth in the back.
>
> Virgil Wade, a thirteen year-old Negro, was shot and killed just outside Birmingham while riding a bicycle. The Jefferson County sheriff's office said "there apparently was no reason at all" for the killing, but indicated that it was related to the general racial disorders.
>
> Another Negro youth and a white youth were shot but not seriously wounded in separate incidents. Four whites, including a honeymooning couple from Chicago, were injured by stones while driving through the neighborhood of the bombing.
>
> Governor Wallace, at the request of city officials, offered a five-thousand-dollar reward for the arrest and conviction of the bombers. None of the fifty bombings of Negro property in Birmingham since World War II had been solved. Mayor Albert Boutwell and other city officials and civic leaders appeared on television station WAPI and urged residents to cooperate in ending "this senseless reign of terror."

Why, the nation wondered, was Birmingham so driven to strife? And when, the world wondered, would the ugly, ungovernable turbulence end? James Reston attempted to find answers in a *Times* article printed on September 20th:

The striking thing about Birmingham to an outsider is that it seems so advanced industrially and so retarded politically. It has seized the scientific revolution and rejected the social revolution of our time. Accordingly, it is engaged in a remarkable and hazardous experiment: it is trying to back full speed into the future.

The visible and audible symbols of the city dramatize this paradox. It lies in a long valley surrounded by lovely flowering hills. Above the forest of smoking chimneys stands on a peak a vast stainless-steel statue of Vulcan, like some hideous modernistic monster out of the German Ruhr. Yet down below in the city the symbols are not of the fires of the future but of the fires of the past. The Confederate flag is painted on the cars and helmets of Governor George Wallace's state troopers, now very much in evidence here, and the biggest clock in town booms out across the city from the tower of the Protective Life Insurance Company a few bars of "Dixie" before it strikes each hour. Look to the industrial future, says the gleaming Vulcan. "Look away, look away, look away, Dixie Land," chimes the clock.

That Birmingham should have become the symbol of southern defiance adds to the paradox, for it did not come out of the tradition of the old agrarian, slave-holding, plantation South. It was not even incorporated until December, 1871, in the decade after the war between the states; it was populated from the North more than almost any southern city, and its commercial and industrial ties now run to New York and Pittsburgh rather than to Atlanta or New Orleans.

Like most industrial cities it does have a tradition of putting private interests above public interests and it does have a history of violence. It was for many years an overgrown mining camp, populated by rough men from all sections of the country. Convict labor from the state prisons worked in the mines until the early 1920's, and National Guardsmen first went on strike patrol during the coal miners' walkout here in 1894. Thus Birmingham is not like any other city in the country. Industrially it is ahead of much of the North; politically it is behind most of the urban South. It pays its Negroes better and in some ways treats them worse than most southern towns, partly because it suffers from some of the worst aspects of both industrialization and segregation.

No generalization about Birmingham is safe, but its history does help suggest one possible explanation about the present attitude of many of its most influential leaders. This is not a city dominated by inherited wealth. More than in most southern cities, Birmingham's commercial and industrial leaders are self-made men, with the self-made man's feeling that others can be just as successful too if they will only work.

Many white leaders here created their own fortunes, others are managers under pressure from northern headquarters to produce the maximum at the minimum cost. As human beings, they are probably no better or worse than business leaders in other cities, but there is something in the history and atmosphere of this place, some relationship between the idea of the supremacy of the dollar and the supremacy of the white man, that has made them feel they could hold out longer against social change. It isn't that they wanted more than other white leaders in Atlanta and elsewhere, but merely that in this particular city they thought they could get away with demanding more.

The result is that the leaders of Birmingham are trapped for the time being in the struggle. For the more they have delayed making concessions to Negro equality, the more the Federal Government has dramatized their dilemma, and the more the Negroes have demanded, and the more business the city has lost. The death of the four Negro children in this week's bombing of a Negro church has merely brought all this to a head. It has shocked the community, but there is little evidence that it has changed the convictions of the white leaders about what they regard as the proper (separate) relations between the races. They merely seem a little more convinced now that the continued uproar here is not good business, and Birmingham wants good business, even if it has to obey the federal law to get it.

The day after the church bombing Charles Morgan, Jr., a thirty-three-old white Birmingham lawyer, was scheduled to speak to the city's Young Men's Business Club. He sat down that morning and wrote out his thoughts about the responsibility for four children's death. This is what he said on September 16, 1963:

Four little girls were killed in Birmingham Sunday. A mad, remorseful, worried community asks "Who did it? Who threw that bomb? Was it a Negro or a white?"

The answer should be "We all did it." Every last one of us is condemned for that crime and the bombing before it and the ones last month, last year, a decade ago. We all did it.

A short time later, white policemen kill a Negro and wound another. A few hours later two young men on a motor bike shoot and kill a Negro child. Fires break out and, in Montgomery, white youths assault Negroes. And all across Alabama, an angry, guilty people cry out their mocking shouts of indignity and say they wonder, "Why?" "Who?" Everyone then "deplores" the "dastardly" act.

But, you know the "who" of "who did it?" is really rather simple. The "who" is every little individual who talks about the "niggers" and spreads the seeds of his hate to his neighbor and his son. The jokester, the crude oaf whose racial jokes rock the party with laughter. The "who" is every governor who ever shouted for lawlessness and became a law violator.

It is every senator and every representative who in the halls of Congress stands and with mock humility tells the world that things back home aren't really like they are. It is courts that move ever so slowly and newspapers that timorously defend the law. It is all the Christians and all the ministers who spoke too late in anguished cries against violence.

It is the coward in each of us who clucks admonitions. We are ten years of lawless preachments, ten years of criticism of law, of courts, of our fellow man, a decade of telling school children the opposite of what the civics books say. We are a mass of intolerance and bigotry and stand indicted before our young. We are cursed by the failure of each of us to accept responsibility, by our defense of an already dead institution.

Sunday, while Birmingham, which prides itself on the number of its churches, was attending worship service, a bomb went off and an all-white police force moved into action, a police force which has been praised by city officials and others at least once a day for a month or so. A police force which has solved no bombings. A police force which many Negroes feel is perpetrating the very evils we decry. And why would Negroes think this?

There no Negro policemen; there are no Negro sheriff's deputies. Few Negroes have served on juries. Few have been allowed to vote, few have been allowed to accept responsibility, or granted even a simple part to play in the administration of justice. Do not misunderstand me. It is not that I think that white policemen had anything whatsoever to do with the killing of these children or previous bombings. It's just that Negroes who see an all-white police force must think in terms of its failure to prevent or solve the bombings and think perhaps Negroes would have worked a little bit harder. They throw rocks and bottles and bullets. And we whites don't seem to know why the Negroes are lawless. So, we lecture them.

Birmingham is the only city in America where police chief and sheriff in the school crisis had to call our local ministers together to tell them to do their duty. The ministers of Birmingham who have done so little for Christianity call for prayer at high noon in a city of lawlessness and, in the same breath, speak of our city's "image." Did those ministers visit the families of the Negroes in their hour of travail? Did any of them go to the homes of their brothers and express their regret in person or pray with the crying relatives? Do they admit Negroes into their ranks at the church?

Who is guilty? A moderate mayor elected to change things in Birmingham and who moves so slowly and looks elsewhere for leadership? A business community which shrugs its shoulders and looks to the police or perhaps somewhere else for leadership? A newspaper which has tried so hard of late, yet finds it necessary to lecture Negroes every time a Negro home is bombed? A Governor who offers a reward but mentions not his own failure to preserve either segregation or law and order? And what of those lawyers and politicians who counsel people as to what the law is not when they know full well what the law is?

Those four little Negro girls were human beings. They have lived their fourteen years in a leaderless city; a city where no one accepts responsibility; where everybody wants to blame somebody else. A city with a reward fund which grew like Topsy as a sort of sacrificial offering, a balm for the conscience of the "good people." The "good people" whose ready answer is for those "right-wing extremists" to shut up. People who absolve themselves of guilt. The liberal lawyer who told me this morning, "Me? I'm not guilty," then proceeded to discuss the guilt of the other lawyers, the ones who told the people that the Supreme Court did not properly interpret the law. And that's the way it is with the southern liberals. They condemn those with whom they disagree for speaking while they sigh in fearful silence.

Birmingham is a city in which the major industry, operated from Pittsburgh, never tried to solve the problem. It is a city where four little Negro girls can be born into a second-class school system, live a segregated life, ghettoed into their own little neigborhoods, restricted to Negro churches, destined to ride in Negro ambulances, to Negro wards of hospitals or to a Negro cemetery. Local papers, on their front and editorial pages, call for order and then exclude their names from obituary columns.

And who is really guilty? Each of us. Each citizen who has not consciously attempted to bring about peaceful compliance with the decisions of the Supreme Court of the United States, each citizen who has ever said "they ought to kill that nigger," every citizen who votes for the candidate with the bloody flag; every citizen and every school-board member and school teacher and principal and businessman and judge and lawyer who has corrupted the minds of our youth; every person in this community who has in any way contributed during the past several years to the popularity of hatred, is at least as guilty, or more so, than the demented fool who threw that bomb.

What's it like living in Birmingham? No one ever really has and no one will until this city becomes part of the United States.

Birmingham is not a dying city; it is dead.

Charles Morgan's words attracted national attention, but the pressure brought by Birmingham on Morgan and his family became insupportable—and they left. But there was, slowly, change. In the summer of 1964—almost a year later—Birmingham seemed to be adjusting peacefully to the new Civil Rights Act, and public facilities were desegregated to a degree that few would have been willing to predict in the embattled days of 1963.

Chapter 11

Mississippi

The revolution that so profoundly changed American race relations between 1954 and 1964 stopped at the borders of Mississippi. Northerners who were concerned with the problem felt, when they visited Mississippi, that they had strayed into another time, another country. There the law that bound other Americans, the law of the Constitution as interpreted by the Supreme Court, was simply ignored. State and even federal judges acted as if the Fourteenth Amendment were not applicable to Mississippi. Evasion, intimidation, violence met Negro attempts to exercise the most elementary rights of citizenship. For any white man, or woman, who dared to dissent from segregationist orthodoxy there was similar harassment. Even more striking than the unimpaired external structure of white supremacy was the emotional atmosphere in the state. "The unscrupulous have virtual immunity so long as they act in the name of segregation," Claude Sitton wrote in the *New York Times Magazine* on April 28, 1963. "Charlatans who would be laughed off the streets in normal times find a receptive audience. History is rewritten, substituting pleasing fiction for unpleasant fact. And the Mississippian, who bows to no man in loyalty to country, lends encouragement or stands by silently while his public officials flirt with sedition."

Sitton's piece, entitled "Inquiry into the Mississippi Mind," traced some of the elements that made the state what it was.

Mississippi was settled by planters and slaves from the worn-out farms of the southern Piedmont. Streaming into the lands of the Choctaw and Chickasaw at the beginning of the nineteenth century, they built an empire on cotton. The state became one of the nation's richest. But much of its wealth was wiped out by the Civil War, subsequent depressions and the boll weevil. It is now the poorest state in the nation. Mississippi had a per capita income in 1961 of only $1,229, compared with a national average of $2,263. The median annual family income of its whites was $4,209, and of its Negroes, $1,444.

The state has the third highest illiteracy rate—4.9 per cent—in the nation, trailing only South Carolina and Louisiana. A total of 32,196 of its Negroes and 8,444 of its whites have never attended school. A far larger number, 119,741 Negroes and 40,274 whites, are considered functional illiterates. Negroes, who once outnumbered whites, now make up only forty-three per cent of the state's population of 2,178,141. Mississippians are still a largely rural people; only thirty-eight per cent live in urban areas. Most of the state's manufacturing jobs are in scattered, small textile and apparel plants. Jackson, the capital and the state's largest city, has a population of 150,000.

Mississippi offers a study in contrasts, especially in the Delta. Greek-revival mansions and rambling ranch houses in groves of shade trees look out on weather-beaten rows of clapboard cabins and tar-paper shacks, most of which have open privies and some of which lack even running water. A planter dressed in expensive western boots and hat gets up from a leisurely meal in a restaurant and displays a rare dime valued at $90 from his coin collection. Less than a mile away, a Negro mother arises and prepares a breakfast of sugar syrup and hoecake for her children, some of whom cannot attend school because they have no shoes.

The state's campaign for economic expansion has reached a promising stage. The International Paper Company plant, whose towering smokestack dominates the tidewater town of Moss Point, the cargo ships and nuclear submarines on the ways in the Ingalls Shipyard in Pascagoula and the Standard Oil refinery under construction at Bayou Casotte offer impressive evidence of progress. Business experts see no evidence that segregation has hampered such industrial growth, but continuing racial unrest is another thing indeed. A leading financial economist in the southeast predicts that Mississippi's number of new plant acquisitions will begin to decline at midyear. "It will continue shrinking for a long time to come, until and unless the state shows that it is willing to rejoin the Union," he says.

High as is the economic cost of intransigeancy, the social cost is higher. A thumbnail sketch of what white supremacy means in Mississippi is provided in a current report of the state advisory committee to the Federal Civil Rights Commission. It should be noted that its members are Mississippians.

"The committee's investigations have indicated that in all important areas of citizenship, a Negro in Mississippi receives substantially less than his due consideration as an American and as a Mississippian. This denial extends from the time he is denied the right to be born in a nonsegregated hospital, through his segregated and inferior school years and his productive years when jobs for which he can qualify are refused, to the day he dies and is laid to rest in a cemetery for Negroes only."

Further, Negroes frequently are denied the most effective recourse from these wrongs—the ballot. The extreme to which disfranchisement goes and the irrational behavior of some whites when confronted by a mere attempt to remedy the situation have just been underscored in Leflore County in the Delta.

More than ninety-five per cent of the county's whites twenty-one years of age and older are registered, but less than two per cent of its Negroes. State law gives voter registrars almost sole discretion in saying who may and who may not vote.

The Justice Department recently instituted a federal court action against registrars in Leflore and six other Mississippi counties. But even under reasonable regulations fairly applied, the ignorance and impoverishment of many Leflore County Negroes would preclude their registration. Thus it would appear that, with the cards so patently stacked in favor of white political supremacy, the registration campaign started there last August would have caused no stir. Not so. Campaign workers have been threatened, harassed, beaten and shot. And such terrorism has not been restricted to Leflore County or to the Delta. The Voter Education Project, an Atlanta-based organization financed by national foundations, has issued a list of sixty-four separate acts of violence and intimidation directed against Negroes since January, 1961, in more than a dozen counties. Virtually all of these incidents were related to registration activities.

Some Mississippians believe that the rest of the nation is on their side and that succor cannot be long in coming. "I found a lot of sympathy in the Midwest for our position, particularly in regard to our respect for states' rights and the Tenth Amendment," said one returning missionary.

What underlies this refusal of white Mississippians to face reality? Undoubtedly, the heritage of slavery, the stark poverty and profound isolation that Mississippi has known have played a part. Another important factor has been the fear of the Negro felt by what until recently was a white minority.

There is also bitter resentment against the North. This was first aroused by abolitionism and reinforced by the North's failure to follow a consistent racial policy, either in its demands made upon the South or in its handling of the problem in its own backyard. In a word, Mississippians consider northerners hypocritical.

The genesis of the current agony, of course, lies in the school desegregation decision of the Supreme Court. Dr. C. Vann Woodward, an authority on the history of the post-Civil War South, has written that Mississippi came forward in 1954 "in her historic role as leader of reaction in race policy, just as she had in 1875 to overthrow Reconstruction and in 1890 to disfranchise the Negro." Significantly, many of the state's present leaders—Governor Ross R. Barnett, House Speaker Walter Sillers and Senator James O. Eastland—grew up in the climate of reaction created by those earlier bench-marks of southern democracy. And they served their political apprenticeships in the school of Senators James K. Vardaman, "The Great White Chief," who advocated repeal of the Fifteenth Amendment as the first step toward saving Anglo-Saxon civilization, and Theodore G. Bilbo, known as "The Man," who plumbed the depths of demagoguery.

Raw material from this background combined with the catalyst of the Court's desegregation ruling to touch off a racial conflagration. The first alarm was sounded in the Delta county of Sunflower, home of Senator Eastland, in the summer of 1954 when the first Citizens Council was founded. This was the initial step toward institutionalized bigotry in a more or less respectable setting.

There followed a campaign of indoctrination with few parallels in American history. The results have been described by Dr. James W. Silver, professor of history at the University of Mississippi, in the *New Mexico Electric News*: "Most organizations and individuals (press, pulpit, politicians, patriots, philosophers) capable of influencing public opinion are militantly arrayed in the indoctrination process. A never-ceasing propagation of the 'true faith' goes on day after day. The constant demand, particularly in emergencies, for a united front requires that potential nonconformists and dissenters from the accepted code be kept under wraps, squelched, or, in extreme cases, run out of the community."

What happens to those who dissent is shown by the case of Ira Harkey, editor and publisher of the *Chronicle* at Pascagoula. Harkey, who resembles a low-key Jimmy Cagney, holds that the rights of every man should be protected, "whether he be white, black, yellow, green or shades in between." One of his most biting editorial commentaries on the Mississippi scene followed publication of a letter from a relative of Governor Barnett who is a

missionary in Africa. She criticized Mississippians for
sending persons to minister to Negroes abroad and then
undercutting the missionaries by mistreating Negroes at
home. To this, the *Chronicle* said: "In Mississippi, a person who attempts to carry Christianity out the church
door, who dares to practice the Christian virtue of tolerance outside the church, is cursed as a liberal, a leftist, a
communist, a nigger-lover. Christ was the greatest champion of the underdog the world has ever known. If He
were to visit us here, now, by whose side would He stand,
beside the brick-throwing, foul-mouthed, destroying, pro-
faning, slavering members of the mob and their 'nice-folk'
eggers-on, or beside the trembling victim of their hate?"

Harkey's rewards have included a bullet through the
Chronicle's front door, a shotgun blast through his office
window, an advertising boycott, "hate" mail and social
ostracism.

The vision of white supremacy in the Mississippi mind was
graphically described in a *Times Magazine* piece November 10,
1963, by Margaret Long, a novelist and former columnist for the
Atlanta Journal. She interviewed Don Barrett, a fraternity boy at
Ole Miss.

"I feel, as do most of the white population of the
South, that the Negro is inherently unequal," Barrett
said. "Now, they say it's lack of opportunity, cause and
result, the reason men first took the fire and light of
learning, that the Nigras never had the need in Africa
because they could just pluck the fruit of the woods and
all, and sustain life on that. But you can't say they didn't
get learning and civilization because of the easy climate,
because they've got a range of all climates and moun-
tains and jungles. They came into contact with the
Saracens in North Africa. And Alexander the Great and
they never did catch the light of learning, nobody in the
region. If they hadn't been taken over by the white
man . . .

"Well, where they're not, they're still eating each
other," he said, his voice vibrant with triumph and dis-
gust.

"But the white South has taken the Neegra, fed, clothed, taught them how to speak and wear clothes and taught him Christianity. Still, look at 'em, their illegitimacy rate!"

Barrett is also apprehensive about treatment of white women under black domination. "If the social system is thrown out of kilter, as moderates would do, there would be more danger than there is now under the patient hand of white leadership. I would certainly take up arms to protect our women. To me there is nothing more wonderful than a southern lady. Gosh! It's really undefinable. But she's cultured, genteel, intelligent, beautiful—usually beautiful, anyway."

In defense of the social and economic system, Barrett would not eat with a Negro, or call one Mr. or Mrs. or Miss, because "it's not socially acceptable, it's not done—any more than I'd cut more than one piece of steak at a time or tuck my napkin under my chin."

The Citizens Councils, as Sitton said, were designed to make bigotry respectable. In Mississippi towns they were like chambers of commerce or civic clubs, including almost all the prominent white businessmen and other leaders. The statewide Council organization had decisive influence on the state government, dominating the legislature and executive, and indeed receiving appropriations from the state to carry on a television program, Citizens Council Forum. In this as in private Council meetings the gospel was preached: The Negro is naturally inferior, integration is being pushed by Communists to destroy America, whites must stand together in unbending resistance. But not with violence—no, the Councils always insisted on respectability. That violence might follow from counsels of unreasoning fear and hate was not their business.

And there was violence in Mississippi. In 1955, the year after the School decision, there were three lynchings in the state—the first in this country since 1951. One victim was a fourteen-year-old Negro boy, Emmett Till, who had been accused of whistling at a white woman.

In 1959 there came another lynching, one that threw unusual light on the quality of Mississippi justice. The victim was Mack Charles Parker, a twenty-three-year-old Negro accused of

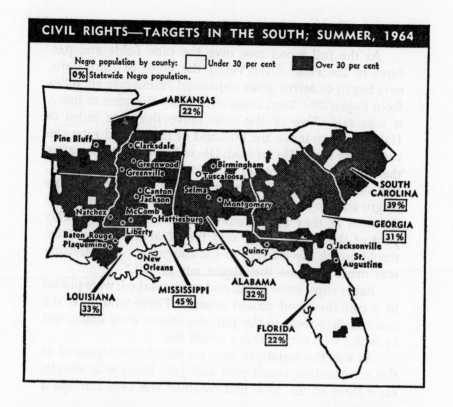

raping a pregnant white woman. The woman picked Parker out of a group of twenty Negroes assembled by the police. Later she said: "When I saw the man, I told these police that I wasn't positive it was him but it looked like him. But the picture in the paper looked exactly like the man."

On April 25, 1959, two days before he was to be tried, Parker was dragged from the Poplarville jail by a mob of masked men. His body was found in the Pearl River on May 4th. What made the case unusual was that the facts of what happened and who was involved were widely known and printed—and the law did nothing. Claude Sitton summarized in the *Times* what was known on January 4, 1960:

> Poplarville residents told a visitor last week that the names of the chief suspects and the details of the lynching had been common gossip in that county seat for some time. Inquiries there and among officials and others elsewhere in the state with a knowledge of the case produced a detailed account of events surrounding Parker's death.

As the full moon rose over the pine fields and pastures of the Pearl River Valley the night of April 24th, cars began to arrive at an unpainted farmhouse six miles from Poplarville. Soon there were thirty-five men or more, it was said. Two of the men drove thirty-six miles to Hattiesburg to invite the husband of the alleged rape victim to join them. He refused. His wife told newsmen after the lynching that Parker should have received a trial. She said she had no objection to being questioned by the Negro attorneys. But this was the point most discussed by the men as they milled around in the hard-packed clay yard of the house. Many said they feared that someone would attack the lawyers in the courtroom. The decision was made to "take the nigger out of jail."

Paper slips, some blank and some marked, were placed in a container and passed around. Those who drew the marked slips went to the jail; the others went home, not knowing who the lynchers would be.

As was the usual practice, no guard was stationed at the combination courthouse and jail. Entry was simple, once three of the men had obtained the keys through a contact.

Parker's fellow prisoners said that nine men disguised in masks and gloves had clattered up the stairway at the rear of the second-floor courtroom and into the cell block. One held a pistol. Others brandished clubs. After a brief scuffle, Parker was dragged struggling and screaming down the stairway. His captors clubbed him on the head repeatedly. His head bounced off the steel treads like "a ping pong ball," it was said. A trail of bloody hand prints was left behind as he clawed frantically at the steps.

Four men tossed Parker into the back seat of a four-door sedan, jumped into the car and drove off. Three others followed in another automobile. The cars raced westward through the tung-tree orchards toward the Pearl River, the boundary between Mississippi and Louisiana. They stopped just short of the bridge over the muddy river, which was swollen by spring rains. Parker was pulled from the car and dumped on the ground. Two shots through the chest ended his life.

The men picked up Parker's body to throw it over the

railing. But the headlights of a car approaching from the
Louisiana side of the bridge frightened them. They threw
the body into the automobile and drove away. It is
thought that they crossed the bridge into Louisiana and
turned around at a livestock inspection station. Driving
back into Mississippi, they dropped the body into the river
on the downstream side of the bridge.

By Saturday afternoon, R.W. Bachman, special agent
in charge of the New Orleans office of the Federal Bureau
of Investigation, and a number of agents had arrived in
Poplarville. Justice Department officials said the investigation that followed was one of the most intensive in the
F.B.I.'s history and cost about $80,000.

The F.B.I. report ran to three hundred and seventy-
eight pages. The Justice Department turned it over to Mississippi Governor J. P. Coleman, who subsequently gave it
to Vernon Broome, Circuit Prosecutor. J. Edgar Hoover,
the F.B.I. director, announced that agents would be
available to testify "should the case be tried in a state
court."

An eighteen-member grand jury was impaneled on
November 2nd by Circuit Judge Sebe Dale in Poplarville.
In his charge to the jury, the judge said that recent
Supreme Court decisions might have been responsible for
the lynching. He referred to the Court as that "board of
sociology, sitting in Washington, garbed in judicial robes."
Three days later the grand jurors went home without
action in the Parker case. They had declined to hear
F.B.I. agents, who had offered to appear without being
subpoenaed. Prosecutor Broome and County Attorney
William H. Stewart indicated that the panel had made
no request for the F.B.I. report. "I have an idea the nation may look down on Mississippi justice now," said
Judge Dale. "But I'm not apologizing."

Those questioned in Poplarville last week said that
residents generally agreed with the grand jury's course.
They pointed out that there would have been practically
no chance of convicting Parker's murderers had they been
indicted. A trial, they contended, would only have em-
barrassed the community. "You couldn't convict the

guilty parties if you had a sound film of the lynching," said one official.

The Attorney General of the United States, William P. Rogers, termed the handling of the case "a travesty on justice, . . . flagrant and calculated." He had said the murder was a matter for state handling, but now he reopened a federal proceeding. The details in the F.B.I. report were presented to a federal grand jury—made up, as the Constitution requires, of local citizens, in this instance twenty whites and one Negro. The Justice Department asked the jury to return an indictment for violation of an old civil-rights act making it a crime to deprive citizens of their constitutional rights. On January 14, 1960, the jurors said they were "unable to arrive at any true bill," having found no "basis for prosecution in the case."

That same year a young staff sergeant in the Air Force completed the second term of his enlistment and received an honorable discharge. A high school graduate who had earned credits toward a college degree while in the service, he enrolled at Jackson State College in Mississippi. By January of 1961 he had decided that the educational opportunities at all-Negro Jackson were inadequate. And so James Howard Meredith applied for a transfer to the all-white University of Mississippi at Oxford. His application was rejected on the grounds that Jackson was not a member of the Southern Association of Secondary Schools, and because he did not have letters of recommendation from five alumni of the university.

On May 31, 1961, Meredith filed suit in the United States District Court for Southern Mississippi, contending that he had been denied admission to the university solely on racial grounds. This was but the first of more than thirty legal actions to be taken by the opposing forces in the struggle over desegregation in the state. James Meredith became the symbol of that clash, its hero and archenemy, and Americans wondered what manner of man he was. In a column headed "Resolute Mississippian," the *Times*, on September 21, 1962, presented the following picture:

> The old man paused a moment to consider the question about his son and then spoke, with a note of pride: "I encouraged him because he wants the higher education that they don't have here for the colored people." This was Moses (Cap) Meredith, a seventy-one-year-old Negro

farmer, talking about his boy, James Howard Meredith. "J.H.," as the family calls him, is one of ten children of Moses and Roxie Meredith. He was born on June 25, 1933, on an eighty-four-acre cotton-and-corn farm scratched out of the rocky bottomland of Attala County in north central Mississippi by his father.

The senior Meredith described himself as the son of a slave. "I was just a poor man," he said, "and I never got beyond the fourth grade." But he was determined that his children would do better. All ten were graduated from high school. Seven went to college.

As a boy, James learned to plow and he helped his father in the fields before and after classes at Tipton High School, a four-mile walk down the road. He hunted and fished a bit and caught crickets and grasshoppers as bait to sell to white anglers. "He was one of the best students," his father recalled, "always reading."

James Meredith has a slight build. He stands 5 feet 6½ inches and weighs 135 pounds. He wears a pencil-line mustache. His demeanor is so quiet it almost masks his zeal to help improve the lot of his race in the State of Mississippi. Asked why he had chosen Mississippi rather than an institution outside the state, he replied: "I am more concerned with the need of Negroes in Mississippi than a personal desire to attain a degree."

In his appearances before state officials and in court he has been described as poised and polite, with a somewhat detached air. One observer spoke of an impression of "almost superhuman courage and some naïveté" in Mr. Meredith. Asked about his safety Meredith said: "It is not by any means the major concern. The major concern is that I get into the school and that I become as nearly as possible just another student."

There is an almost mystical urge impelling James Meredith. He has implied that unless he accomplishes his goal he either will not have existed or might as well not have existed. Speaking of his application, he said: "I think this is going to help the nation solve its race problem."

He was reared, like his brothers and sisters, as a Methodist, but he now describes his beliefs as a mixture of Judaeo-Christian ideas and, possibly, Buddhism. While in service he met his wife, Mary June, in Gary, Indiana. He took her with him to Japan, where she worked as a civil-service employee for two years. They have a son, James, Jr., born in 1960.

Meredith's suit was dismissed by Federal District Judge Sidney C. Mize of Mississippi on the ground that no racial discrimination had been proved. But in June, 1962, the United States Court of Appeals for the Fifth Circuit found that Meredith had been rejected "solely because he was a Negro," reversed Judge Mize's decision and directed Meredith's admission to Ole Miss. A summer of frantic legal maneuvers followed. The Fifth Circuit's ruling, by a panel of three judges, was stayed by another member of the court—Judge Ben F. Cameron of Mississippi, a dedicated segregationist who had said in opinions that the Fourteenth Amendment should not be enforced in the South. The panel that had decided the case vacated the stay, but Judge Cameron issued three more in succession. Finally, in September, the issue of a stay was put to Justice Hugo L. Black of the Supreme Court, acting as Circuit Justice for the Fifth Circuit. He ordered the judgment of the circuit panel into effect at once. The showdown was at hand for Mississippi.

The state's governor at this moment of truth was a far-out racist whom northerners found difficult to believe rational, Ross Barnett. Following the discredited path of Orval Faubus in Arkansas and Jimmie Davis in Louisiana, he announced that he would stand against the enforcement of federal law. On September 18, 1962, the United States Government entered the Meredith lawsuit as a friend of the court. The legislators, judges and executive officials of the State of Mississippi declared war. The Associated Press summarized the events of the next two weeks in a dispatch that appeared in the *Times* on October 1, 1962:

> September 20—Chancery Judge W. T. Horton, Hinds County, Mississippi, enjoined Meredith from enrolling.
>
> September 20—The Mississippi legislature passed a bill prohibiting the enrollment at any institution of higher learning of students who have been convicted or have pending against them criminal charges involving moral turpitude.

September 20—Justice of the Peace Homer Edgeworth of Jackson, Mississippi, convicted Meredith in absentia of falsely testifying on a vote-registration application. The charge was one involving moral turpitude. Meredith was sentenced to a year in jail.

September 20—The Federal Court of Appeals invalidated the Horton injunction, the legislature's bill and Meredith's conviction.

September 20—Meredith made a first attempt to register at the Ole Miss campus in Oxford. Governor Barnett personally blocked his way.

September 21—The Court of Appeals ordered the Mississippi college board, plus the university's three top officials, to appear at a contempt hearing.

September 24—The Court of Appeals said that the board and officials were in contempt but withheld judgment when they agreed to obey the court mandate and register Meredith.

September 25—The Court of Appeals issued a sweeping restraining order against Governor Barnett and practically all district attorneys and sheriffs in Mississippi, telling them not to interfere.

September 25—Governor Barnett blocked Meredith's entry to the college board office. The Court of Appeals ordered him to show cause September 28 why he should not be held in contempt.

September 26—Lieutenant Governor Paul B. Johnson prevented Meredith from enrolling; the appeals court ordered Johnson to appear at a contempt hearing September 29.

September 27—The Justice Department abandoned a fourth attempt to register Meredith when federal marshals accompanying him were called back because of the possibility of "major violence and bloodshed."

September 28—Barnett was found guilty of civil contempt and was ordered by the Court of Appeals to purge himself or face arrest and a fine of $10,000 a day.

September 29—President Kennedy, acting at midnight and after holding three telephone conversations during the day with Barnett, called Mississippi's National Guard into federal service and dispatched troops of the

United States Army to Memphis to stand in reserve in the event more forces were needed. He issued a proclamation calling on the government and the people of Mississippi to "cease and desist" all their obstructing actions and to "disperse and retire peaceably forthwith." The Court of Appeals declared Lieutenant Governor Johnson in contempt of court for his part in blocking Meredith's admission and ordered him to pay a fine of $5,000 a day unless he obeyed the court's desegregation orders.

In Washington, officials were genuinely afraid that the issue would end in an armed conflict between American soldiers and Mississippi law-enforcement officers and citizens. But finally, after more telephone conversations with the President and his brother, Attorney General Robert F. Kennedy, Governor Barnett agreed to the admission of James Meredith. He promised— and reiterated this vital pledge—that he would use the forces of the State of Mississippi to maintain order.

On Sunday night, September 30th, Meredith was flown to Oxford from Memphis in a federal plane. He was met at the university airport by Deputy Attorney General Nicholas deB. Katzenbach and driven to the campus in a convoy of automobiles and military trucks. There to protect him were three hundred federal marshals, carrying riot clubs and tear-gas cartridges, and a large force of Mississippi state troopers. Governor Barnett, as planned, made a statement indicating that his resistance was over. President Kennedy made an address televised to the nation but aimed directly at the students and people of Mississippi, urging them to comply with the law. "You have a new opportunity to show that you are men of patriotism and integrity," he said. "For the most effective means of upholding the law is not the state policemen or the marshals or the National Guard. It is you. It lies in your courage to accept those laws with which you disagree as well as those with which you agree."

But even as the President spoke, riot raged on the Ole Miss campus. As the federal marshals moved in ahead of Meredith, students gathered in "The Grove," a tree-shaded grassy mall in front of the university administration center, the Lyceum Building. They began to heckle the marshals, shouting "nigger-

lover" and "We don't want Bobby Kennedy." The state highway patrol, which was supposed to keep outsiders off the campus,
withdrew from the entrances; then cars filled with roughly
dressed white men drove in, many showing out-of-state licenses.
Crowds began moving in on the marshals, and there was gunfire. At the crucial moment the state troopers whom Governor
Barnett had pledged to have on hand just drove off. The marshals
were nearly overwhelmed before federalized Guardsmen and
regular army units called in by Deputy Attorney General Katzenbach arrived. By then two men were dead. Claude Sitton painted
the scene in a story filed the early morning of Monday, October 1:

> Clouds of tear gas billowed around the Lyceum Build-
> ing. The tree-dotted mall had the appearance of a battle-
> field as students and adults massed behind Confederate
> battle flags and charged repeatedly toward the marshals.
> Travel to and from the campus was extremely danger-
> ous. Roving bands of students halted cars and questioned
> their occupants to determine if they were friend or foe.
> The troops were bombarded with bricks and sticks, and
> obscenities were shouted at the men.
>
> Five minutes later students brought a bulldozer up
> from a construction site. A yell went up from a nucleus
> of about two hundred students among a milling throng of
> more than one thousand. Students and others moved in
> behind the bulldozer, which aimed straight for the main
> door of the administration building. The plan seemed to
> be to abandon the machine at full throttle and let it
> plow wildly into the troops. But the dozer stalled and was
> quickly swallowed up in the clouds of tear gas. Later,
> however, the students and their adult reinforcements re-
> trieved the bulldozer and sent it crashing against the
> steps at the entrance of the building. Others in the
> mob stole a fire truck and drove it around and around
> through the trees. At one point its driver sent it careen-
> ing down the drive in front of the building, drawing a bar-
> rage of tear-gas grenades.
>
> Aside from the marshals, the chief targets of the
> rioters were newsmen. One of the dead was Paul Gui-
> hard, a correspondent for Agence France Presse. The
> other man killed was Ray Gunter, twenty-three years

old, a juke-box repairman from nearby Abbeville, Mississippi. Guihard received a bullet wound in the back. Gunter was shot in the forehead. A sniper fired three quick shots at Karl Fleming, a reporter in the Atlanta bureau of *Newsweek* magazine, but the bullet struck the doorway of the Lyceum. Other newsmen were attacked and beaten. Gordon Yoder, a Telenews cameraman from Dallas, and Mrs. Yoder were set upon by the mob. State troopers rescued them.

Virtually all the street lights were shot out or broken by rocks early in the evening. Observers edging as close to the action as the tear gas and prudence would permit got a view of shadowy forms racing back and forth behind Confederate battle flags. Snipers operated under the cover of darkness, aiming blasts of birdshot and pistol and rifle fire at the marshals and others.

One of the mob's charges on the Lyceum followed a harangue by former Major General Edwin A. Walker from the pedestal of a Confederate monument across the mall from the Greek-revival structure of white columns and brick masonry. General Walker, who resigned his commission after being reprimanded for rightist political activity, arrived in Oxford saying there was a "spontaneous movement" of sympathetic southerners to come here. "Protest! Protest! Keep it up!" Walker shouted. He did not advocate violence. But he told the students that help was coming from out of the state. He accused Mississippi officials of a "sellout."

The Reverend Duncan M. Gray, rector of St. Peter's Protestant Episcopal Church, stepped up on the pedestal and called on the students to end the violence, Some grabbed him and roughed him up. He was led through the mob by an unidentified law-enforcement officer.

Walker then told the students he would give them his "moral support." He turned and strode up a walkway toward the Lyceum with one hundred students following behind.

"Sic 'em, John Birch," a student shouted from across the street.

The former general and his followers were greeted

with a volley of tear gas after some among them had begun throwing rocks and bottles at the marshals. One newsman said a man wearing a policeman's uniform was throwing bottles and rocks.

A force of two hundred state troopers, used by Governor Barnett to block one of Meredith's three previous attempts to register, stood by on and around the campus. The troopers made no effort to break up the mob at the Lyceum; and some made it plain that they sided with the students.

The three hundred or more deputy marshals who ringed the Lyceum Building fired a barrage of tear gas to force back the mob, led by General Walker, as it surged toward them. A flaming missile was hurled atop a big army truck used to transport the marshals. Its canvas cover began to burn. As a soldier climbed up and put the fire out, members of the mob aimed squirts from a fire extinguisher at him. The students then turned on a station wagon, which was loaded with equipment. They smashed its windows, ripped off its license plates and kicked dents in its sides. Students let air out of the tires of three army trucks parked in front of the Lyceum Building and tossed lighted matches at them.

Several state troopers looked on and laughed. Others walked away as the students charged in toward the deputy marshals, who were forced to fire the tear gas to protect themselves. At 9:10 P.M. the troopers climbed into their patrol cars and left the campus.

The riot lasted fifteen hours. By Monday night five thousand soldiers and Guardsmen were on duty in the streets of Oxford, whose population in ordinary times was just six thousand five hundred.

Open warfare was over. But to assure the safety of one brave man, James Meredith, a federal presence remained on campus—a dwindling number of troops, then marshals. Their life was relatively uneventful; some said later that they were most surprised by the foul language of the coeds, supposedly examples of white southern womanhood at its most bellelike. The federal men protected Meredith from physical harm. But they could not, as Claude Sitton noted in a dispatch printed

January 17, 1963, extend their protection "to Meredith's sympathizers among the faculty and students, or to those whose only departure from segregationist orthodoxy has been to discourage further disorder." For racists on the Oxford campus, as elsewhere, the rights of dissent and free association that they so frequently invoke for themselves did not extend to those who disagreed with them. Sitton wrote:

> Slander, intimidation and threats have been directed at moderates and liberals on the campus. And the campaign shows no sign of abating. The family of one student who had befriended Mr. Meredith reportedly was pressed to such lengths recently that it sought to ease the situation by saying the youth had suffered a "nervous breakdown" and therefore was not responsible for his actions.
>
> Faculty members have received threatening telephone calls and scurrilous letters. The area of the university cafeteria in which they usually sit is referred to by students as "the Communist section." The little daughter of a professor who had invited Mr. Meredith to dinner received a black doll last month at a school party. The accompanying card read, "a nigger-lover."
>
> One weapon of the extremists is an anonymous weekly publication that refers to itself as the "rebel underground." No one with a prominent role in the effort to maintain compliance with the federal court orders under which Meredith was admitted September 30th has escaped its slanderous brush. The publication, which has urged the execution of President Kennedy, has labeled its targets variously "criminal goons," "Marxist monster," "conscious communist," "fellow conspirators," "satanic professionals of the party," "comsymps," "the betrayers," "that erstwhile pink prof," "quisling," "foul wrench," "liar," and "murdering paranoid."
>
> In a few cases the segregationists have employed more direct methods. One of the chief objects of torment now is William J. Temple, a lanky eighteen-year-old blond freshman from Washington. On the wall outside his door in Howry "B" Dormitory are scrawled the words, "Temple Lies Here." A flower pot once rested beneath the mock epitaph.

Squatting on a chair with his arms wrapped around his knees, Temple recounted some of the incidents that have befallen him since he ate dinner with Meredith last November in the university cafeteria. As he talked, a student in an adjoining room rapped on the wall. A radio was turned up full blast. Then a music box was heard near the door playing "Dixie." The glass transom over the door had a jagged hole. A soda bottle had smashed through it the night before, grazing Temple's forehead. A visitor hitched his chair out of the line of fire as voices rose in the hallway.

Craig Knobles, eighteen, of Meridian, Mississippi, and James Definbaugh, eighteen, of Gulfport, Mississippi, planned the dinner with Meredith, according to Temple. They and several other students wanted to change the public impression of Ole Miss that had been left by rowdy student demonstrations in October. Temple was invited to come along. "We figured people would make sly remarks, but we expected nothing like this," he recalled.

The night of the dinner someone entered the room he shared with Knobles, dumped books, records and clothing on the floor and poured water over them. A student leader visited him and offered him time on the campus radio station to apologize for having eaten with Meredith. Pressures stemming from the incident led Knobles to withdraw from the university. Temple said administration officials had implied it might be wise for him to leave, too, but he refused. Since the dinner, he said, hardly a night had passed without bottles or other missiles being smashed against the wall outside his door. Shortly before the Christmas holidays, three "cherry bomb" firecrackers were rolled into a wash-room stall occupied by the student.

The half-dozen students gathered outside in the hallway said his attitude was responsible for the trouble in the dormitory. "He wouldn't have no friends even if Meredith wasn't on the campus," one asserted.

The conversation got down to basics as one in the group, head bowed in concentration, struck matches and threw them on the floor. "The big thing is the nigger immortality in the South," observed a shirtless sophomore, rubbing his bare stomach thoughtfully.

"The what?"

"The immortality. They ain't got no morals at all."

For the university's only Negro student and his sympathizers, the sophomore added a prediction. "Meredith won't never break into this social clique at Ole Miss," he said confidently. And, as any freshman here will tell you, social acceptance is prized above all things at Ole Miss.

On January 30, 1963, James Meredith appeared at a press conference. The spring semester was about to begin, and it was widely believed that he would not choose to return to the tension and hostility of another term. "After listening to all arguments, evaluations and possibilities, and weighing all this against my personal possibilities and circumstances," he said, "I have concluded that the 'Negro' should not return to the university."

A southern radio news reporter applauded.

"However," Meredith continued, "I have decided that I, J. H. Meredith, will register for the second semester."

Meredith was accompanied at the press conference by a man whose personal counsel had been a bulwark during the two years since he first applied to the university. He was Medgar Evers, secretary of the N.A.A.C.P. in Mississippi. For Evers, Meredith's admission to Ole Miss had been a major victory. His next campaign was in the city where he made his home—Jackson, the state capital. There, with other Negro leaders, he was striving to win a promise from the municipal government to hire some Negro policemen and to appoint a bi-racial committee. On June 1, 1963, the *Times* selected him as the "Man in the News," and printed this story under the heading, "Quiet Integrationist":

> Medgar Wiley Evers likens his feeling during a racial demonstration to the reaction of a varsity football player. "I played football in college for four years," he said, "and no matter how many games you play, there is still a certain amount of butterflies. But the first time you tackle a man, your fear disappears. You're just in it." The husky thirty-seven-year-old Negro is now at the center of racial turmoil in his city. For nine years, he has served here as state field secretary for the National Association for the Advancement of Colored People.

Whether speaking to rallies or arranging bail for N.A.A.C.P. members arrested for picketing downtown stores, Evers gives evidence of his college training in business administration. He talks quietly and attends to small details. But his strong feelings, like his unexpected smile, are never fully submerged by his methodical manner.

Evers was born on July 2, 1925, in Decatur, Mississippi. He went through school in Newton County, Mississippi, and entered the United States Army in 1943. At the war's end, he enrolled at Alcorn A. & M. University in southwestern Mississippi. Working as an insurance salesman after graduation, he joined the N.A.A.C.P. in 1952 and became a member of its staff two years later.

He recalls one college experience that left a deep impression: "The president of Alcorn, a Negro, had discouraged us from trying to register to vote. He said we had no contribution to make to the community. I couldn't forget that."

Evers has other memories of practices he wants to eliminate before his own children repeat his experiences. "A close friend of my dad's was lynched when I was fourteen or so." He continued: "He was supposed to have insulted a white woman. His clothes stayed out in the pasture where they killed him for a long time afterward. You'd see the blood turning rust color."

The white officials who deal with Evers consider him an effective organizer. Although the name of his organization is anathema to them, they describe Evers as a reasonable and dependable man. This grudging respect has not protected him from police harassment, however. "During the first sit-ins here in 1961," he said, "I went to the trial and applauded the defendants. The police lunged in, and I was beaten over the head with a snub-nosed revolver."

On another occasion, in 1960, Evers was visiting a cousin when a judge ruled against a Negro in a civil-rights case. Sitting in the kitchen of his cousin's house, Mr. Evers wrote a statement condemning the decision and called the news services. When the statement appeared in print, he was arrested, fined $100 and sentenced to thirty days in jail for contempt of court. The conviction was reversed by the Mississippi Supreme Court.

"When my sons are grown," he said in a tone that was faintly challenging, "they're going to find Jackson even better than New York City."

Eleven days later, as he walked from his automobile to his home, Evers was struck by a bullet from a high-powered rifle. Claude Sitton reconstructed the events in the following report in the *Times* of June 13th:

> Evers left a mass meeting at a church last night, stopped at the residence of a Negro lawyer, and then drove to his home on the city's northern edge. Before leaving the church, he remarked to a newsman that "tomorrow will be a big day."
>
> He arrived at his neat, green-paneled and buff-brick ranch-style home on Guynes Street shortly after midnight. He parked his 1962 light blue sedan in the driveway, behind his wife's station wagon. As he turned to walk into a side entrance opening into a carport, the sniper's bullet struck him just below the right shoulder blade. The slug crashed through a front window of the home, penetrated an interior wall, ricocheted off a refrigerator and struck a coffee pot. The battered bullet was found beneath a watermelon on a kitchen cabinet.
>
> Evers staggered to the doorway, his keys in his hand, and collapsed near the steps. His wife, Myrlie, and their three children rushed to the door.
>
> The screaming of the children, "Daddy! Daddy! Daddy!" awoke a neighbor, Thomas A. Young. Another neighbor, Houston Wells, said he had heard the shot and the screams of Mrs. Evers. Wells, according to the police, said he had looked out a bedroom window, saw Mr. Evers' crumpled body in the carport and rushed out into his yard. He crouched behind a clump of shrubbery, fired a shot into the air and shouted for help.
>
> The police, who arrived a short time later, helped neighbors place Evers in Wells's station wagon. As the station wagon sped to University Hospital, those who accompanied the dying man said he had murmured weakly, "Sit me up," and later, "Turn me loose."

On the day of Evers' funeral in Jackson, June 15th, the misery and resentment of the Negroes he had helped to lead broke out in a demonstration that almost brought more bloodshed. Claude Sitton reported:

Mayor Allen Thompson temporarily lifted a ban on parades today to allow thousands of mourning Negroes and some fifty sympathetic whites to march a mile and a half through the city behind a hearse bearing Evers' body. He will be buried next week in Arlington National Cemetery. The police, often Evers' opponents in life, provided an eight-man motorcycle escort for him in death. Some two hundred other officers sealed off the line of march from the Masonic Temple, site of the funeral services, to the Collins Funeral Home. The parade permit stipulated that the procession be a silent one. But as the group of younger Negroes and whites crossed West Capitol Street, the main thoroughfare, they broke into the hymn of the protest movement: "We Shall Overcome."

After the last of the four-block-long line of marchers had reached the funeral home on North Farish Street, the younger Negroes apparently decided to make an attempt to demonstrate in the white business district. They began singing and chanting: "Before I'd be a slave, I'd be buried in my grave, and go home to my Lord and be free." At a signal from one of them, two hundred and fifty surged southward toward West Capitol Street. Other persons spilled out of the small shops, taverns and restaurants along the street and fell in behind them.

Four motorcycle patrolmen let them through one intersection, but Deputy Chief A. L. Ray met them with twenty officers as they approached the main thoroughfare. "Your leaders said you wanted to have a private, mournful march, and we agreed under those circumstances," he shouted over an electric bullhorn. Then he ordered the group, now numbering approximately one thousand, to disperse.

"We want the killer! We want the killer! We want the killer!" chanted the leaders. "We want equality! We want freedom!"

Demonstrators in the rear began stamping their feet

and shouting "Freedom! Freedom! Freedom!" in staccato cadence.

Officers using police dogs moved in at this point, driving some of the Negroes and a group of fifty or more white newsmen back down the street. One demonstrator after another was grabbed and hustled into waiting patrol wagons. White and Negro merchants along Farish Street quickly bolted their doors.

With newsmen out of the way, the police went to work in earnest to clear the area. A television cameraman caught in a doorway said a Negro man who did not move fast enough was struck in the face with a shotgun butt by a deputy sheriff. Another deputy cut a soundman's microphone cable. The cameraman said a Negro woman was clubbed by a policeman. She fled to a car, but was dragged out and clubbed again. Two men in one camera crew said the police had threatened to turn a police dog on them if they did not move out of the area quickly.

By this time, most of the Negroes had been sealed off in a one-block area. They began throwing bricks, bottles and other missiles at the police. Most fell short of the mark. Deputy Chief Ray called over the bullhorn to the rioters: "You came here to honor a dead man and you have brought dishonor. You have brought dishonor, dishonor."

The crowd, many of whose members were in their twenties and thirties, screamed back at him. The growling and barking of the police dogs, the crash of bottles on the pavement and the cursing of the policemen added to the uproar.

At about this time, Mayor Thompson broadcast a special bulletin over Jackson radio stations, urging residents to stay out of the downtown area. "Let the Justice Department see this," called Deputy Chief Ray to a Columbia Broadcasting System cameraman. "Let this cameraman up there so he can get pictures of how they're acting."

The Department's John Doar approached at this point, and the police official shouted to the rioters, "This is Mr. Doar with the Justice Department."

The federal official strode down the middle of the street, shifting slightly now and then to dodge bottles and brickbats.

"You're not going to win anything with bottles and bricks," Mr. Doar called to the rioters. He could hardly be heard over the roar of the crowd, which began to encircle him, the camera and crew and a reporter. "Hold it!" shouted Mr. Doar. "Is there someone here who can speak for you people?" A Negro youth emerged from amid the rioters and joined the federal official in the street.

"This man is right," he said, pointing to Mr. Doar. The youth began berating hoodlums who had taken refuge behind a group of women and were throwing bottles into the street.

"My name is John Doar—D-O-A-R," the official kept calling to the rioters. "I'm from the Justice Department, and anybody around here knows I stand for what is right."

Other Negroes then began joining the effort to calm the mob. The hard-core troublemakers, apparently convinced that they would not have an opportunity to engage the police, began hurling their bottles to the pavement or through plate-glass windows. Within a short time, the street was clear. The police removed barricades set up to keep whites out of the section, and the motorized street sweeper began whisking up the debris.

But the mood of the Negroes was still one of bitterness and anger.

"The only way to stop evil here is to have a revolution," muttered a young man in a doorway. "Somebody have to die."

The significance for Mississippi of the Medgar Evers murder was described in the *Times Magazine* of June 23, 1963, by Hodding Carter, editor of the *Delta Democrat-Times* of Greenville:

Whatever the motive for the murder, it is fair to comment upon the poisoned atmosphere in which Medgar Evers died.

Jackson is a pretty town. It has made remarkable

strides in industrialization. Its population has more than doubled in twenty years; and it enjoys cultural advantages not present in some of the smaller Mississippi cities and towns. But it is a town obsessed with a determination to maintain existing relationships between the races. Its politics and social order are monolithic. One can count on two hands those Jacksonians who are willing to speak out against any status quo. It is the seat of a state government whose legislature, which meets too frequently, represents probably the lowest common denominator of any political assembly in the United States.

Almost the sole source of the city's newspaper information comes from a morning and afternoon combination owned by a family whose animation can only be described as an admixture of fundamentalism, furious racism and greed.

Rare is the Jackson citizen of any prominence, or even of no consequence, who does not belong to the Citizens Council. In short, only an intensely dedicated man, white or Negro, who differs with the almost proslavery interpositionist sentiment of a John Calhoun would choose to lift his voice above a slight whisper in Jackson, Mississippi. And hardly a week has gone by for many months in which some agency—political, journalistic and even clerical—has not issued an inflammatory statement of defiance or contempt for government, the United Nations or any idea of world order.

Surely the residual guilt must rest with what any impartial poll would determine to be the most inflammatory newspapers, the sorriest legislature and the most weak-kneed citizenry in our nation. No one can know now whether their joint influence added to the compulsion of one man to kill another. But it is a fair supposition that it did.

It may be—let it be said hopefully—that the struggle between moderates and extremists of both races will eventually be resolved in favor of the moderates. If it does not, God help us all. Mississippi's population, almost evenly divided between these two groups, may learn from the Ole Miss riot and the murder of Medgar Evers that violence, political atavism and notions discarded almost everywhere else in the world can help none of us.

I believe many Mississippians, though not yet a majority, are coming around to this viewpoint. Our state is almost an island today. We know it. We don't like it. We are discovering that a bloody conflict on the university campus can denude that campus of a great many of its best teachers. We are learning fast that the Negro will no longer bow his back to the lash. We are even beginning to discover that most of the rest of our country doesn't endorse old southern credos.

It may be that Medgar Evers has not died uselessly.

Claude Sitton also saw signs of change in Mississippi. In the *Times Magazine* of April 28, 1963, he wrote:

> There are harbingers of a new day: voting applicants standing patiently at the courthouse door in Greenwood for hour on endless hour, a Justice Department attorney shaking hands with a Negro while a white woman shivers with rage, the songs of freedom rolling out of the little Negro churches into the blackness of the Delta night, and a white man, trapped by a system he inherited, smiling sadly and saying, "We would like to be more responsible than we can afford to be."
>
> Sitting in his modernistic office overlooking Jackson, a prominent lawyer spoke of the state's responsible citizens and their weariness with racism and its fruits. "The human mind can accept just so much of this type of thing, then it seeks relief," he said. It seems evident that Mississippi cannot long delay some compromise with the legitimate demands of its Negro citizens. The hazards of the present situation are implicit in the mounting evidence of widespread bitterness. In the crowded sanctuary of a Negro church one warm spring night, a speaker at a voter-registration rally referred with sarcasm to "the good white people." A voice from the audience shouted: "They ain't no good! None of them!"

One measure of any change in Mississippi would be the seriousness of any attempt to find and prosecute Medgar Evers' killer. On June 24, 1963, a white man from Greenwood,

Mississippi, Byron de la Beckwith, was charged with the murder. A profile printed in the *Times* the next day said he "could have stepped from a William Faulkner novel about the decaying traditions of the southern aristocracy."

Beckwith's family ties reach back to the gracious plantation life of the Old South and to family friendships with Jefferson Davis. A fertilizer salesman, Beckwith lives alone in the rambling, three-story family home that was once a showplace but now is dilapidated and weather-beaten, unpainted for years. The yard is barren. The profile described him as "a man of southern charm, tasteful dress and lively gait. He is also a man of contrasts— pleasant on most matters, stinging and bitter of the racial issue."

Most observers, and Beckwith himself, expected a *pro forma* trial and a quick acquittal by the jury, but it did not turn out that way. The prosecutor, thirty-seven-year-old Bill Waller, a seventh-generation Mississippian, set out to get a conviction. He reckoned with the jurors' prejudices—but with a view to overcoming them. John Herbers of the *Times* reported an exchange on January 29, 1964, during the selection of a jury.

> "Do you think it is a crime for a white man to kill a nigger in Mississippi?" Waller asked a prospective juror.
>
> "What was his answer?" inquired the judge, Leon F. Hendrick.
>
> "He's thinking it over," Waller said.

On February 7th the case ended in a mistrial when the jury could not agree. It was divided seven-to-five for acquittal. In most areas, that would not have been regarded by friends of a murder victim as a triumph for justice, but in Mississippi even the Negroes thought it was a long advance. The very fact that Prosecutor Waller thought his political future would be served by a genuine effort to convict Beckwith was interesting. A second jury was also unable to agree on a verdict.

Another eye-opener early in 1964 was the attitude of Mississippi's new Governor, former Lieutenant Governor Johnson. He had run as a militant segregationist, but on taking office on January 21, 1964, he warned that Mississippi was "a part of this world, whether we like it or not." He said,"We are Americans as well as Mississippians." He set out on a low-key policy of trying to keep people from getting mad at Mississippi.

Before the year was over, it was clear that Mississippi was approaching the day of ultimate decision on its future—the decision on whether to go down in blood and violence, resisting all change, or to begin the process of accommodation to the second American revolution. A critical test was at hand with the arrival of hundreds of northern students in the state for a summer of civil-rights activity. Just a few days after the start of the summer project, on June 21st, there was tragedy. Two visiting white students, Michael Schwerner and Andrew Goodman of New York, and a local Negro boy, James Chaney, disappeared into the night after their arrest on a "speeding" charge in the city of Philadelphia. Six weeks later, on August 4th, the F.B.I. found their bodies buried in an earthen dam nearby. They had been shot.

In the *Times Magazine* of July 19, 1964, Professor James W. Silver of the University of Mississippi, author of *Mississippi: The Closed Society*, described the forces at work in the state. The article was entitled: "Mississippi Must Choose."

The united front that has been strong enough to nullify the United States Constitution since 1875 is officially as solid as ever. But every knowledgeable Mississippi segregationist looks to the future with foreboding. He knows, in short, that the time is fast running out when the country will longer tolerate this enclave of feudalism within the United States, and that his only choice is to make the inevitable transition peaceable or bloody. . . .

The social order that former Governor Barnett defended with such satisfaction rests upon the stubborn determination of the white population to keep Mississippi a white man's country. Those in power or near it refuse to acknowledge any serious challenge to the doctrine and system of white supremacy. Their beliefs are sustained by the unconditional and unwavering acceptance of an interlocking sequence of discredited assumptions:

1. The biological and anthropological "proof" of Negro inferiority (which would keep him a second-class citizen forever).

2. The presumed sanction of God as extrapolated from the Bible.

3. The present state of affairs as one that is desired and endorsed by Negroes and whites alike.

4. The repeated assurance that only through segregation can law and order prevail.

5. A view of history which declares that there has been a century of satisfactory racial experience in Mississippi.

6. A constitutional interpretation which denies the validity of the Supreme Court desegregation decisions and the 1964 Civil Rights Act.

Nowhere in the prevailing thought is there admission that nearly everyone in the civilized world has long since abandoned these premises, without which the Mississippi way of life founders in its own absurdity.

A philosophical foundation, even if intellectually respectable, would not furnish the massive support necessary for the continuation of the closed society in an antagonistic world. Beyond its fundamentalist creed, the society has two engines designed to insure the maintenance of white supremacy: the distortion of Mississippi's past and the distortion of Mississippi's present.

The first of these is composed of the ante-bellum myth —the Old South as a classical Golden Age; the Confederate myth—the South as a humane society risen in spontaneous self-defense of its sanctified institutions, its family and country life, against wanton northern aggression; and the Reconstruction myth—a society laid waste by an unprovoked war, become a federal garrison, oppressed by an insolent Yankee inquisition and finally redeemed by virtuous southern patriots (the intruder is expelled and the Negro is saved from himself by returning him to his old security through segregation and new and beneficent forms of his old tasks).

The present view of life is distorted by the claim of Negro contentment, by the notion that all racial troubles originate outside the state, by the politics of segregation (the asserted usurpation of Mississippi's sovereignty by a federal civil-rights-and-school-desegregation conspiracy based in Washington and not so obscurely related to the international Communist plot to destroy America), and by the almost absolute support of the status quo by the makers of public opinion—the press, the pulpit and the politicians.

With such powerful forces of indoctrination at work, it would be strange indeed if whites and blacks alike did not grow up prepared to accept and extol their heritage. But there are still stronger means by which the closed society is entrenched. Every lawmaking body and every law-enforcing agency is completely in the hands of those whites who are faithful to the orthodoxy. From governor to constable, from chief justice to justice of the peace, every officer of the society is dedicated to upholding and maintaining the status quo by whatever means are necessary.

The white man is educated to believe in his superiority and the Negro is educated to accept his position of subservience and inferiority. In the civic and service clubs, the educational institutions, the churches, the business and labor organizations, the patriotic, social and professional fraternities—all individuals who would advance themselves in any of these are oriented from infancy in the direction of loyalty to the accepted code. In times of stress the Legal Educational Advisory Committee, the State Sovereignty Commission, the Citizens Councils, the Women for Constitutional Government, Patriotic American Youth and dozens of similar new groups spring up to man the ramparts against outside encroachment and internal subversion. The nonconformist learns the advisability of keeping his mouth shut, or is silenced in one way or another, or he finds it expedient to quit the state.

The closed society of Mississippi thus swears allegiance to a prevailing creed with over a hundred years of homage behind it. Based on antique assumptions no longer tenable and on a legendary past, the doctrine of white supremacy is guarded by a bureaucracy, by ceaseless, high-powered and skillful indoctrination employing both persuasion and fear, and by the elimination, without regard for law or ethics, of those who will not go along. Within its own borders the closed society of Mississippi comes as near to approximating a police state as anything we have yet seen in America.

And yet the closed society is not absolutely closed. In Mississippi there are legislators (very scarce), editors,

lawyers, labor leaders, ministers, educators and businessmen who sometimes protest against the prevailing orthodoxy. And now there is Negro leadership.

In fact, the most remarkable development in Mississippi history is the indigenous Negro leadership in evidence since 1954 when one hundred Negroes flatly
refused to endorse Governor Hugh White's plans for
separate-but-really-equal school facilities. It is not just
Medgar and Charles Evers, the Robert L. T. Smiths, not
just Aaron Henry, J. H. Meredith and Clyde Kennard, but
hundreds of developing leaders such as the three hundred
social-science teachers I talked with in Jackson a few
months back. By themselves these stalwarts could do
very little, but it is increasingly evident that they are not
alone, that indeed the rest of the country is rapidly throwing its weight behind them. And this phenomenon is not
just a summertime thing.

Mississippi's great hope economically is the industrialization of the state. Here some progress has been made.
The businessman, however, has been too engrossed in
making money to think clearly about the consequences
of industrialization, but neither he nor anyone else is
magician enough to freeze the social status quo while
revolutionizing the economic order. Many now regret the
turning over of the Negro problem to the extremist leadership in the Citizens Councils, and are beginning to
understand that a healthy modern industrial structure
cannot be raised upon the sands of segregation, minimum
wages (for whites only), poor schools, anti-intellectual-
ism, Negrophobia, meager social services, anti-unionism
and a general policy of "hate the Federal Government."
The pressing need now is for a substantial number of
prudent and imaginative representatives of the power
structure—which has, until now, failed the state—to become sufficiently aroused by recent events to band together for the purpose of withdrawing their support from
Mississippi's self-inflicted closed society.

Several years ago the Mississippi Economic Council
(the state's chamber of commerce) spoke out strongly
for keeping open the public schools even with integration.
The Jackson Chamber of Commerce has recently advised

the local owners of hotels, restaurants and theatres that
they must obey the new Civil Rights Law (though the
Robert E. Lee Hotel chose to close its doors) in spite of
the anguished cries and threats of the white supremacists.
Sons and daughters of northern owners of industry
brought into the state by its famous Balance Agriculture
With Industry program are now teaching in the summer
Freedom Schools and this is bound to have an eye-opening
effect.

Our country is now in the midst of an authentic revolution. The promises of the Declaration of Independence
and the Emancipation Proclamation are beginning to become reality for twenty million black Americans. These
promises will not be denied to a million citizens just because they happen to live in Mississippi. The long predicted turn is upon us.

As the tensions of the long summer ahead accumu-
late in both North and South, the outlook is divided between the certainties of concealed resistance and sporadic
terror and the more distant "new society." Perhaps in Mississippi the new society can be seen only as a matter of
faith, as something beyond a wide and temporal Jordan.
If this is the case, the fault, while Mississippian enough,
is shared beyond the borders of my state.

The shock around the nation over the disappearance
of the three student workers and the continuance of their
work by their colleagues and others make it inevitable,
however, that Mississippians will one day break out of
the blind patterns of resistance required by the convul-
sive imperatives of white supremacy.

Chapter 12

The North

$\mathbf{A}$s the racial revolution developed in the South, there was a certain amount of sanctimoniousness in the North. That northerners should feel morally superior on the racial issue was understandable, for they did not live in a society which was officially, legally dedicated to treatment of the Negro as a separate and inferior being—a society like the old South. The legal premise in the North was the opposite: Government was pledged against racial discrimination. And the political remedy was open to the northern Negro; he could vote, and in many places he had political power. But all this was unimportant to so many Negroes in New York and Chicago and Boston and Philadelphia and the other great cities of the Northeast. Reality was life in a slum, education in ancient schools, a job as a bus boy—or no job at all. And so northern righteousness had a hollow ring to it.

The smugness of some northern white readers of the *New York Times Magazine* must have been shattered on March 12, 1961, when they read an article by James Baldwin. He was identified as "an American Negro writer," and the name was probably new to most of the readers; he had not yet achieved his fame as essayist, novelist, playwright. But Baldwin's great gifts were immediately apparent, especially his savage talent for clearing away illusions.

The article began by alluding to a recent event that Baldwin said had "shocked and baffled most Americans." It was a wild demonstration in the United Nations General Assembly in New York over the murder of Patrice Lumumba, former premier of the Congo. Fifty persons, most of them Negroes, interrupted Adlai Stevenson's maiden U.N. speech with cries of "Vive Lumumba," and then grappled with guards in the worst riot in United Nations history. Baldwin noted that the riot had been widely described as Communist-inspired, the rioters as "merely a handful of irresponsible, Kremlin-corrupted *provocateurs*." Then he wrote:

> I find this view amazing. It is a view which even a minimal effort at observation would immediately contradict. One has only, for example, to walk through Harlem and ask oneself two questions: Would *I* like to live here? and, Why don't those who now live here move out?
>
> The answer to both questions is immediately obvious. Unless one takes refuge in the theory—however disguised—that Negroes are, somehow, different from (i.e., inferior to) white people, I do not see how one can escape the conclusion that the Negro's status in this country is a cruel injustice and a grave national liability.
>
> Now, I do not doubt that, among the people at the United Nations that day, there were pro-Communists and professional revolutionists acting out of the most cynical motives. Wherever there is great social discontent, these people are to be found sooner or later. Their presence is not as frightening as the discontent which creates their opportunity. What I find appalling—and really dangerous—is the American assumption that the Negro is so contented with his lot here that only the cynical agents of a foreign power can rouse him to protest.
>
> This is a notion which contains a gratuitous insult, implying, as it does, that Negroes can make no move unless they are manipulated. It forcibly suggests that the

southern attitude toward the Negro is also, essentially, the national attitude. When the South has trouble with its Negroes—when they refuse to remain in their "place"— it blames "outside" agitators and "northern interference." When the nation has trouble with the northern Negro, it blames the Kremlin.

This, by no means incidentally, is a hazardous thing to do. We give credit to the Communists for attitudes and victories which are not theirs. We make of them the champions of the oppressed, and they could not, of course, be more delighted.

If, as is only too likely, one prefers not to visit Harlem and expose oneself to the anguish there, one has only to consider the two most significant movements among Negroes in this country today.

At one end of the pole is the Negro student movement. The people who make up this movement really believe in the America of "liberty and justice for all." They really believe that the country is anxious to become what it claims to be.

We, therefore, all of us, have a grave responsibility to these young people. Our failure, now, to rise to the challenge they represent can only result in the most unimaginable demoralization among them, and among their children; and I would rather not think of the probable effects of such demoralization on the life of this country and on the role we play in the Western world.

The movement does not have as its goal the consumption of overcooked hamburgers and tasteless coffee at various sleazy lunch counters. Neither do Negroes, who are the principal proof and issue of miscegenation, share the white man's helplessly hypocritical attitudes toward the time-honored and universal mingling. The goal of the student movement is nothing less than the liberation of the entire country from its most crippling attitudes and habits. It is of the utmost importance for white people to see the Negroes as people like themselves. Otherwise, the whites will not be able to see themselves as they are.

At the other pole is the Nation of Islam movement, which, daily, becomes more powerful. It is not the only Muslim group in the city or the nation, but it seems to be the best organized and the most articulate.

The Muslims do not expect anything at all from the white people of this country. They do not believe that the American professions of democracy or equality have ever been even remotely sincere. They insist on the total separation of the races. This separation is to be achieved by the acquisition of land from the United States. The land is owed the Negroes, say the Muslims, as "back wages" for the labor wrested from them when they were slaves, and for their unrecognized and unhonored contributions to the wealth and power of this country.

The student movement depends, at bottom, on an act of faith, an ability to see, beneath the cruelty and hysteria and apathy of white people, their bafflement and pain and essential decency. This is superbly difficult. It demands a perpetually cultivated spiritual resilience, for the bulk of the evidence contradicts the vision. But the Muslim movement has all the evidence on its side. Unless one supposes that the ideal of black supremacy has virtues denied to the idea of white supremacy, one cannot possibly accept the deadly conclusions a Muslim draws from this evidence. On the other hand, it is quite impossible to argue with a Muslim concerning the actual state of Negroes in this country; the truth, after all, is the truth.

This is the great power a Muslim speaker has over his audience. His listeners have not heard the truth about their daily lives honored by anyone else. Almost all others, black or white, prefer to soften the truth, and point to a new day which is coming in America.

But this "new day" has been coming for nearly one hundred years. Viewed solely in the light of this country's moral professions, the lapse is inexcusable. Even more important, however, is the fact that there is desperately little in the record to indicate that white America ever seriously desired—or desires—to see this day arrive.

Usually, for example, those white people who are in favor of integration prove to be in favor of it later, in some other city, some other town, some other building, some other school. The rationalizations with which they attempt to disguise their panic cannot be respected.

Northerners proffer their indignation about the South as a kind of badge, as proof of good intentions; they never suspect that they thus increase, in the heart of the Negro they address, a kind of helpless pain and rage—and pity.

Negroes know how little most white people are prepared to implement their words with deeds, how little,
when the chips are down, they are prepared to risk. And
this long history of moral evasion has had an unhealthy
effect on the total life of the country, and has eroded
whatever respect Negroes may once have felt for white
people.

We are beginning, therefore, to witness in this country a new thing. "I am not at all sure," states one prominent Negro, who is *not* a Muslim, "that I *want* to be integrated into a burning house."

"I might," says another, "consider being integrated
into something else, an American society more real and
more honest—but *this*? No, thank you, man, who *needs*
it?"

And this searching disaffection has everything to do
with the emergence of Africa: "At the rate things are
going here, all of Africa will be free before we can get
a lousy cup of coffee."

Of course, it is easy to say—and true enough, as far
as it goes—that the American Negro deludes himself if
he imagines that he is capable of loyalty to any country
other than the United States. He is an American, too,
and he will survive or perish with the country.

This seems an unanswerable argument. But, while I
have no wish whatever to question the loyalty of American Negroes, I think this argument may be examined
with some profit. It is used, I think, too often and too
glibly. It obscures the effects of the passage of time, and
the great changes that have taken place in the world.

In the first place, as the homeless wanderers of the
twentieth century prove, the question of nationality no
longer necessarily involves the question of allegiance. Allegiance, after all, has to work two ways; and one can
grow weary of an allegiance which is not reciprocal.
I have the right and the duty, for example, to vote in my
country; but it is my country's responsibility to protect
my right to vote.

People now approaching or past middle age, who have
spent their lives in such struggles, have thereby acquired

an understanding of America and a belief in her potential which cannot now be shaken. (There are exceptions to this, however—W.E.B. DuBois, for example. It is easy to say he was duped by the Communists, but it is more interesting to consider just why so intelligent a man became so disillusioned.)

But I very strongly doubt that any Negro youth, now approaching maturity and with the whole, vast world before him, is willing, say, to settle for Jim Crow in Miami, when he can—or, before the travel ban, *could*—feast at the welcome table in Havana. And he need not, to prefer Havana, have any pro-Communist—or, for that matter, pro-Cuban or pro-Castro—sympathies: he need merely prefer not to be treated as a second-class citizen.

These are extremely unattractive facts, but they *are* facts, and no purpose is served by denying them. Neither, as I have already tried to indicate, is any purpose served by pretending that Negroes who refuse to be bound by this country's peculiar attitudes are subversive. They have every right to refuse to be bound by a set of attitudes that are now as useless and as obsolete as the pillory.

Finally, the time is forever behind us when Negroes could be expected to "wait." What is demanded now is not that Negroes continue to adjust themselves to the cruel racial pressures of life in the United States, but that the United States readjust itself to the facts of life in the present world.

One of these facts is that the American Negro can no longer, nor will he ever again, be controlled by white America's image of him. This fact has everything to do with the rise of Africa in world affairs.

At the time that I was growing up, Negroes in this country were taught to be ashamed of Africa. They were taught it bluntly by being told, for example, that Africa had never contributed "anything" to civilization.

Or one was taught the same lesson more obliquely, and even more effectively, by watching nearly naked, dancing, comic-opera cannibalistic savages in the movies. They were nearly always all bad, sometimes funny, sometimes both. If one of them was good, his goodness was proven by his loyalty to the white man.

A baffling sort of goodness, particularly as one's own father, who certainly wanted one to be "good," was more than likely to come home cursing—cursing the white man.

One's hair was always being attacked with hard brushes and combs and Vaseline; it was shameful to have "nappy" hair. One's legs and arms and face were always being greased, so that one would not look "ashy" in the wintertime. One was always being mercilessly scrubbed and polished, as though in the hope that a stain could thus be washed away. I hazard that the Negro children, of my generation, anyway, had an earlier and more painful acquaintance with soap than any other children, anywhere.

The women were forever straightening and curling their hair, and using bleaching creams. And yet it was clear that none of this effort would release one from the stigma and danger of being a Negro; the effort merely increased the shame and rage. There was not, no matter where one turned, any acceptable image of oneself, no proof of one's existence. One had the choice either of "acting just like a nigger" or of *not* "acting just like a nigger"—and only those who have tried it know how impossible it is to tell the difference.

My first hero was Joe Louis. I was ashamed of Father Divine. Haile Selassie, shown in a newsreel, was the first black emperor I had ever seen; he was pleading vainly with the West to prevent the rape of his country. And the extraordinary complex of tensions thus set up in the breast, between hatred of whites and contempt for blacks, is very hard to describe. Some of the most energetic people of my generation were destroyed by this interior warfare.

But none of this is so for those who are young now. The power of the white world to control their identities was crumbling as these young Negroes were born; and by the time they were able to react to the world, Africa was on the stage of history.

This could not but have an extraordinary effect on their own morale, for it meant that they were not merely the descendants of slaves in a white, Protestant, and

Puritan country; they were also related to kings and princes in an ancestral homeland, far away. And this has proven to be a great antidote to the poison of self-hatred.

It also signals, at last, the end of the Negro situation in this country as we have known it thus far. Any effort, from here on out, to keep the Negro in his "place" can only have the most extreme and unlucky repercussions. This being so, it would seem to me that the most intelligent effort we can now make is to give up this doomed endeavor and study how we can most quickly end the division in our house.

The Negroes who rioted in the United Nations are but a very small echo of the black discontent now abroad in the world. If we are not able, and quickly, to face and begin to eliminate the sources of this discontent in our own country, we will never be able to do it in the world at large.

The white man of the North was suddenly made aware, toward the end of the decade, of the misery and frustration of the Negroes in his own community. He became aware of the great migration of Negroes from the rural South to the urban North. He was also brought face to face with his own prejudice. For when a man with black skin sought more than legal rights—when he sought acceptance as another human being—it turned out that there were racial instincts in the North, too. And heartlessness.

In the *Times Magazine* of April 17, 1960, Wilma Dykeman and James Stokely compared the racial attitudes in a rural community of the South—Clinton, Tennessee—and in a northern suburb—Deerfield, Illinois. They found the irony that Clinton, "with most of its citizens admitting that they do not believe in or want integration, is nevertheless partially integrated, while Deerfield, with the majority of its citizens assuring the world that they believe in integration, is nevertheless totally segregated." Of Deerfield the authors wrote:

> Deerfield is actually a "bedroom" of Chicago; the majority of its residents are families of junior executives whose daily work is carried on in the nearby metropolis. They commute to suburban homes in which they have invested an average of twenty-three thousand dollars apiece. Their average take-home income is a little more

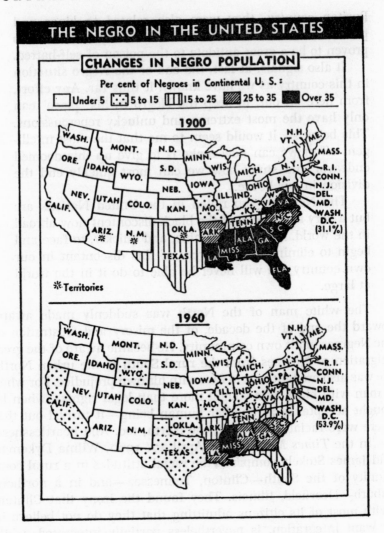

THE NEGRO IN THE UNITED STATES

CHANGES IN NEGRO POPULATION

Per cent of Negroes in Continental U. S.:

Under 5 · 5 to 15 ‖ 15 to 25 // 25 to 35 ■ Over 35

1900

WASH. DC. (31.1%)

* Territories

1960

WASH. D.C. (53.9%)

than nine thousand dollars a year. Most are college graduates.

The town has had the usual problems of any fast-growing suburb: schools, local government, parks. Yet, as one Deerfield man pointed out not long ago, "Many of the people who live here haven't come so they can assume new responsibilities, but so they can escape old problems."

In this town, in July and August, 1959, a Chicago

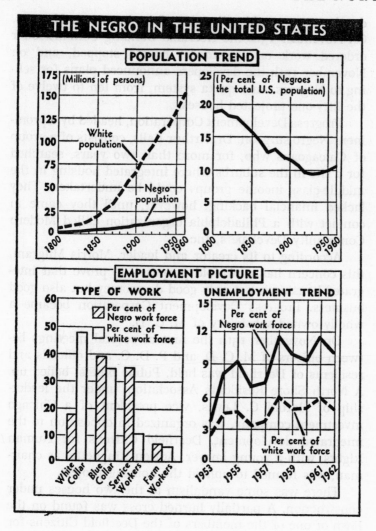

THE NEGRO IN THE UNITED STATES

POPULATION TREND

(Millions of persons)

White population

Negro population

(Per cent of Negroes in the total U.S. population)

EMPLOYMENT PICTURE

TYPE OF WORK

Per cent of Negro work force
Per cent of white work force

White Collar · Blue Collar · Service Workers · Farm Workers

UNEMPLOYMENT TREND

Per cent of Negro work force

Per cent of white work force

group, the Progress Development Corporation, acquired sites for construction of a housing project to consist of fifty-one homes costing between thirty thousand dollars and forty thousand dollars. Building permits for two model homes were obtained and their construction in the Floral Park subdivision was begun.

On November 11th the Reverend Jack Parker of St. Gregory's Protestant Episcopal Church informed the Deerfield Village Board that he had learned that the new development would sell some of its houses to Negroes. On November 13th the Deerfield Building Commissioner ordered work on the model homes stopped, and on November 15th the developers announced plans for selling to Negroes, on a quota system, from ten to twelve of the fifty-one projected houses.

Progress Development Corporation, headed by a prominent Negro surgeon, Dr. Arthur Falls, consists of a group of Chicagoans who, for more than two years, searched for a site in the suburbs where integrated housing in the middle-class income groups could be undertaken. They lacked financial backing, however, until they came in contact with a Philadelphia organization called Modern Community Developers, Inc.

According to its creator and leader, Morris Milgram, this concern has a twofold purpose—to prove that integrated housing is not only good democracy but also good business. Progress Development Corporation became a wholly owned subsidiary of M. C. D.

On November 15th the first of several meetings between officers of M. C. D. and P. D. C. and officials and residents of Deerfield was held. Public protest boiled up. A North Shore Residents Association, under the leadership of Harold C. Lewis, vice president of a Chicago investment company, was organized in opposition to the integrated development. Deerfield Citizens for Human Rights, with a young lawyer, Adrien Ringuette, as chairman, was formed to uphold the housing project.

There was some vandalism at the two houses under construction. A partially burned cross was found on the lawn of one of the members of the Deerfield Citizens for Human Rights. "Nigger Lover, why the hell don't you just move out of Deerfield?" an anonymous fellow townsman wrote a minister who favored the housing project. "Go ahead and live with those black apes and let your children marry one of them and present you with a nice dark brown grandson or daughter."

Fundamental antagonism to interracial housing was overlaid with anger at the developers. The Deerfield Park Board, which had previously sought and been denied bond issues for public parks, decided the time was ripe for obtaining such facilities. They told the developers to sell their land for parks, or condemnation proceedings would be started. December 21st was set for a referendum asking five hundred and fifty thousand dollars with which to acquire six park sites.

Those who opposed and those who favored obtaining the house sites for parks knew the issue at stake was Deerfield's attitude toward racially integrated housing. A young housewife said, "One of my neighbors told me, when I spoke out against the bond issue, that she might not mind living next door to a nigger, but she wouldn't want to live next door to any nigger-lover."

Another woman voiced the feelings of a particularly frustrated group of citizens: "We moved to Deerfield from Glencoe—some call it Glencohen now, you know— to get away from the Jews, and now here we are with the Negro problem in our lap."

The main arguments used against the housing development, however, were its effect on property values and the methods of its builders. "Now, I'm not denying any of the Negroes' rights," one of the town's businessmen said recently, "but I am saying people can talk about brotherhood all they want till it moves next door. I've put everything I have into my home here and I don't want to lose it to a bunch of do-gooders."

An attractive young married couple explained, "We're all mortgaged up to here. And although we've got most of our money tied up in our homes, we don't expect to live in them really very long. Some of the junior execs expect to become seniors and move a few miles east to the real North Shore, and a lot of us will be transferred all over the United States. When this happens, we want to be sure our homes have resale value."

Other arguments used for passage of the park bond issue were critical of the builders. "Interlopers" and "Eastern money interests" who act in "suspicious secrecy" were denounced. There were hints of Communist influence. Elizabeth Dilling spoke to a group gathered at a private home and handed out material entitled "The Red Hand Over Deerfield."

Shortly before the referendum one young matron

called together some of the members of the Residents Association and the local ministers. Chief topics of discussion were the high crime rate among Negroes, venereal disease and lawlessness in Chicago's ghettoes. (It was also suggested that everyone associated with the developers should be asked to take a loyalty oath.) "No one present seemed to understand that Negroes who can pay thirty thousand dollars to forty thousand dollars for a home aren't starting ghettoes," a member of one church congregation said.

On December 21st in a record turn-out of voters, the village decided, 2,635 to 1,207, in favor of acquiring the land for parks.

In the North the Negro has the legal formalities of equality and in recent years he has taken giant strides toward full political and economic participation in society, but even here he has not wholly won his freedom. He has been subjected to new tensions, subtler, better camouflaged, even more frustrating at times than the sharply defined barriers in the South. For example, while segregation in housing in the North has been more and more outlawed during the last ten years, it has become more and more real.

Housing, in fact, is the key to northern segregation. The separate-but-equal laws and customs that afforded the South a technique of togetherness while still maintaining a superior-inferior relationship can only be approximated in the North by segregated housing. In short, the North has arrived at the point of total commitment to democracy a little earlier than the South. And suddenly, under the Yankee accents, are echoes of Dixie. Under the protests against integrated housing are the cries against integrated schools: "They're trying to force instant and compulsory integration on us." "They're pushing too fast; racial good will has been set back years." "The Negroes themselves don't want integration. It's a few troublemakers among them. They don't want to go where they're not wanted."

This final rationalization, spoken in both the North and South, reveals a fundamental inadequacy of either region to meet the situation. Professor A. D. Albright of the University of Kentucky has said, "Integration is more important to Negroes than the white man realizes, and segregation is more important to whites than the Negro realizes." The accuracy of this observation is reflected in the shock with which white people react to each new Negro push for full equality, and the surprise on the part of many Negroes at the tenacious white resistance to any extension of that equality.

The prejudices of both regions are deeply rooted in insecurity. In southern towns much of the bitter antagonism toward Negro equality has come from the lower-income group whose economic security is most directly threatened by Negro competition. In northern suburbs much of the protest against Negro equality has come from members of the recently arrived middle class whose social status is most insecure, who feel their prestige would be jeopardized by association with Negroes.

Basic to this insecurity and to the fundamental prejudice, North or South, is one belief: that white is superior to black.

One of the most significant implications in the Dykeman-Stokely article was its picture of the confused insularity of the northern white in the early 1960's. Unlike the southerner, he conducted many of his daily activities side by side with Negroes—at lunch counters, in parks, in trains and buses, in theatres and sports arenas, and in department stores and factories. During the day his eye saw more evidence of integration than of segregation, and more of racial equality than of a codified caste system. At night he went home to his suburban bedroom, traveling in trains or on highways that went under, around or over the black ghettoes. Although he was impersonally aware of the Harlems and the Southsides, he did not become involved with them first-hand—not in the overcrowding, the exorbitant rents, the deplorable health conditions.

The gulf between white and Negro in the North was dramatized by a curious meeting between James Baldwin and Attorney General Kennedy, held in the Kennedy family's apartment on Central Park South in New York on May 24, 1963. At Kennedy's suggestion, Baldwin gathered a group of Negroes, mostly intellectuals—Lorraine Hansberry, the playwright; Kenneth B. Clark, professor of psychology at City College, and singers Lena Horne and Harry Belafonte, among others—and a few white persons. They met with the Attorney General and his assistant for civil rights, Burke Marshall.

It was a disaster. Early in the meeting one of the Negroes made a sarcastic reference to "the Kennedys." Another said he would not fight for the United States if the tension with Cuba came to arms. Kennedy bristled, and tempers rose. When Marshall told in his self-effacing way about the near-miracle he had just accomplished in negotiating the Birmingham riots to a peaceful settlement, someone laughed: Why hadn't the Federal Government used troops to protect Negroes instead of words? When the Attorney General tried to explain his belief that a federal police force would be dangerous, he might have been speaking in Urdu. When Baldwin and the others talked about how Negroes felt, Kennedy kept saying: "What is it you want me to do?"

The whole affair was steeped in irony. Robert Kennedy had been one of the first public officials to warn about the potential explosiveness of the racial situation in the North. Two years before that meeting he had said that the individual injustice found in the North would be harder to solve than the South's official discrimination, and might be more dangerous. Part of his reason for thinking so was the marginal usefulness of law to cure the diseases of the North—private prejudice, Negro ignorance and social backwardness. He did not think a federal Attorney General could solve those problems by lawsuits, or by troops. His audience that day on Central Park South understandably thought him insensitive, unable to understand. But Professor Clark did say later: "The fact that Bobby Kennedy sat through such an ordeal for three hours proves he is among the best the white power structure has to offer. There were no villains in that room—only the past of our society."

As the summer of 1963 approached, the country became increasingly aware of the electric quality of the racial protest movement, no longer a merely southern phenomenon. Plans were made for a great national demonstration, a March on Washington. The idea worried many responsible persons. Could the Negro leaders really persuade as many as one hundred thousand people to come to Washington for such a rally? They had used that figure, and anything less would look like a flop. Could that many people descend on the capital without disorder of some kind, possibly real rioting? A violent march would do the cause of civil rights permanent harm.

But the plans went forward, under the leadership of A. Philip Randolph and Bayard Rustin. It was to be a March for Jobs and Freedom—goals that expressed the Negro's discontent in the North and South. The March took place on August 28, 1963. E. W. Kenworthy reported it the next day in the *Times*:

More than two hundred thousand Americans, most of them black but many of them white, demonstrated here today for a full and speedy program of civil rights and equal job opportunities. It was the greatest assembly for a redress of grievances that this capital has ever seen.

One hundred years and two hundred and forty days after Abraham Lincoln enjoined the emancipated slaves to "abstain from all violence" and "labor faithfully for reasonable wages," this vast throng proclaimed in march and song and through the speeches of their leaders that they were still waiting for the freedom and the jobs. There was no violence to mar the demonstration. In fact, at times there was an air of hootenanny about it as groups of schoolchildren clapped hands and swung into the familiar freedom songs.

But if the crowd was good-natured, the underlying tone was one of dead seriousness. The emphasis was on "freedom" and "now." At the same time the leaders emphasized, paradoxically but realistically, that the struggle was just beginning.

On Capitol Hill opinion was divided about the impact of the demonstration in stimulating Congressional action on civil-rights legislation. But at the White House, President Kennedy declared that the cause of twenty million Negroes had been advanced by the march.

The march leaders went from the shadows of the Lincoln Memorial to the White House to meet with the President for seventy-five minutes. Afterward, Mr. Kennedy issued a four-hundred-word statement praising the marchers for the "deep fervor and the quiet dignity" that had characterized the demonstration. "The nation," the

President said, "can properly be proud of the demonstration that has occurred here today."

The main target of the demonstration was Congress,
where committees are now considering the Administration's civil-rights bill. At the Lincoln Memorial this afternoon, some speakers, knowing little of the ways of
Congress, assumed that the passage of a strengthened
civil-rights bill had been assured by the moving events
of the day. But from statements by Congressional leaders,
after they had met with the march committee this morning, this did not seem certain at all. These statements
came before the demonstration.

Senator Hubert Humphrey, one of the fifteen or more senators who participated in the demonstration, put it another way
as he stood on the steps of the Lincoln Memorial and looked
down on the jammed Mall. "All this probably hasn't changed
any votes on the civil-rights bill," the Minnesota Democrat said,
"but it's a good thing for Washington and the nation and the
world."

Russell Baker of the *Times* reported that "no one could remember an invading army quite as gentle as the two hundred
thousand civil-rights marchers who occupied Washington today."
He continued:

> For the most part, they came silently during the night
> and early morning, occupied the great shaded boulevards
> along the Mall, and spread through the parklands between
> the Washington Monument and the Potomac. But instead
> of the emotional horde of angry militants that many had
> feared, what Washington saw was a vast army of quiet,
> middle-class Americans who had come in the spirit of the
> church outing. And instead of the tensions that had been
> expected, they gave this city a day of sad music, strange
> silences and good feeling in the streets.
>
> It was apparent from early morning that this would
> be an extraordinary day. At eight A.M. when rush-hour
> traffic is normally creeping bumper-to-bumper across the
> Virginia bridges and down the main boulevards from
> Maryland, the streets had the abandoned look of Sunday
> morning. From a helicopter over the city, it was possible
> to see caravans of chartered buses streaming down New

York Avenue from Baltimore and points north, but the downtown streets were empty. Nothing moved in front of the White House, nor on Pennsylvania Avenue.

For the natives, this was obviously a day of siege and the streets were being left to the marchers.

By nine-thirty the number of marchers at the assembly point by the Washington Monument had reached about forty thousand, but it was a crowd without fire. Mostly, people who had traveled together sat on the grass or posed for group portraits against the monument, like tourists on a rare visit to the capital. Here and there, little groups stood in the sunlight and sang. A group of seventy-five young people from Danville, Virginia, came dressed in white sweatshirts with crudely cut black mourning bands on their sleeves.

"We're mourning injustice in Danville," explained James Bruce, a fifteen-year-old who said he has been arrested three times for participating in demonstrations there.

Standing together, the group sang of the freedom fight in a sad melody with words that went, "Move on, move on, move on with the freedom fight; move on, move on, we're fighting for equal rights."

Other hymns came from groups scattered over the grounds, but there was no cohesion in the crowd. Instead, a fairgrounds atmosphere prevailed. Marchers kept straggling off to ride the elevators to the top of the monument. Women sat on the grass and concentrated on feeding babies.

As the crowd on the steps thickened and gradually became an impassable mass, the extraordinary politeness that characterized the day was dramatized every time an elbow was crooked. People excused themselves for momentarily obstructing a view, excused themselves for dropping cigarette ashes on shoeshines.

When the marshals called for a clear path, hundreds hastened to fall aside with a good will rarely seen in the typical urban crowd. The sweetness and patience of the crowd may have set some sort of national high-water mark in mass decency.

At one fifty-nine the official speaking began. For those

who listened it was full of noble statement about democracy and religious sincerity, but the crowd was dissolving
fast now. Those who left early missed two of the emotional high points of the day. One was Mahalia Jackson's
singing, which seemed to bounce off the Capitol far up
the Mall. The other was the speech of the Reverend Dr.
Martin Luther King, Jr., president of the Southern Christian Leadership Conference.

The vibrant moments of Dr. King's address were captured
in E. W. Kenworthy's report. "He ignited the crowd," said the
Times reporter, "with words that might have been written by
the sad, brooding man enshrined within the Memorial." The
story continued:

When Dr. King arose, a great roar swelled up from
the crowd. When he started to speak, a hush fell.

"Even though we face the difficulties of today and tomorrow, I still have a dream," he said. "It is a dream
chiefly rooted in the American dream. I have a dream
that one day this nation will rise up and live out the true
meaning of its creed: 'We hold these truths to be self-
evident, that all men are created equal.'

"I have a dream . . ." The vast throng listening in-
tently to him roared.

". . . that one day on the red hills of Georgia, the sons
of former slaves and the sons of former slave-owners will
be able to sit together at the table of brotherhood.

"I have a dream . . ." The crowd roared.

". . . that one day even the State of Mississippi, a state
sweltering with the heat of injustice, sweltering with the
heat of oppression, will be transformed into an oasis of
freedom and justice.

"I have a dream . . ." The crowd roared.

". . . that my four little children will one day live in
a nation where they will not be judged by the color of their
skin but by the content of their character.

"I have a dream . . ." The crowd roared.

". . . that one day every valley shall be exalted, every
hill and mountain shall be made low, the rough places will
be made plain, and the crooked places will be made
straight, and the glory of the Lord shall be revealed and all
flesh shall see it together."

As Dr. King concluded with a quotation from a Negro hymn—"Free at last, free at last, thank God Almighty"— the crowd, recognizing that he was finishing, roared once again and waved their signs and pennants.

James Reston of the *Times* said:

The question of the day was raised by Dr. King's theme: Was this all a dream or will it help the dream come true?

No doubt this vast effort helped the Negro drive against discrimination. It was better covered by television and the press than any event here since President Kennedy's inauguration, and, since indifference is almost as great a problem to the Negro as hostility, this was a plus.

James Baldwin, the author, summed up the day succinctly. The day was important in itself, he said, and "what we do with this day is even more important." He was convinced that the country was finally grappling with the Negro problem instead of evading it; that the Negro himself was "for the first time" aware of his value as a human being and was "no longer at the mercy of what the white people imagine the Negro to be."

Above all, the Negro leaders got over Lincoln's point that "the necessity of being ready increases." For they left no doubt that this was not the climax of their campaign for equality but merely the beginning, that they were going to stay in the streets until they could get equality in the schools, restaurants, houses and employment agencies of the nation, and that, as they demonstrated here today, they had found an effective way to demonstrate for changes in the laws without breaking the law themselves.

But the promise of that happy day in Washington could not be kept. No realist could have expected that there would be only polite demonstrations from then on, or that the economic and social barriers to Negro advancement would politely be dropped. What happened as the decade ended in 1964 was that protest tactics grew more militant—some would say less rational. Demonstrators chained themselves together at construction sites to demand employment of Negroes; one was tragically run over and killed by a bulldozer. They threatened a "stall-in" to paralyze traffic near the New York World's Fair—a threat that was condemned by most of the established Negro leadership and that fortunately did not work.

In a sense the persons responsible for such tactics were anarchists. They had given up on our system and were ready to destroy it. They cared little for the danger of alienating the sympathy of the whites, who were ninety per cent of the American population. One vital question in 1964 was whether such extremists would capture the support of the northern Negro community.

The ultra-militants tended to dominate the headlines because of their extreme measures. On March 6, 1964, a small band of demonstrators made New York City's Triborough Bridge the scene of protest. They sat down on the roadway, blocking all traffic, and littered the area with garbage. They would not move until they were forcibly removed by the police. On March 8th, in an editorial headed "Disservice to Civil Rights," the *Times* commented on the protest:

> It might help if the sit-downers took time out to read a perceptive analysis of the equal-rights problem in the current issue of *The Atlantic* by Professor Oscar Handlin of Harvard, whose studies of the absorption of minorities into the American mainstream have won him wide acclaim. His conclusion is that sit-ins and street demonstrations are the sole recourse in those areas of the South where Negroes are still excluded from political decisions and due process of law, but that they are self-defeating in such cities as New York, Chicago, Philadelphia and Boston, where Negroes do have legitimate means of making their wants and needs felt.
>
> The battle for equality of opportunity is the common responsibility of all New Yorkers; it will not be won by tactics that tear the community apart.

New Yorkers were puzzled and dismayed by such episodes. And the phenomenon was not local. Lawrence E. Davies of the *Times* reported from San Francisco on March 19, 1964:

> A shocked city, cast by civil-rights advocates in a new, unexpected role, is talking of little else these days.
> Many residents cannot get used to the idea that San

Francisco, long pictured as cosmopolitan, sophisticated and tolerant, is deeply involved in racial troubles. The Negro leadership is split over civil-rights demonstrations that have led to about four hundred arrests in recent weeks. Religious leaders, although sympathetic to campaigns to end discrimination and provide more jobs for Negroes, are divided over the use of civil-disobedience methods in seeking the objectives.

Civil-rights leaders have declared a two-week truce on demonstrations involving disobedience of the law. Attorneys threaten to demand a trial by jury for every demonstrator who has been arrested. If the demand is granted, judges say, the courts would be clogged for months.

The city will long be arguing over "the night the civil righters seized the palace." Civil rights, a widely held view insists, took a severe beating when more than one thousand chanting, marching, sitting, door-blocking demonstrators carried out a tumultuous all-night siege of the Sheraton-Palace Hotel March 6th.

Governor Edmund G. Brown, an avowed champion of civil rights, is partial to that view. With many other supporters of the Rumford Housing Act, he believes that such mass demonstrations will backfire and damage the chances of defeating in November an initiative measure that would nullify the anti-discrimination act. The act applies to eighty per cent of California's housing.

The hotel demonstrations on two consecutive weekends, like those previously at the drive-in supermarkets of Lucky Stores, Inc., where demonstrators filled and then abandoned shopping carts, have been aimed at allegedly discriminatory hiring practices. In each case the company involved has entered a disclaimer.

The Bank of America, believing itself to be marked as an early target of demonstrations, defended its employment methods last week. It warned it would file charges against participants in any disruptive demonstrations. Since then bank representatives and officers of the Congress of Racial Equality have had a "frank and fruitful" exploratory meeting.

Much of the controversial talk has revolved around the youth leadership in the hotel demonstrations. The participants have been mostly white youths. Of the more than one hundred and sixty arrested, fewer than a dozen were Negroes.

Dr. Thomas N. Burbridge, now head of the N.A.A.C.P. chapter, took the position that "if the situation calls for it, civil disobedience is the proper tactic to apply in getting civil rights."

However, Donald Warden, a young Negro lawyer who heads the Afro-American Association, called the hotel demonstration "a battle for headlines that was splitting civil-rights groups." He held that most of the demonstrators had little concern for the Negroes as a whole.

The most notable new protest technique of 1964 was the school boycott. On February 3rd, in the largest civil-rights demonstration to date, four hundred and sixty-four thousand pupils stayed out of New York City's public schools in a peaceful one-day boycott. That was nearly forty-five per cent of the enrollment. In numbers it was impressive, but in concrete results it was less so. For no protest could solve the real problems of education in New York. Most experts thought that deliberate mixing of the races in the city's schools so that racial percentages would be equal everywhere—mixing that would have to be accomplished in good measure by long bus trips—would drive more middle-class white families into the suburbs and destroy the city school system. The experts thought that what was most desperately needed was not "integration" but better education in the slums: Replacement of ancient buildings, more money for intensified instruction of children made backward by their environment, new techniques in pre-school education.

Every attempt to deal with the racial problem in the school showed how intractable it was. Fred Powledge of the *Times* described in the *Times Magazine* of May 10, 1964, the conflict over a proposal to "pair" two schools six blocks apart in the middle-class borough of Queens—one with eighty-seven per cent white pupils, the other ninety-seven per cent Negro. The latter was built in 1910 but, interestingly, could never get on the list for early renovation until after the authorities proposed the pairing plan, under which the enrollments of the two schools would be mixed. The idea for the pairing came from white leaders, but it brought reactions of intense bitterness among

the white parents. A city-wide committee now began speaking of
a *white* school boycott if modest plans for further integration
were carried out.

It remained to be seen how the New York School Board,
already short of funds and battered by angry Negro and fearful
white parents, would resolve the tensions. One thing shown by
its experience—and similar problems in other northern cities—
was the inability of law as such to deal with the North's racial
discrimination. An attempt was made to establish through lawsuits the doctrine that the Constitution not only forbade officially
imposed racial segregation in schools but put a responsibility on
officials for affirmative action to eliminate "de facto segregation" caused by residential patterns. But the lower courts
rejected that view, and on May 4, 1964, the Supreme Court refused to review one such decision, from Gary, Indiana. As the
law stood, then, the state could not put its official weight behind discrimination. But neither was it required to compel integration. Law and the courts, for so long the instruments of
the drive for Negro equality, were not enough in the North.
The rescuing of the Negro child from the cycle of the deprived
family and the slum school was a job not for the Constitution
but for social policy.

Social reform depends upon the willingness of politicians and
their constituents to spend money and engage in experiments
and make sacrifices. That is why the tension between northern
white and Negro communities, so readily observable in 1964,
seemed to many observers so unhappy a portent.

On April 22nd demonstrators drowned out President Johnson
when he spoke at the World's Fair. He was asked the next
day what his reaction had been. "Frankly, one of compassion,"
he said. "Somehow all of us must learn understanding. Even
though it is difficult, it is still possible. I believe the basic good
will of the American people is strong enough to carry us through
the strains."

Not everyone could be as optimistic as the President. There
were reports from Harlem of gangs of anti-white youths. And in
the white North there were signs of "backlash"—the unfavorable
white reaction to the intensity of Negro demands for equal treatment and personal acceptance. Governor George Wallace of Alabama, peddling racism with a thin coating of "states' rights,"
entered three Democratic Presidential primaries and won thirty-

four per cent of the vote in Wisconsin, thirty per cent in Indiana and forty-three per cent in Maryland. Analysts noted that the districts which were ordinarily the backbone of liberal Democratic strength—the areas of union members, Italian and Polish and German and Irish Catholics—had gone for Wallace, presumably feeling the economic threat of the Negro. In Gary, Indiana, a steel city where Negroes had sued to end racial imbalance in the public schools, Wallace carried every white precinct.

Then, in the summer, came race riots, and the estrangement of the whites and Negroes of the North worsened. The first outbreak came in Harlem, on Saturday night, July 18th. Two days later a remarkable insight into how such riots happen was provided in a *Times* article by Paul Montgomery, who gave the history of that night in Harlem.

A few minutes before seven o'clock Saturday night, a young woman from the Congress of Racial Equality set up a rickety blue cafe chair and a child's American flag on the southwest corner of 125th Street and Seventh Avenue. A desultory crowd of a hundred gathered in the steaming early evening and the rally began. There was impatience with the heat, and anger over the shooting of a fifteen-year-old Negro boy by an off-duty white police lieutenant in Yorkville two days before. But the crowd was not unruly, nor was there any air of violence.

Seven hours later screaming mobs, numbering in the thousands, thrashed back and forth through the center of Harlem, breaking windows, looting smashed storefronts, menacing policemen, and threatening or assaulting the few white people in the area. Thousands of other residents watched in awe from their tenement windows or from sheltered places on the streets. More than four hundred policemen who had sped to the scene fired thousands of shots in the air in an effort to control the crowd. Many who resisted police attempts to disperse the mobs were clubbed until they ran, or could no longer run.

At 123rd Street and Seventh Avenue a jeering crowd of six hundred, several with bloodied heads, faced a grim group of white-helmeted troops from the Tactical Patrol Force. Bottles and garbage cans and garbage smashed around the policemen. They crouched and fired volley after volley into the air, aiming just above the roofs. The night became acrid with gunsmoke.

"Go home, go home," a sweating red-faced captain shouted through a bullhorn.

A scream came back from a man in the mob: "We are home, baby."

What happened between the C.O.R.E. rally on Saturday night and the grim dawn of Sunday morning?

The rally was sponsored by three militant C.O.R.E. chapters—Downtown, East River and South Jamaica. Its purpose had originally been to protest events in Mississippi, but the theme shifted after Thursday morning, when Lieutenant Thomas Gilligan shot and killed fifteen-year-old James Powell in an apartment-house doorway on East 76th Street. The police say that the boy, who was taking a voluntary remedial reading course at the Robert F. Wagner Junior High School nearby, moved toward the lieutenant with a knife. Several Negro witnesses have disputed this story and say the killing was unprovoked.

On the Harlem street corner Saturday night, a dozen patrolmen lounged and watched from nearby stations as Judith Howell, a seventeen-year-old member of Bronx C.O.R.E. spoke to the crowd from the blue chair. "James Powell was shot because he was black," the girl said. The crowd murmured assent and applauded. "We got a civil-rights bill," she went on, "and along with the bill we got Barry Goldwater and a dead black boy."

The shifting crowd had grown to about two hundred. Several of them heckled the C.O.R.E. speakers who followed. "White people dictate your policy," one man yelled. Chris Sprowal, chairman of Downtown C.O.R.E. said: "It is time to let 'the man' [white people] know that if he does something to us we are going to do something back. If you say, 'You kick me once, I'm going to kick you twice,' we might get some respect." Charles Saunders of South Jamaica C.O.R.E. followed with the charge that "forty-five per cent of the cops in New York are neurotic murderers." The crowd grew more excited, but not unruly. Then C.O.R.E. turned the blue chair over to speakers in the crowd.

At about eight P.M. the Reverend Nelson C. Dukes of

the Fountain Springs Baptist Church, 15 West 126th Street, mounted the makeshift podium and gave a twenty-minute speech. Declaring it was time to stop talking and to act, he shouted that the people at the rally should march on the police station and present their demands. The crowd became more animated. There were shouts of "Let's go" and "Let's do it now." A scar-faced man wearing a white sports shirt followed the preacher, saying "We have got to act now."

The meeting broke up at 8:35 P.M. "Let's go to the precinct," Mr. Dukes and the other man shouted. About a hundred spectators and C.O.R.E. people followed them down Seventh Avenue to 123rd Street, walking silently on the sidewalk. They turned right at 123rd Street, moving toward the 28th precinct station house, halfway up the block on the uptown side. There they tried to force their way in, but were turned back and herded across the street by a squad of policemen.

A few bottles and garbage-can covers sailed toward the police. The policemen donned helmets and faced the crowd. The crowd began taunting the policemen as some patrolmen rushed to the rooftops to stop the bottle throwing.

"Murphy must be removed," the crowd shouted. "Killers, murderers. Murphy's rats."

The patrolmen did not move. The precinct captain was asked how many men he had out. "Enough," he replied. There were about twenty.

Meanwhile Mr. Dukes, Ernest Russell of East River C.O.R.E., and a group of hangers-on presented their demands to Inspector Thomas V. Prendergast, who was in charge. They said they wanted Commissioner Murphy to come to Harlem and announce the suspension of Lieutenant Gilligan. They said they would not move until he did so.

At about nine-twenty—just at dusk—a truck carrying police barricades pulled up. As the barricades were being set up between the crowd and the police a scuffle broke out. It was the first violence of the long night. About twenty-five patrolmen and demonstrators went down in a welter of flailing arms and legs. "That's it," said Inspec-

tor Prendergast. "Lock them up." The crowd by this time
had grown to several hundred. Sixteen demonstrators—
including two C.O.R.E. speakers from the rally—sat down
on the sidewalk. All were rushed roughly across the street
and into the station. Those from C.O.R.E. took the characteristic non-violent position of demonstrators—arms
over the ears, knees tucked up to the chest. Others who
had not had training were dragged into the station.

The crowd began shouting. The rain of bottles and
debris increased. Dozens of policemen poured out of the
station, buckling on holsters as they ran. One was struck
on the head by a bottle and was sent to the hospital. The
force began pushing the crowd toward the Seventh and
Eighth Avenue ends of 123rd Street amid a rain of bottles.
A bus rolled up, and forty-eight members of the Tactical
Patrol Force—the police shock troops—scrambled out.

Mr. Dukes looked on, shaking his head. "This has got
out of hand," he said. "If I knew this was going to happen,
I wouldn't have said anything." Then he walked away.

The fresh police forces established barricades on
Seventh and Eighth Avenues and cleared 123rd Street
between them. An emergency truck with a searchlight
blocked the Seventh Avenue end and was surrounded by
white-helmeted policemen. A crowd of five hundred had
formed by the searchlight and was constantly growing.
Groups of youths stopped cars on Seventh Avenue on the
downtown side. They picked out a car with a white couple
in it and began pounding on it with their fists. One older
man came up and broke a headlight with a bottle. The
car finally got free of the fifteen people surrounding it
and careened away.

It was a little after ten o'clock and Deputy Chief Inspector Harry Taylor had assumed command. Off-duty
policemen, detectives and forces from other precincts
began arriving. Between the barricades, 123rd Street was
clogged with police vehicles. At Seventh Avenue, the
police determined to break up the mob. Two squads of
the Tactical Patrol Force, brandishing nightsticks and
shouting "Charge!" leaped over the barricade and into
the crowd. In a turmoil, the mob broke into sections that

eddied and flowed on Seventh Avenue between 122nd and 124th Streets.

The first shots were fired at ten-thirty at 125th Street and Lenox Avenue. A youth hurled a bottle of flaming gasoline at a squad car, and a sheet of flame spread on the street. A patrolman was burned, and his four companions emptied their revolvers into the night air. The shots sounded like strings of firecrackers, except that there were flashes from the pistols. It was a sound that was to become familiar the rest of the night.

From eleven to midnight there was a lull in the area on Seventh Avenue, and it seemed that a near-riot had ended. Actually, five blocks away to the northeast, other groups on Lenox Avenue were breaking store windows and pillaging goods.

A drunken woman lay down on the northbound side of Seventh Avenue at 125th Street. Staring at the sky through an alcoholic haze, she said she just felt like lying down. "They walked all over me in Greenville, South Carolina," she said. "They might as well run over me here."

The crowd of several hundred on the corners attached a different interpretation to the scene. "Did you see that?" a man asked his companion. "They shot that woman down in cold blood." He glared at the handful of patrolmen near the resting woman.

"Women and children, beating up women and children," another remarked. A stout woman in a blue knit suit shouted to her group: "They are trying to pick us off one by one."

Just after midnight a tremendous volley of shots sounded from the northeast corner of 125th Street and Seventh Avenue. A dozen patrol cars, sirens screaming, raced down 125th Street to Lenox Avenue to answer an "assist patrolman" call. Hundreds of people poured down 125th Street following the sirens. They raced along, shouting wildly as rock 'n' roll music floated down from a third-story dance hall. Older people, puffing and mopping their brows, trotted along to keep up.

The corner of 125th Street and Lenox Avenue was a disaster area. The ground was littered with broken glass and debris. Screaming crowds occupied each corner, pushing toward a ring of police cars and patrolmen crouched behind them. The police fired volley after volley into the air and over the roofs as the crowd raced wildly back and forth. Police reinforcements arrived and patrolmen began charging into the mobs on the corners. Some policemen had apparently reached the end of their patience. Anyone who did not move immediately when charged was set upon and clubbed.

Shuttles of squad cars took away youths holding their heads. There were smears of blood up and down the sidewalks. These scenes were repeated up Lenox Avenue to 135th Street. Screens protecting the windows of stores were ripped off and the stores looted. Every rifle in two pawnshops on 135th Street was gone. Grocery stores, an insurance agency, a men's clothing store and many others were sacked. Volleys of shots rang up and down the avenue and the spent cartridges littered the pavement. A woman who had been struck by a hit-and-run driver lay on 125th Street, surrounded by friends and policemen. The rain of bottles continued and the crowds shouted, "Murderers!" at the police.

About two A.M. the main thrust of the riot seemed to have been spent, although there were sporadic incidents until dawn. The 28th precinct communications were snarled by the avalanche of call. False alarms were frequent and fire equipment raced here and there.

Sometime after four a figure stumbled through the the police barricade at 123rd and Seventh Avenue and went toward the precinct house. He was a white youth with a bloody mouth and glazed eyes. He sobbed uncontrollably. Through numbed lips he told police that he was a sailor who had got off at the wrong subway stop. He had been set upon by a group of youths, he said. "They beat me. They beat me and took my watch and I yelled. I'm a sailor from California, and I took the wrong subway train."

The issue in 1964 was more than race. It was the unity of the country. Lyndon Johnson, a man who cared especially about national unity and was uniquely situated to maintain it, faced the most difficult problems imaginable. The overwhelming, bipartisan endorsement of the civil-rights bill by Congress gave renewed hope for that unity and for continued faith among Negroes in the orderly processes of government. But the savage opposition to the bill of the Republican candidate for President, Senator Barry Goldwater of Arizona, raised the terrible prospect of race as a political issue in a national campaign. In the summer of 1964, the peaceful, cheerful spirit of the March on Washington, just a year earlier, seemed long, long ago.

In all the discouraging difficulty of the northern racial situation as the decade ended there was one constructive element: the removal of illusion. The pretense that discrimination existed only in the South was gone, and it was better to face the truth, however painful. It was healthier, too, to have Negro and white talking frankly about each other's faults.

On May 31, 1964, the *Times Magazine* printed a white man's critical appraisal of the Negro protest movement—indeed of the Negro community. Daniel Bell, professor of sociology at Columbia University, wrote:

> The Negro protest movement in the North is in a crisis phase. The established leadership finds itself in danger of being stampeded (the National Urban League the other week withdrew from direct-action tactics in collaboration with other organizations because it feared it might be sucked into ever wilder adventures). New leaders are quickly "thrown up" as the movement spreads from civil rights to schools, to rent strikes, to claims for preference in jobs. New pressure tactics, such as the stall-ins or lay-downs, have alarmed the older Negro leadership, as well as the white liberals. Indeed, as Edward H. Levi, the provost of the University of Chicago put it recently, the Negro protest movement and law enforcement are running on a collision course. Unless one makes the unlikely assumption that the protest movement may, in its trajectory, become overtly revolutionary (as some extremist Negro leaders dream) or that the tensions may explode into a racial war (as some hotheads on both sides are spoiling for) some method of institutional compromise has to be established. How can this be done?
>
> There are two preconditions for successful political bargaining in the American system: one is that the Negro

community has to choose its political spokesmen in a responsible way (in the way the farm groups have done); the other is that the Negro community has to specify its priorities and demands, so that we know what to bargain about. In short, there has to be a consensus about the ends desired—and such a consensus is not simply a list of slogans.

So far the Negro community is struggling with both problems. A story in this newspaper earlier this year highlighted one situation: "Almost every week a new civil-rights organization with a new philosophy is born in the metropolitan area and another man or woman is acclaimed as a civil-rights leader. . . . Experience, education and social standing are not necessary for this kind of leadership. What is necessary is the ability to articulate the desperate feelings of the impatient members of the community."

The situation is exacerbated, as Whitney Young of the Urban League has pointed out, by the irresponsibility of the press and television. As we saw in the threats before the opening of the World's Fair, many lesser-known leaders are moved to make extreme statements in the knowledge that in this fashion they can catch attention. Yet at the same time the carefully worked out programs for social change by the established organizations go unreported.

A second point is that most Negro leaders now find it difficult to speak out against "militancy" even when they know that militancy can become self-defeating, for in the protest movement (and often among white liberals who feel guilty in not being militant enough) "militancy" is accounted as an intrinsic good. Yet militancy is a means not an end in itself; and its use—and sometimes one may have to be quite militant—should only be proportionate to the problem at hand.

It is not only that the Negro leadership is in danger of becoming fragmented but its efforts to deal concretely with practical problems are often overridden by these "militant" leaders in their efforts to catch attention, publicity and power. A case in point is that of the Reverend Milton Galamison, the organizer of the New York school boycotts. From the start Mr. Galamison raised the single abstraction of "integration" with little heed to plan or method or recognition of the fact that his demands might simply wreck the educational system.

As an article in a recent issue of *New America*, the organ of the Socialist party, summed it up: "Galamison opposed the development of any plan by the civil-rights groups. He said that it was the job of the Board of Education to propose a plan. And even beyond this, he was opposed to introducing demands to improve ghetto schools, as he felt this would de-emphasize the integration issue. . . . He never accepted any of the concrete plans offered by the Urban League and other groups. As a result the movement was left with a few abstractions and an emphasis on busing."

To call attention to these situations is not to exculpate the New York City Board of Education, which failed to provide any consistent proposals and which was divided among itself. Nor can we neglect the fact that the failure of Congress and municipal agencies to act feeds a nihilistic sentiment in the Negro community. But the simple point is that bargaining is a two-way process and that the Negro community has a responsibility to organize itself so that the bargaining may proceed effectively.

Obviously such a course will not be an easy one. At the moment, Negro emotions understandably ride high, and the mood of released anger encourages bolder, and even wilder, pitches of feeling. The exacerbated climate is favorable to demagogues—in fact, some of the influential Negro leaders have quietly stepped back from overt involvement with immediate issues and are waiting for calmer times—and these have been quick to emerge, abetted by such wily politicians as Adam Clayton Powell, who dreams of becoming "the grand old man of the Black Revolution."

There are, it seems to me, three conditions for a responsible self-organization and political bargaining to emerge. The first is a clear indication by the country of its willingness to act decisively to meet legitimate Negro demands—actions such as the school-integration plan presented by the special commitee of the New York State

Commissioner of Education, John Fischer, Kenneth Clark and Judah Cahn, or the quick passage of the Congressional civil-rights bill before the summer.

The second is a willingness on the part of the responsible Negro leadership to speak out openly, when the situation presents itself, against its demagogic elements. And third, the presence of skilled "political brokers" or mediators—just as in the industrial-relations experience —who can quietly explore the limits of settlements and bring about agreements.

This does not mean that the Negro community must create a monolithic political organization for bargaining; no community can. There is, within the Negro community, a wide range of legitimate political differences over goals and tactics, from the skillful patience of a Whitney Young to the radical convictions of a James Farmer. But on specific issues, a consensus on immediate priorities has to emerge, if effective change is to take place.

In the political bargaining that will necessarily take place in the coming years, the most difficult question will be that of "preferential rights," which many Negroes are now beginning to ask for—preference in school, in jobs, in housing, and the like. The claim has much force to it. The argument is that because of previous discrimination, the Negro is already disadvantaged, so that when there is a formal equality of opportunity—as in the competitive examinations to the special high schools in the city—the Negro child is bound to lose out; and thus the vicious cycle of deprivation is reinforced.

The issue goes to the root of the American philosophical creed—the idea of equality as an individual right. For what the new claim asserts is that rights and opportunities should inhere to one on the basis of a group, not an individual, status. Historically, the chief pride of democracy has been equality before the law on an individual basis. After all, the rancor of the French Revolution against the feudal system was that such a system gave differential legal privileges to a person on the basis of his birth. But in practice every social system, the American no less, has recognized group rights and acted to protect the interests of specific groups.

In this country tariffs protect infant (and large) industries; maritime and aviation companies have received—and still receive—direct financial subsidies; farmers get price supports; labor receives minimum wages, and, for many years, war veterans have received extra points or outright preference in the claim to civil-service jobs. But all these are "functional" or created groups to which anyone can be admitted. The present claim for preference is for a "natural" group, defined by birth alone. (Though how one would legally define an American Negro is a complex anthroplogical question, particularly in the light of some of the southern miscegenation laws.) The paradox is that the Negro community, in demanding, for example, an equal-accommodations clause in civil-rights legislation, wants to end discrimination on the basis of an arbitrary category such as color, insisting that all men are to be recognized individually; yet, in making a claim for preference in schools or jobs, it is asking for the recognition of that same arbitrary category.

The statement of abstract principle only shows the contradiction. It cannot lead to a resolution of the problem. The need for special subsidy, especially in nursery-school and elementary education, is clear, and the effort is a legitimate one that few can oppose.

The Administration's poverty program offers one general line of attack. By the formal definition which the Council of Economic Advisers has adopted (i.e., the figure of three thousand dollars as a yearly income for a family of four), about forty-five per cent of the Negro families in the United States are poor. And the poverty program, with its emphasis on retraining, literacy and higher job skills, can improve the chance of a Negro to compete for a job. So, on "subsidies" there is little argument.

But when one asks for special quotas or preference, particularly in the cases of schools or jobs where places are limited, such a request serves to discriminate against others. And this is a much more difficult question, morally and practically, to solve.

As a practical fact, many colleges in the Ivy League have established such quotas and even preferences for Negroes. Historically, these schools have had geographical quotas, in order to make them more truly "national" rather than "provincial." (And certainly there are "athletic" quotas, with differential academic standards for these boys.) A special Negro quota, and even preference to the less qualified Negro boy, is a recognition of the responsibility to help the Negro community, as well as to add an extra dimension to the quality of the school.

But these are private institutions. What of the city colleges, which as public institutions are pledged to operate on universalist standards? Making a special place for a less qualified Negro student may eliminate an equally poor Italian or Jewish boy. What then? It is easy to say we must expand the schools, but there are limits of space, numbers of qualified teachers and other resources which are not easily commanded. Much of this dilemma can be attributed to a lack of foresight and planning; and it points the way toward a more comprehensive conception of what our future social needs will be. But this does not give us solutions for the present. Any solution is bound to be an imperfect and an unsatisfactory one. Yet this has to be publicly aired, discussed and "bargained" over.

It would be foolish and illusory—especially for the Negro community—to assume that all solutions, even the most important ones, can be reached by political means alone. The most fundamental ones—the structure of Negro family and communal life—cannot.

In their book, *Beyond the Melting Pot*, Nathan Glazer and Daniel P. Moynihan call attention to one strategic fact: of the 353,000 Negro families in the New York metropolitan area in 1960, one-fourth were headed by women, as against one in ten for white families. This statistic, illustrating the one-sided nature of much of Negro family life, sheds enormous light on the limited economic resources, the inadequate motivational patterns and other social handicaps of the Negro community. In the "cool world" it is the Negro boy who bears the burden. Lacking a regular father, he suffers psychologi-

cal difficulties; lacking a consistent model, his aspirations, understandably, are unrealistic and his self-image
is impaired.

Or, to take a topic that is largely taboo, consider the
extraordinarily high rate of illegitimacy in the Negro
world. In 1961 (according to the September, 1963, issue
of *Indicators*, published by the United States Department of Health, Education and Welfare), about twenty-
two per cent of all Negro children were born out of
wedlock (about 1,800,000 children) as against 2.5 per
cent of white children.

In the central section of one major northern city,
it is estimated that 37.5 per cent of all Negro children
are born illegitimate. This is not a case of the seduction
of ignorant young girls, but more often a regular pattern of Negro women setting up common-law house-
holds with new husbands after the legal husbands have
decamped. One might say, in mitigation, that this represents simply a sociological form of divorce and remar-
riage without the ponderous procedures of the law. Yet
this is only partially the case. The large rise in the number of aid-to-dependent-children cases indicates the
more common patterns of desertion and instability.

The question of a stable family life depends, in large
measure, on regular income, good jobs, decent housing
and the like. But these are the conditions, not the
guarantors, of a good community. Much depends on the
community leadership itself, particularly the middle
classes. One of the most striking aspects of the Negro
community, in comparison with other ethnic groups, is
the lack of any "infrastructure," other than the churches.
A cursory acquaintance with Jewish communal life
in New York City, for example, reveals the dense network of community organizations and services set up
by the Jewish community itself: hospitals, child-care
centers, old-age homes, recreational organizations, credit
unions, community centers, burial societies, landschafts-
men organizations, and such central-service organizations as the Federation of Jewish Philanthropies, the
B'nai B'rith, Workmen's Circle, American Jewish Com-

mittee, National Community Relations Advisory Committee and the like.

Compared to the complex organizational structures of other ethnic groups, there is little organized self-help within the Negro community. And the reason, in great measure, is that these tasks have been shirked or ignored by the Negro middle class. As the late Franklin Frazier, Negro sociologist, pointed out a decade ago in his bitter book, *Black Bourgeoisie*, the Negro middle class has contributed little in money, organization or involvement in Negro social problems; it has been more eager to escape identification with them than to help.

It is probable, as Glazer and Moynihan point out, that no investment of public and private agencies in delinquency and crime-prevention programs would equal the return from an investment by Negro-led and Negro-financed agencies themselves. And these are tasks that no one but the Negro can do.

In short, in the North a new phase in Negro leadership must soon begin. There is a limit—in New York, for example, where the Negroes have achieved a measure of political weight and influence—to what "protest" *alone* can bring. (In the North, the "protest" orientation has long been dominant in the Negro community; in the South, where the Negro leadership sought accommodation to an exploitative white world, the protest leadership, beginning with Martin Luther King in 1958, has only now come to the fore.)

Protest leadership in the North, without an adequate social base in its own community—a set of organized structures, not just the "masses"—will increasingly find itself confronting irrational, shrill and irresponsible competitors who can only be provocative of intensive counter-reaction. There has to be a new phase in which the resources of the Negro community are turned inward, toward the building of communal institutions, as well as outward to more effective political bargaining.

But the question of whether this is possible rests not only on the Negro leadership, but on the white liberal community as well. This can only start when the Negro has begun to achieve his legitimate political demands, and then undertakes the building of a communal life of his own.

The following Sunday, June 7th, the *Times Magazine* printed what was not an answer to Professor Bell but was a candid statement by a Negro to white men, of a kind that would not have been in a general-circulation magazine ten years earlier. The piece was by John Oliver Killens, a Negro novelist, and it was headed "Explanation of the 'Black Psyche.'"

When I was a boy in Macon, Georgia, one of the greatest compliments a benevolent white man could give a Negro was usually found in the obituary column of the local newspaper: "He was a black man, but he had a white heart." And the burden of every black man was supposedly just a little easier to bear that day. It was a time when many of us black folk laughed at the antics of Amos 'n' Andy and wept copious tears at a ridiculous movie, very aptly titled *Imitation of Life*. Most of us looked at life through the eyes of white America.

The great fictional and filmic masterpieces on the American racial theme usually fell into two categories. One theme dealt with the utter heartbreak of the mulatto, who rejected his black blood and was in turn rejected by his white blood. A variation of this theme was the shattering experience of "passing." The other theme was the "Uncle Tom," or what I like to call the "Gunga Din," theme. This one also had many variations, but over all there was the image created by that great apologist for colonialism, Rudyard Kipling, of a man who—

> *. . . For all 'is dirty 'ide*
> *'E was white, clear white, inside*
> *When 'e went to tend the wounded*
> *under fire!*

With some "additional dialogue" by Hollywood, dear old "white inside" Gunga was a marvelous figment of Western man's wistful imagination, the personification of his wish fulfillment. Gunga was a water boy for the British regiment and, in the movie, finally blew the bugle against his own people. And how "whiter" inside could a "noble savage" be?

I am waging a quiet little campaign at the moment to substitute the term "Gunga Din" for that much maligned character "Uncle Tom," in designating the contemporary water boys who still blow the bugles for ol' Massa, better known these days as "Mister Charlie." For, although Mrs. Stowe's beloved "Uncle Tom" was indeed an Uncle Tom, as we understand the term today, he, nevertheless, in the final confrontation chose death rather than blow the bugle against his people.

Variations of the Gunga Din theme were seen in a rash of movie epics like *Gone With the Wind* and *Virginia* and *Kentucky*, et cetera, ad infinitum, ad nauseam, always played magnificently with tongue in cheek by such stalwarts as Hattie McDaniel and Louise Beavers. In the great emotional scene the black mammy was usually in the big house, weeping and moaning over little pure-white-as-the-driven-snow Missy Anne, who had just sneezed, while mammy's own young 'un was dying of double pneumonia, unattended down in the cabins. All in all, the slaves were presented as carefree and contented in their idyllic degradation. If the black man *really* believed in this romantic version of American slavery, he would have long since wasted away, pining for those good old happy-go-lucky days of bondage.

Last year I did considerable research on that bygone utopian era, and I got a very different picture, slightly less romantic. I found that the slaves were so happy that most of the plantation owners could not afford the astronomical rates of fire insurance. Those rapturous slaves were setting fire to the cotton patches, burning down the plantations, every day the good Lord sent them. They organized countless insurrections, killed their masters, poisoned their mistresses, put spiders in the big-house soup. They demonstrated their contentment in most peculiar ways.

I shall never forget an evening I spent in a movie house in Hollywood, watching a closed-circuit television broadcast of the first Patterson-Johansson fight, and the great shame I felt for my white countrymen that night, as they began to smell a possible victory for the white foreigner over the black American. Forgotten entirely was the fact that soft-hearted Floyd Patterson was a fellow countryman. Color superseded patriotism. As I sat there hearing shouted exhortations like, "Kill the nigger!", I felt that Patterson and I were aliens in a strange and hostile country, and Ingemar was home amongst his people.

In fairness to my countrymen in the closed circuits of America that night, their reactions were not intellectual, not even willful. They were spontaneous, not unlike a conditioned reflex. This ecstasy at the sudden emergence of a new white hope came from the metaphoric guts of them; from their hearts, their souls, their bellies. This was their white insides reacting.

It has been rationalized to me that this incident had no racial implications at all, that these rabid Johansson fans were merely in the Old American tradition of rooting for the underdog. Well, I was also rooting for the underdog, and I knew that, win or lose, the underdog in America was Floyd Patterson, Harry Belafonte, Emmett Till, Rosa Parks, Meredith, Poitier, the black American *me*. The words, "Kill the nigger!" could not possibly have come screaming from my throat, subconsciously, unconsciously or otherwise.

Just as surely as East is East and West is West, there is a "black" psyche in America and there is a "white" one, and the sooner we face up to this social and cultural reality, the sooner the twain shall meet. Our emotional chemistry is different from yours in many instances. Your joy is very often our anger and your despair our fervent hope. Most of us came here in chains and most of you came here to escape your chains. Your freedom was our slavery, and therein lies the bitter difference in the way we look at life.

You created the myth of the faithful slave, but we know that the "loyal slave" is a contradiction in terms. We understand, though, that the master must always make himself believe in the undying love of his slave. That is why white America put words in the black man's mouth and bade him sing—improbable lyrics like

All de darkeys am a-weepin'
Massa's in de cold, cold ground.

But my great-grandmother told me differently. "We wept
all right, honey! Great God Almighty! We cried for joy
and shouted hallelujah," when old master got the cold,
cold ground that was coming to him.

In order to justify slavery in a courageous new
world which was spouting slogans of freedom and equality and brotherhood, the enslavers, through their propagandists, had to create the fiction that the enslaved
people were subhuman and undeserving of human rights
and sympathies. The first job was to convince the outside
world of the inherent inferiority of the enslaved. The
second job was to convince the American people. And
the third job, which was the cruelest hoax of all, was
to convince the slaves themselves that they deserved to
be slaves.

The propagandists for American slavery (the creative
writers of the time) tackled these tasks with alacrity and
a great measure of success, the effects of which still
remain with us today, a hundred years after the Emancipation Proclamation, almost two hundred years after
the Declaration of Independence. Thus, the Negro was
invented and the American Revolution thwarted. Knock
on any door in Harlem. Ask any black man or woman
in Alabama or Mississippi: Was 1776 for real?

Ironically enough, the fathers of our magnificent
Revolution, Washington and Jefferson, themselves owned
hundreds of human chattels, and even though the great
Thomas Jefferson made many speeches against the peculiar institution, he was never able to convince himself
to the extent of manumitting his own slaves during his
own lifetime.

Surely the great irony of the situation did not escape
my ancestors back in the days of the Revolution. And
now, today, it does not escape their great-great-grandchil-
dren. When we black folk hear one of our white leaders
use the phrase, "the free world," even though the same
white leader may very well be the Governor of the State
of Mississippi or Alabama, or any other state, for that
matter, we—as the slaves of Washington and Jefferson
must have done—stare at him incredulously and cannot
believe our ears. And we wonder how this word "free-

dom" can have such vastly different meanings, such conflicting connotations.

But the time has come for you (white America) and me (black America) to work this thing out once and for all, to examine and evaluate the differences betwen us and the differences inside of us. Time is swiftly running out, and a new dialogue is indispensable. It is so long overdue it is almost half past midnight.

My fight is not to be a white man in a black skin, but to inject some black blood, some black intelligence into the pallid main stream of American life, culturally, socially, psychologically, philosophically. This is the truer deeper meaning of the Negro revolt, which is not yet a revolution—to get America ready for the middle of the twentieth century, which is already magnificently here.

This new epoch has caught our country (yours and mine) napping in a sweet nostalgia for the good old days. Our country slumbers in a world of yesteryears, before Africa and Asia got up off their knees and threw off the black man's burden; the good old days when you threw pennies to the "natives" and there were gunboats in the China Sea and Big Stick Policies and Monroe Doctrines and "Old Coasters" from the U.K. sipped their gin-and-tonics in Accra and Lagos and talked about the "natives," as they basked in their roles of Great White Fathers in that best of all possible worlds.

That world is gone forever, and black and brown men everywhere are glad, deep in their hearts, but most Western men are chagrined, which is the understatement of the century. This is why the world is becoming much too much for Western men, even for most of you liberal Western men, even you radical Western men, whoever you are, and wherever. But the world is becoming more and more to my liking, to my taste and in my image. It gladdens my heart to see black and brown men and women come with dignity to the United Nations in affirmation of the manhood and the selfhood of the entire human race.

The American Negro, then, is an Anglo-Saxon invention, a role the Anglo-Saxon gentlemen invented for the black man to play in this drama known euphemistically as the American Way of Life. It began as an economic expedient, frankly, because you wanted somebody to work for nothing. It is still that, but now it is much more than that. It has become a way of life within a way of life, socially, economically, psychologically, philosophically.

But now, in the middle of the twentieth century, I, the Negro, am refusing to be your "nigrah" any longer. Even some of us "favored," "talented," "unusual" ones are refusing to be your educated, sophisticated, split-leveled "nigrahs" any longer. We refuse to look at ourselves through the eyes of white America. We are not fighting for the right to be like you. We respect ourselves too much for that. When we fight for freedom, we mean freedom for us to be black, or brown, and you to be white and yet live together in a free and equal society. This is the only way that integration can mean dignity for both of us.

I, for one, am growing weary of those well-meaning white liberals who are forever telling me they don't know what color I am. The very fact that they single me out at the cocktail party and gratuitously make me the beneficiary of their blessed assurances gives the lie to their pronouncements.

My fight is not *for* racial sameness but for racial equality and *against* racial prejudice and discrimination. I work for the day when my people will be free of the racist pressures to be *white like you*; a day when "good hair" and "high yaller" and bleaching cream and hair-straighteners will be obsolete. What a tiresome place America would be if freedom meant we all had to think alike and be the same color and wear the same gray flannel suit!

If relationships are to improve between us Americans, black and white and otherwise, if the country is to be saved, we will have to face up to the fact that differences do exist between us. All men react to life through man-made symbols. Even our symbolic reactions are different from yours. To give a few examples:

In the center of a little southern town near the border of Mississippi, there is a water tower atop which is a large white cross, illumined at night with a lovely (awesome to Negroes) neoned brightness. It can be seen for many miles away. To most white Americans who see it for the first time it is a beacon light that symbolizes the Cross upon which Jesus died, and it gives them a warm feeling in the face and shoulders. But the same view puts an angry knot in the black man's belly. To him it symbolizes the very, very "Christian" K.K.K.

To the average white man, a courthouse, even in Mississippi, is a place where justice is dispensed. To me, the black man, it is a place where justice is dispensed with.

Even our white hero symbols are different from yours. You give us moody Abraham Lincoln, but many of us prefer John Brown, whom most of you hold in contempt and regard as a fanatic; meaning, of course, that the firm dedication of any white man to the freedom of the black man is *prima facie* evidence of perversion and insanity.

You look upon these times as the Atomic Age, the Space Age, the Cold War era. But I believe that when the history of these times is written, it will not be so important who reached the moon first or who made the largest bomb. I believe the great significance will be that this was the century when most of mankind achieved freedom and human dignity. For me, this is the Freedom Century.

So now it is time for you to understand us, because it is becoming increasingly hazardous for you not to. Dangerous for both of us. As Richard Wright said in his *Twelve Million Black Voices*, voices you chose not to heed: "Each day when you see us black folk upon the dusty land of your farms or upon the hard pavement of your city streets, you usually take us for granted and think you know us, but our history is far stranger than you suspect, and we are not what we seem."

The Reverend Ralph Abernathy of Montgomery placed the question humorously when he said that the new Negro of Montgomery had stopped laughing when he wasn't tickled and scratching when he didn't itch.

In a word, we are bringing down the curtain on this

role you cast us in, and we will no longer be a party to
our own degradation. We have become unbelievers, no
longer believing in the absolute superiority of the white
man's juju. You have never practiced what you
preached. Why would we want to be like you? We have
caught you in too many lies. You proud defenders of the
chastity of womanhood, you champions of racial purity,
you are, if I may coin a phrase, "the last of the great
miscegenators."

Yes, we are different from you and we are not
invisible men, Ralph Ellison notwithstanding. We are
the most visible of Americans. We are both Americans
and Negroes. Other Americans, for the most part, ex-
cepting Puerto Ricans and Mexicans, are just Americans. But we are more than just Americans, not because
of our color but because of how America exploited
our color. We are different, not because we willed it, but
because America set us apart from the rest of the community for special exploitation. And so we are special,
with extraspecial insights.

In the summer and fall of 1961 I traveled in a
Land-Rover twelve thousand miles through Africa. I talked
to people in the cities, on the farms, in the villages. I
talked with workers, farmers, artists, market women,
ministers of state, politicians, teachers, and the same
question was asked me everywhere I went, with variations: "How can we believe your country's professions of
good will to us, with whom they have not lived, when
they deny human dignity to you who come from us and
have lived with them for centuries and helped to build
their great civilization?"

It is a question America has to answer to the entire
New World of Africa and Asia. The only way we Americans, black and white, can answer this question affirm-
atively is to make freedom and democracy work *here*
and *now*. Just as most Negroes still believe that the ultimate solution for us is in America, I am firmly convinced that the ultimate salvation of America is in the
Negro. The Negro loves America enough to criticize
her fundamentally. Most of white America simply can't be
bothered. Ironically enough, in the middle of the

twentieth century, the Negro is the new white hope. To live castrated in a great white harem and yet somehow maintain his black manhood and his humanity—this is the essence of the new man created out of the Negro Invention. History may render the verdict that this was the greatest legacy handed to the New World by the West.

Western man wrote *his* history as if it were the history of the entire human race. I hope that colored men all over the world have watched Western man too long to commit the fatal folly of writing history with a colored pencil. For there is great wisdom in the old Ghana proverb which says: "No one rules forever on the throne of time."

We black folk have learned many lessons during our sojourn in this place. One of them is the truth of another Ghana proverb that says: "Only a fool points to his heritage with his left hand." We are becoming prouder and prouder of our heritage in America and Africa. And we know the profound difference between pride and arrogance; the difference, if you will, between James Meredith and Ross Barnett, both of Mississippi. . . . Yes, we black people stand ready, eager, willing and able to make our contribution to the culture of the world. Our dialogue will not be protest but *affirmation* of the human dignity of all people everywhere.

I know there are white folk who want America to be the land of the free and the home of the brave, but there are far too few of them, and most of them are seldom brave. And I, too, cherish old John Brown and Garrison and William Moore. Let the winter patriots increase their ranks. Let those who truly love America join the valiant Negro Revolt and save the beloved country.

Chapter 13

The Law

On September 19, 1963, twelve Negro residents of Clinton, Louisiana, wrote letters to the mayor and the district attorney requesting the appointment of a bi-racial committee on community relations. They suggested respectfully that such a committee could give "careful consideration of the many problems facing our community" and would help "to avoid civil domestic disturbances of racial tension." One of the writers was a seventy-five-year-old woman, a lifelong resident of the area; another was the husband of the superintendent of the local Negro schools.

The response came on December 3rd, when the twelve Negroes were arrested. The charge was intimidating public officials; bail was set at four thousand dollars each. Somehow the defendants managed to raise the money; but they must await trial.

In Itta Bena, Mississippi, a group of Negroes marched to the home of the deputy sheriff on the night of June 18, 1963, to ask for police protection against harassment of a voter-registration campaign. Fifty-seven were arrested and charged with disturbing the peace. After a night in jail, forty-five of them—all but those less than fifteen years old—were tried by a justice of the peace. They had no lawyer, and no evidence was introduced connecting any individual defendant with illegal action. It took just over an hour for the trial, conviction and sentences. Every man was given a sentence of six months in jail and a fine of five hundred dollars. (The fine amounted to five and one-half months more in jail, at the Mississippi rate of three dollars a day to work off fines, because these impoverished people could not pay.) Each woman was sentenced to four months and two hundred dollars.

To go free while they tried to appeal, the defendants had to produce appeal bonds—fixed at seven hundred and fifty dollars for the men, five hundred dollars for the women. They could not raise that money, and so they were imprisoned, some in the quarters and conditions of chain gangs. They were finally released two months later, after the National Council of Churches had raised some money for them and a New York insurance company had written a bond at the personal urging of Attorney General Kennedy. At a new trial before a jury they were convicted again. They then appealed to a circuit court. If they lose there, they must go next to the Mississippi Supreme Court. Then they can seek review in the Supreme Court of the United States.

The events in Clinton and Itta Bena were not isolated incidents. Again and again today Negroes in certain parts of the South find themselves caught up in the machinery of the criminal law because of entirely innocent acts—that is, acts that would be innocent anywhere else. A man appeals for help to an official, supposedly his public servant. The next thing he knows he is charged with a crime, arrested, convicted on no evidence of anything that constitutionally can be a crime, held on bail that is difficult or impossible for him to raise, forced to go through a long and frustrating and expensive legal process before someone—probably the Supreme Court—ends the lawless course of law.

The Clinton and Itta Bena cases illustrate a particularly disturbing aspect of southern resistance to change in race relations—corruption of the processes of law. Corruption is not too strong a word; it is used by a gentle man given to understatement, Burke Marshall, the head of the Justice Department's Civil Rights Division, who often gets appeals for help from persons caught up in this kind of southern justice. Not all of the South has forgotten this country's commitment to law; but in Mississippi, Alabama and sections of some other states today, men sworn to exalt the law ruthlessly and cynically misuse it in order to repress the Negro's demand for rights.

The cynicism can be so pervasive that it seems absurd and outrageous. Consider what has happened in the last few years to Aaron Henry, a Negro pharmacist in Clarksdale, Mississippi, and a local official of the National Association for the Advancement of Colored People. In 1961, after some freedom riders tried to desegregate the railroad waiting room in Clarksdale, the county prosecutor, Thomas Pearson, called Mr. Henry in for questioning about his asserted attempts to "disturb" existing race relations. In January, 1962, when Negroes held off buying from Clarksdale stores that discriminated against them, Mr. Henry was charged with a conspiracy in restraint of trade; the prosecution is still pending. In March of that year he was accused of an indecent assault on an itinerant eighteen-year-old white youth who had allegedly hitched a ride with him; he was convicted and sentenced to two months in jail, but the Supreme Court agreed to review the conviction the next term. Mr. Henry accused Prosecutor Pearson and the Clarksdale police chief, Benford Collins, of dreaming up that charge, and they promptly sued him for libel; a jury awarded them all they asked, forty thousand dollars, the Mississippi Supreme Court affirmed that judgment and the case is now pending in the U. S. Supreme Court. In June, 1962, Mr. Henry's wife was dismissed from her job as a local public-school teacher; she brought suit in a federal court, and the case is still pending. In March, 1963, Mr. Henry's home was bombed. Two men admitted the crime, but one was acquitted by a jury and the charge against the other was then dropped; the district attorney in charge of the prosecution complained in open court that Prosecutor Pearson had tried to persuade a witness not to testify against the arsonist. In June, 1963, Mr. Henry was convicted of "parading without a permit" when he picketed City Hall to protest segregation; that conviction is on appeal. After the bombing of his home, Mr. Henry obtained a permit for a revolver and hired a private watchman at his home. On the night of July 30, 1963, Police Chief Collins arrested the watchman for possession of a concealed weapon—the revolver, which he had left on the seat of a car parked in the driveway—and confiscated the revolver.

It is not only stubborn Negro leaders of civil-rights organizations who meet such tactics. "A very proper midwestern law professor," as he was once described, ran into them in the summer of 1963. He was Charles Oldfather of the University of Kansas, a white man who had never before imagined the world in which some southern Negroes live. His daughter Felicia, president of the student body at Carleton College, went down to Albany, Georgia, to help the Negro movement that summer. She was arrested and charged with "vagrancy," and Professor Oldfather went down to Albany to help her. He watched the trial and was surprised to find her convicted despite testimony that he was supporting her. Felicia decided to leave Albany, and Professor Oldfather drove her car over to the Negro section to pick up her belongings. This is what happened next, in his words: "As I was heading back downtown, I was motioned over to the curb by two officers in a county police car. After my driver's license was examined, I was instructed to get out of the car and to put my hands on the roof. I was frisked, my wrists were handcuffed behind my back and I was driven to the county jail in the police car. . . .

"Inquiry disclosed that I was being arrested for driving a car with a bad muffler, and that the car was impounded. . . . The arresting officer, when he had finished questioning me, walked across the room to a desk where he engaged another man in conversation. He punctuated the end of his conversation by taking a sap [blackjack] out of his hip pocket, slamming it onto the top of the desk and looking meaningfully at me."

When Professor Oldfather told the police that he was planning to leave Albany with his daughter, he was immediately released and the car returned to him. He is not likely to forget that in the year 1963, in the United States, he was arrested in handcuffs for supposedly driving a car with a faulty muffler.

Physical brutality is not only threatened by law-enforcement officials. John Frazier, a Negro college student from Greenville, Mississippi, took a bus from Atlanta to Greenville on August 26, 1960. He sat up front despite warnings from the driver. At several stops in Mississippi the driver got off. Then, at Winona, the sheriff and a deputy met the bus, and they said: "Nigger, we want to see you." According to Frazier's sworn testimony, the deputy began beating him with a blackjack and the sheriff with his fists, one of them saying: "You had no business sitting at the front of that bus. You know you are a Mississippi nigger, and that does not work here." Mr. Frazier lost consciousness during the beating and came to in a police car on the way to jail. There a doctor treated him. He was charged with disturbing the peace and resisting arrest. The next morning he was allowed to telephone a friend in Jackson to ask for a lawyer's help, but as he started to tell the story of what had happened the telephone was taken from his hand and he was beaten again. The doctor came back and stopped a nose bleed. Mr. Frazier was eventually tried, convicted and released on two thousand dollars' bond pending appeal.

When John Frazier took that bus ride, it had been the law of this country for fourteen years that racial segregation could not be practiced in interstate commerce. The sheriff who arrested him and the judge who convicted him knew that that was the law, but they were not interested. Like so many of their brethren in that part of the South they were dedicated to defeating that federal law and preserving the white supremacy called for by the unconstitutional statutes and customs of Mississippi.

Law in these instances has become the instrument of the ruling class in a caste system. It has become, really, the Marxist idea of law, as officially defined by the Soviet Union in 1938: "Law is a combination of the rules of behavior established or sanctioned by state authority, reflecting the will of the ruling class—rules of behavior whose application is assured by the coercive power of the state for the purpose of protecting, strengthening and developing relationships and procedures suitable and beneficial to the ruling class."

It is important to recognize that defiance of federal law is not just an occasional aberration by an occasional southern police officer. There are places where there is a wholesale perversion of justice, from bottom to top, from police force to supreme court.

The police, for example. On May 8, 1963, a gasoline bomb was thrown into the home of a leading Negro citizen of Holmes County, Mississippi, who headed a voter-registration campaign.

The next day he and his common-law wife were arrested and charged with arson of their own home; four student workers were charged with the same crime, and one with obstructing the investigation by photographing the burned house. Eventually the arson charges were dismissed for lack of evidence—there never had been any. By then the man and his wife had gone through a formal marriage ceremony some months earlier. But the local grand jury that looked into the fire indicted them for unlawful cohabitation. Although they were advised that this charge could not legally apply so far back in time, they decided it would be easier to plead guilty and pay a hundred-dollar fine.

And mayors. In Ruleville, Mississippi, on August 6, 1963, Mayor Charles Dorrough arrested three Negro student voting workers because they were accompanying frightened local Negroes to the polls. The mayor was acting in the capacity of police chief, and the formal charge he placed was conspiracy to commit an unstated offense. The students were taken to the town hall, tried by the mayor in his capacity as police magistrate, convicted, given a sentence of thirty days and a fine of one-hundred dollars each. At the "trial" the mayor commented that there was no need to take any testimony, since everyone knew what had happened. The cases were then appealed.

And voting registrars. Among others there is the story, told in Chapter 8, of John Hardy—the student who was pistol-whipped by the registrar when he tried to help two Negroes register in Walthall County, Mississippi.

And prosecutors. In Americus, Georgia, on August 8, 1963, four student civil-rights workers, white and Negro, were charged with "insurrection" under a Georgia statute that the Supreme Court had held unconstitutional in 1937. Because this offense was punishable by death, they were denied bail. After they had been in jail two months, the prosecutor, Stephen Pace, stated frankly that he had brought the charge in the hope not of obtaining constitutional convictions but of discouraging civil-rights activities. He said: "The basic reason for bringing these charges was to deny the defendants, or ask the court to deny them, bond. We were in hopes that by holding these men, we would be able to talk to their lawyers and talk to their people and convince them that this type of activity is not the right way to go about it." The defendants stayed in jail until a federal court ordered them released in January, 1964.

And judges. Judge Durwood T. Pye of Atlanta conducted a
series of trials in 1963 and 1964 of persons charged with trespass
for sit-in demonstrations. He sentenced Ashton Jones, a sixty-
seven-year-old white minister from California, to a year and a half
in prison and a thousand-dollar fine for helping some Negroes
attempt to gain entry to a white church. Then Judge Pye set
bail at twenty thousand dollars. The Georgia Supreme Court
found that excessive and ordered it reduced to five thousand
dollars. Mr. Jones's wife came from California with five thousand
dollars, but Judge Pye refused to accept cash, saying only Georgia
real estate would do for bond. After Mr. Jones had been in
prison seven months, a white Atlanta woman pledged her property for the bail and he was released.

Judge Pye also gave an eighteen-month sentence—six in the
common jail and twelve on the public works—to an eighteen-
year-old white girl, Mardon Walker of Connecticut College for
Women. She was convicted of trespass after a sit-in attempt at a
restaurant. Despite the Georgia Supreme Court's bail ruling in
the Reverend Walker's case, he fixed her bond at fifteen thousand
dollars. Two citizens of Atlanta put that up.

The prosecutions of freedom riders in Jackson, Mississippi,
show how an entire local system of courts can work with lawless
law-enforcement officials to make federal rights virtually meaningless. In 1961, three hundred and three persons were arrested
in Jackson for trying to use the interstate bus terminal on a desegregated basis. Everyone knew that segregation in the terminal
was unlawful; in addition to the constitutional decisions of the Supreme Court as to any state-enforced racial discrimination, the
Interstate Commerce Commission had issued specific rules against
terminal segregation. The freedom riders who tried to exercise
these rights were charged with breach of the peace. Eventually, as
anyone must have known, the charges could not stand because
there was simply no evidence to support them. But the Mississippi
court system made it clear that anyone who really wanted to
enforce his federal rights would have to go all the way to the
Supreme Court of the United States—and that it would take a
long time, and much expense and trouble, to get there.

The authorities insisted that every one of the arrested persons
have a separate trial, although there was no legally relevant
difference in the facts of the cases. This meant that, instead of
a single test case, every defendant had to retain a lawyer and

personally return to Jackson for a trial—and then, if he persisted, a new trial on appeal. Counsel mostly had to be brought from far away also, for no white lawyer in Mississippi will handle a civil-rights case and there are only four Negro lawyers who will. The Mississippi courts also fixed bail of fifteen hundred dollars in most cases, a total of $372,000 for the group. The three hundred and four licensed Mississippi surety companies refused to write bail bonds.

Fifty-six of the defendants gave up in the face of these tactics, accepted suspended sentences and paid two-hundred-dollar fines for their crime of believing that federal law applied in Mississippi. The others fought on. Most drew sentences of four months in jail and a five-hundred-dollar fine. Their cases had to go through the city court, county court, circuit court and supreme court of Mississippi. On June 13, 1964, the first twenty-nine petitioned the Supreme Court of the United States. They were able to do so at last because their convictions had been affirmed by the Mississippi Supreme Court in an opinion saying that no "abject surrender" of racial customs "should be expected, much less demanded."

Among state supreme courts, Alabama's has a particularly notable record for cynical disregard of federal law. For more than six years it prevented a final ruling on the right of the National Association for the Advancement of Colored People to operate in Alabama—and during that time the N.A.A.C.P. was barred by a "temporary" restraining order from doing business in the state. The ground advanced by the state for ousting the association, that it had not signed a registration form and paid a ten-dollar fee, was found patently unconstitutional by the Supreme Court of the United States in June, 1964. But that was the fourth Supreme Court decision required in the case, and there was no assurance that more may not be needed. Once the Alabama Supreme Court threw out an N.A.A.C.P. appeal on the ground that the wrong form of writ had been used. The U.S. Supreme Court found that ground frivolous, but the Alabama court at first refused to follow the ruling, saying the Supreme Court had been misinformed. A second Supreme Court decision was followed by years of delay, a third warning from Washington and, finally, the first hearing for the N.A.A.C.P. in Alabama. The state supreme court then again refused to pass on the merits of the case, finding this time that the association's lawyers had written their brief in the wrong order. When the case was argued before the U.S. Supreme

Court, the lawyer for Alabama found himself embarrassedly unable to explain his own court's decision.

And governors. Again and again such southern governors as George Wallace of Alabama have told their people that federal law need not be obeyed, that decisions of the highest court in the land are not binding, that there is some "legal" way to resist laws one does not like. They have made lawlessness respectable.

And legislators. The legislatures of several southern states attempted to deal with federal measures against racial discrimination by passing transparently invalid statutes purporting to make the exercise of federal rights a state crime. A Mississippi statute declared it a crime to make false statements to any federal official; it was left to state law-enforcement processes to decide what was "false," and the statute added that the assertedly false statement need not be "material" to be punished. When Mississippi officials invoked this statute against two Negroes who testified in the federal courts about voting discrimination, the Justice Department moved to block the state prosecution as an unconstitutional attempt at intimidation.

And all state officials, it must be remembered—legislators and governors and prosecutors and judges—are bound by oath to support the Constitution of the United States.

The public, the white public, played its part as the jury in the legal process. In the same areas where the law was otherwise used as an instrument of white supremacy, almost no Negroes were ever called as jurors—although the Supreme Court had held since the year 1880 that exclusion of jurors because of race is unconstitutional. The white juries took part readily in the mockery of justice that sent civil-rights workers to jail for "vagrancy" or passing a stop sign in their car or some such mythical offense.

What a jury could do—with assistance from judges—was illustrated in the New York Times libel case decided by the Supreme Court in 1964. The Times and four Alabama Negro ministers were sued for libel by a Montgomery, Alabama, city commissioner, L. B. Sullivan, because of an advertisement generally critical of southern law enforcement that appeared in the Times and carried the ministers' names among others. The trial was conducted in a segregated courtroom before an all-white jury. It returned a verdict for five hundred thousand dollars— all Mr. Sullivan had demanded—although he was not mentioned in the ad and his own witnesses had testified that his reputation was not damaged. The *Times* fortunately had the money and the patience to take the case to the Supreme Court, which found the award unconstitutional. But there were many similar cases in the South—against other newspapers, wire services, television networks—and they continued. They had been brought not really in the hope of collecting any damages but to discourage aggressive race-relations reporting by harassment.

Misuse of the law, it should be repeated, was a phenomenon found not throughout the South but in particular areas. These were the same areas where voting discrimination was practiced and Negroes were excluded from the political process, where most newspapers presented a distorted, white-supremacist view of life, where most ministers were unwilling or felt themselves unable to speak out for racial justice. In the words of Professor James Silver of the University of Mississippi, they were the areas of the "closed society." There was, therefore, no realistic hope of dealing locally with abuses of the law. No jury would bring in a verdict for false arrest or police brutality; no Negro would have been foolish enough to sue. Leaders of the bar might have spoken out, but what was heard from them in many areas was a deafening silence.

Burke Marshall of the Justice Department summarized what disturbs those who cherish our legal system in a lecture at Columbia University in 1964. "It is difficult for anyone concerned with corruption of the law to say that corrections are not needed," he said. "Negro disenfranchisement over decades has created a system of all-white courts, staffed by all-white officialdom. The apparent inability of the bar to bring itself to provide counsel in cases with racial implications is by itself one proof that our basic assumptions about the workings of justice in state courts are wrong. The unavailability of normal sources of bail is another. Examples of abuse of authority are a third. They are compounded by repeated exclusion of Negroes from juries, enforced segregation and racial abuses in courtrooms and other evidences of the weight of state authority thrusting imbalance into the processes of justice where racial customs are threatened."

Lawlessness is bound to have effects more serious than the short-run intimidation and cruelty that shock us. In the long run such tactics can only infect all of those involved—perpetrators and victims of injustice, white and black—with contempt for the law. This country is rightly concerned by outbreaks of Negro violence in northern cities. There is no excuse for it, whatever the emotional causes. But we are surely in a poor position to condemn private lawlessness when a system of official illegality operates with such ruthless efficiency in another part of the country.

Justice Brandeis warned of the consequences of official lawlessness in a great Supreme Court opinion in 1928. "In a government of laws," he said, "existence of the government will be imperiled if it fails to observe the law scrupulously. Our government is the potent, the omnipresent teacher. For good or ill, it teaches the whole people by its example. Crime is contagious. If the government becomes a law-breaker, it breeds contempt for law; it invites every man to become a law unto himself; it invites anarchy."

Official lawlessness in these southern areas also threatened to damage a vital aspect of this country's federal system of divided governmental powers—our tradition of leaving most law enforcement to local authorities. For the Federal Government was inevitably pushed to take corrective steps. Civil-rights groups in fact repeatedly demanded that the Justice Department actually take over law-enforcement responsibility in large sections of the South by putting marshals or even troops on permanent duty. These demands were resisted by Attorney General Kennedy and his associates, who deeply feared the idea of a national police power. But lesser extensions of federal authority did begin, called forth to meet the abuses. The longstanding rules of comity between state and federal courts, which usually forbid federal interference with state court proceedings, were eroded. For example, the Justice Department sought and obtained a federal injunction to prevent Mississippi from prosecuting John Hardy, the student who was pistol-whipped by the registrar of Walthall County. Federal judges, unwilling to let civil-rights defendants be dragged for years through biased state courts before obtaining a federal forum in the Supreme Court, began to invoke an old and never-before-used statute allowing removal of criminal cases from state to federal courts when a fair state trial is unlikely.

As long as southern judges and prosecutors and juries and police and legislators and town officials continue to misuse their power—to use it as an expression of force, not law, to maintain a caste system—then the extension of federal protection will continue. Congress and the executive branch and the federal courts will move deeper and deeper into the province once left to local law enforcement. And when the process has gone irreversibly far, some years from now, the southern officials whose disregard for law brought it on will undoubtedly be heard decrying the decline of "states' rights."

While some areas in the South thus engaged in silent rebellion against federal law, there was no stopping the development of that law in its condemnation of racial discrimination. The Supreme Court did not pause with *Brown v. Board of Education;* inexorably, over the next ten years, its decisions applied the rule against discrimination to more and more aspects of national life.

Within a year of the School decision the Court held that a state could not segregate its parks. Then came libraries, trolleys, buses, golf courses, sports arenas, courtrooms. The Court dealt with these cases summarily, usually elaborating no reasons but simply citing the *Brown* case. That drew some criticism from legal scholars: After all, the *Brown* opinion had emphasized the special nature of education and the way children were affected by segregation; what had that to do with adults riding the buses in Montgomery, Alabama? But it soon became evident that *Brown v. Board of Education* rested on something broader than the articulated grounds. The Court was saying that for a state to segregate human beings by color was inherently invidious, wherever done.

And so all *state* discrimination was forbidden. But there was the next problem: What was the "state," constitutionally? The Fourteenth Amendment says that "no state shall" deny equal protection. That language has always been read to exclude purely private discrimination from its coverage. The Supreme Court said in 1883: "It is state action of a particular character that is prohibited. Individual invasion of individual rights is not the subject matter of the amendment."

But the line between private and official action, like so many others in the Constitution, is not self-defining. The Supreme Court has attempted to draw it, but the problem is so slippery that there has never been any definite solution. In one notable case the Court said that state enforcement of private discrimination could bring the latter within the ambit of the Constitution; that was the Restrictive Covenants case, holding that state courts could not enforce private real-estate agreements to exclude Negroes. In another, the Court found that a privately owned activity may become so public in its scope that it is constitutionally public; a company town was held subject to constitutional limitations just like an ordinary municipality.

The complex problem of state-versus-private action came to a climax during the decade 1954-64. Eschewing nicer formulas, the Supreme Court adopted the eclectic approach that an activity was covered by the Constitution if there was significant state involvement in it. A Wilmington coffee shop located in space leased from a Delaware public garage had to stop excluding Negroes. And the Supreme Court in 1964 let stand a Fourth Circuit Court of Appeals decision of large import, requiring private hospitals in the South to admit Negro patients and doctors because the hospitals had had various forms of state aid.

The sit-in demonstrations posed the problem most acutely. Thousands of students who demanded service at lunch counters and other privately owned public accommodations were convicted of trespass. Could the convictions stand? The answer depended on whether what had happened was merely private discrimination—like the choice of a citizen not to admit Negroes to his home or his club—or partook of an official, community character.

In the tradition of postponing difficult constitutional questions the Court disposed of all its sit-in cases through June of 1964 without resolving the fundamental legal issue.

Because of the large number of defendants involved, the sit-in cases put an enormous burden on the remarkable organization that operated before and after 1954 as the main legal arm of the civil-rights movement—the N.A.A.C.P. Legal Defense and Educational Fund. It was the Fund's great counsel, Thurgood Marshall, who headed the list of lawyers arguing the School Segregation cases. In 1961 President Kennedy appointed him to the Court of Appeals for the Second Circuit, and he was succeeded by another expert in the law of race relations, Jack Greenberg. It might be more accurate to say creators of race-relations law rather than experts in it, for the Fund's lawyers over the years framed most of the civil-rights cases that gave concrete meaning to the Constitution's generalities. And much of the time the Fund worked nearly alone, a rather small and understaffed private organization matched against the resources of the southern states; only recently has the Justice Department become a major partner in the enterprise.

In the decade after 1954 the biggest job for the N.A.A.C.P. Fund's lawyers was to make the School decision more than a remote ideal to the Negro children of the South. It was an endless job, often heartbreaking, and it is by no means completed yet. In fact, implementation of the *Brown* decision has posed one of the greatest challenges to the legal process that this country has seen.

The South made a number of attempts by law to escape altogether from the mandate to end school segregation. There persisted for an astonishingly long time the idea that somehow shrewd lawyers could find a way to defeat the Supreme Court decision "legally." The schemes did not work, but they posed a graver threat than may be remembered now that time has deflated their pretensions.

The critical tests for these efforts at open legal resistance came in the school year 1958-59. As it began, a *Times* observer in Washington commented that the momentum of events was running strongly against compliance with *Brown v. Board of Education*. In Little Rock, Federal Judge Harry J. Lemley had ordered a suspension of the embattled desegregation program because of community opposition. In Prince Edward County, Virginia, Federal Judge Sterling Hutcheson had set 1965—seven years later—for a start on desegregation. And elsewhere in Virginia, Senator Harry Byrd's policy of Massive Resistance was in full flower, providing inspiration to all those in the South who hoped there were respectable, "lawful" ways to block implementation of the Supreme Court's decision. President Eisenhower made clear that he proposed to do nothing to rally moderate southern opinion behind the Court.

That may well have been the low point of the decade for supporters of the School decision. The tide soon turned and began moving toward compliance. The Supreme Court stepped in itself that fall with its decision in the Little Rock case. Local antagonism, the Court said, could not be a reason for abandonment of declared constitutional rights. Judge Lemley's order was reversed.

The Virginia issue took longer to resolve. Federal court orders to begin school desegregation became effective that fall in Norfolk, Charlottesville and Front Royal, Virginia. The response of the Governor, J. Lindsay Almond, was to close the nine affected

schools under the state's Massive Resistance legislation. For five
months nearly thirteen thousand children were without education. The Federal Government did nothing. Massive Resistance
seemed to be winning, if it was a victory to have no school at
all rather than admit a handful of Negro children to classes
with whites.

Governor Almond was a good enough lawyer, and a good
enough human being, to know the folly in which his state was
engaged. At a press conference on September 16, 1958, he was
asked why he did not personally seize one of the closed schools
and reopen it on a segregated basis in his sovereign capacity as
governor. He replied: "I would be delighted to do that, . . . but
there's a little difficulty in the offing. . . . That is, the state could be
enjoined, the Governor could be enjoined, his agents could be enjoined from operating in violation of the federal decrees. . . .
You're getting back to interposition, . . . and interposition does
not [work]."

Publicly, Governor Almond felt he had to remain faithful to
the intransigeant position of Senator Byrd, master of the Democratic machine that had managed Virginia politics for a generation. Privately, he has since disclosed, he expected the federal
courts to end the school closings promptly. But they did not, and
community pressure mounted to reopen the schools. Finally the
Governor instigated a friendly lawsuit in the Virginia Supreme
Court of Appeals to test whether the state could validly shut
down selected schools under its own constitution. Another test
case was brought by some Norfolk parents before a three-judge
federal district court.

On January 19, 1959, both courts—their judges had been in
touch with each other—handed down their decisions. The state
and federal tribunals found violations, respectively, of the state
and federal constitutions. Now was the time for Lindsay Almond
to give way gracefully. But he paid one last debt to Senator
Byrd. The next night the Governor went before television cameras
and excoriated even the slightest touch of racial mixing, saying
"no price is too high to pay" for maintaining the principle of
segregation. When Lindsay Almond, now a judge, gave an interview in 1964, this was the one act of his governorship for which
he expressed real regret. "I don't know why I made that damned
speech," he said. "If I had listened to my wife, I wouldn't have."

Just eight days after that television speech Governor Almond

addressed the Virginia legislature and in effect called off Massive
Resistance. The schools reopened, and the process of desegregation proceeded smoothly. Harry Byrd never forgave Almond.
When President Kennedy nominated him to the Court of Customs
and Patent Appeals in 1962, Senator Byrd's chill reaction delayed
confirmation a year and a half.

One county in Virginia remained faithful to Massive Resistance. This was Prince Edward, deep in the racist Southside
of Virginia, from which one of the original School cases decided
in 1954 had come. Judge Hutcheson's choice of 1965 for an
actual start on desegregation was set aside on appeal, and 1959
was fixed as the date instead. But rather than comply, Prince
Edward closed all her public schools. An "academy" was set up
for white children, supposedly private, actually supported in large
part at first by state tuition grants to the parents and county tax
rebates. The Negroes had no schools. And so things remained
through years of mishandled litigation. The Negro children finally
had a chance at education again in the year 1963-64, when
private gifts, some inspired by Attorney General Kennedy, supported a superb Free School Association in the county. That was
for the one school year only, until the lawsuit was resolved. And
the Supreme Court did resolve it, holding in May of 1964 that no
state can escape responsibility for the denial of public education
in a county while schools everywhere else in the state remain
open. Prince Edward authorities were ordered to appropriate
school funds again, and state officials were on notice that—if all
else failed—they might have to provide schools in Prince Edward. No one was optimistic about the chances for a really adequate integrated educational system in the county, but at least
there was some hope now for an end to what Solicitor General
Archibald Cox had called "this experiment in ignorance."

The Virginia experience essentially exhausted the tactic of
frontal legal resistance to the Supreme Court decision. There
were terrible episodes in Louisiana and Mississippi in later years,
and there was Governor Wallace's charade at the University of
Alabama. But all except the completely self-deluded knew that
game was up. It became clear that in an open contest with a
state, federal law inevitably must prevail. Inevitable was the
word that the South came to understand about desegregation.
When the crisis at the University of Mississippi was coming to
a head in September, 1962, someone asked Attorney General

Kennedy whether Mississippi officials would eventually admit James Meredith. With an air of genuine surprise that anybody would raise such a question, he replied: "They don't have much choice, do they?"

But if desegregation could not be stopped cold, it could be slowed to a centipedal crawl by sufficiently sophisticated tactics of evasion. That is the conclusion one would have to draw from the decade's statistics on the actual admission of Negro children to white schools in the eleven states of the old South. In mid-1964 nearly three million Negro children attended public schools in those states. Only a few more than thirty thousand were in classes with white children—one per cent.

This tokenism was accomplished by what Jack Greenberg of the N.A.A.C.P. Legal Defense Fund called "pettifoggery." The chief weapon was the pupil placement plan, which required every Negro child whose family wanted him in a white school to apply for a transfer, pass a battery of achievement and psychological tests and then file an individual lawsuit if the school board said no. The separate white and Negro school systems continued except for the few unusual souls who could get past the barriers of expense and inertia and fear.

Pupil placement was often used in combination with a grade-a-year plan, allowing transfers in only one grade the first year and one additional grade each year afterward. Atlanta, for example, had a plan for "desegregation" by transfer at the rate of one grade a year from the top down. It would not be until after 1970 that the plan would reach down to the first grade and all pupils entering the system would be assigned to schools without regard to race.

The courts at first upheld pupil placement and similar devices so long as they did not appear to be discriminatory. The result was to permit long delays in meaningful desegregation. There is an ironic illustration in a comparison of Virginia and North Carolina. While Virginia stood for Massive Resistance, North Carolina invented pupil placement and won national applause for permitting some desegregation. In 1964, a little over one-half of one per cent of North Carolina's Negro children were in classes with white children; the percentage in Virginia was three times as high. Fabian tactics had worked.

At the end of the 1954-64 decade, the federal courts looked through the mask of intricate southern school schemes and

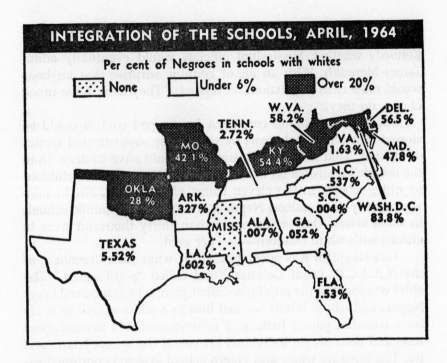

began demanding genuine equality. The Courts of Appeals outlawed the practice of making Negro students take transfer tests
not given to whites. In some instances they found one grade a
year too slow a pace. In the spring of 1964 the Supreme Court
heard an Atlanta case in which the N.A.A.C.P. Fund attacked
the whole idea of maintaining separate school systems with desegregation by transfer only. Counsel for Atlanta candidly conceded that some past devices designed to make desegregation
publicly acceptable had been illegal, and he said the School Board
was taking further steps to hasten the process. The Supreme
Court then sent the case back for examination of the new
plans, but it added a warning: The time for "deliberate speed"
was over. Ten years after *Brown v. Board of Education,* something more was required.

One thing learned in those ten years was that the law as
laid down by the Supreme Court is not self-executing. Even apart
from the overt legal devices used by the South there are significant impediments to progress toward the constitutional rule
of non-discrimination. In the areas of white supremacy it may
be dangerous even to sign a petition for desegregated schools—
dangerous to one's livelihood and one's life. Lawyers in a state
supposedly as civilized as Virginia have found themselves charged

with professional misconduct because they encouraged poor Negro families to bring a school suit. In the most resistant areas federal judges are themselves likely to share white-supremacist attitudes. Civil-rights organizations were distressed at the way four of President Kennedy's southern judicial appointments turned out. Some Eisenhower and Truman appointees were also given to delay and obstruction of civil-rights litigation, although it should be said that most federal judges in the South have performed superbly in placing Constitution above custom.

The feeling that the Supreme Court and the judicial process generally now needed help was a major reason for the Civil Rights Act of 1964. It was the judgment of Presidents Kennedy and Johnson, and finally of Congress, that the power of the Federal Government must be thrown more directly into the struggle. And so the Justice Department was authorized to move against discrimination in schools, employment and public accommodations—and more forcefully against exclusion of Negroes from voting.

But the 1964 act still relies on the courts as its operating mechanism: Government officials are authorized to bring more lawsuits. In a way, the statute may mark the end of an era—the exhaustion of legal remedies for the blight of racism. For by 1964, most of all in the North, America had come to recognize the limitations of law in the struggle against racial discrimination. Not that law was useless, as President Eisenhower had suggested; it was just not enough. The Negro child in New York, protected from cradle to grave by laws against discrimination, was still the innocent victim of generations of discrimination and ignorance and social backwardness. In addition to law, we now know, we need money and effort and love to make the color of an American's skin truly irrelevant.

But without the law there could have been nothing. However discouraged one may be at the continuing reality of discrimination, he should remember that this country is at least on the right course—and that the law put it there. In the face of doubts and provocations, a conservative Congress in 1964 overwhelmingly approved the most comprehensive legislative assault on racial inequity ever seriously proposed. It did so because it was in a current of history set in motion ten years before by the Supreme Court of the United States.

The first decade of the revolution in race relations has also been a decade of great experiment in the law. The Supreme Court has changed sharply in outlook, taking a much more vigorous and expansive part in the protection of individual liberties than it ever has before. And the racial issue has played a large part in the enlargement of the Court's role.

The efforts of Alabama to discover the membership of the N.A.A.C.P. and suppress its activities led to landmark decisions in support of freedom of association. South Carolina's refusal to let Negroes carry on a protest march outside the legislature brought new safeguards for free speech. The award of five hundred thousand dollars by Alabama jurors and judges in the *New York Times* libel case resulted in an historic advance for freedom of the press—a new rule that a newspaper (or anyone) may criticize public officials without fear of libel unless the criticism is deliberately malicious.

Those decisions arose in a racial context but are not limited to that context in application: The *New York Times* case will protect editors and speakers in Wisconsin as well as Alabama, and on any subject. An even more telling example of how overreaching are some of the decisions made because of racial discrimination—and how they may lead to decisions with broader connotations for freedom—is provided by the Tuskegee case.

In 1957 the Alabama legislature redrew the boundaries of the city of Tuskegee, changing it from a square to a dragon-shaped object with twenty-eight sides. No reason was given, but the effect made the reason obvious. All but five of some four hundred Negroes registered to vote in Tuskegee were now outside the new city limits, while no white voters were excluded. When a legal challenge to the new boundaries reached the Supreme Court in 1960, it was thought to present difficult problems because the Court had held in the past that political districting was beyond its competence. But the facts in the Tuskegee case were just too compelling to ignore, and the Court unanimously upset the boundary change. Two years later, in 1962, the Court had before it the old districting question without the racial context. After the Tuskegee case it was not so easy to dismiss the whole subject as too "political" for the Court, and the justices for the first time held that they could pass on the fairness of legislative districts. In 1964, in a decision of the greatest national importance of any since the School cases a decade earlier, the Court held that citizens are entitled to equality of representation in both houses of every state legislature.

Of course the Tuskegee case provided only a minor link between the racial decisions and the new issue of legislative apportionment. More important than any direct connection, for the apportionment and other libertarian decisions, was the indefinable influence on the Court itself of what it had dared in race relations. It had dared greatly, on a moral issue from which the other institutions of government had run, and it had been right.

The Supreme Court started a social revolution in 1954, one whose achievements and costs we cannot yet reckon. It also enlarged, in a way that will probably not be undone, the already extraordinary role in American society of law and the courts.

Acknowledgments

Index

ACKNOWLEDGMENTS

The following is a list of the articles reprinted from the *New York Times*. The date is the day of publication. An asterisk indicates that the article appeared in the Sunday *Times Magazine*.

CHAPTER	PAGE	AUTHOR/TITLE	DATE
1	5	HODDING CARTER *"Segregation's Way in One Southern Town"*	*April 5, 1953**
	7	MARGARET ANDERSON *"Clinton, Tennessee: Children in a Crucible"*	*November 2, 1958**
	12	DR. MARTIN LUTHER KING, JR. *"The Case Against Tokenism"*	*August 5, 1962**
3	3	CABELL PHILLIPS *"Integration: Battle of Hoxie, Arkansas"*	*September 25, 1955**
	37	GEORGE BARRETT *"Desegregation: The Clinton Story"*	*September 16, 1956**
4	49	BENJAMIN FINE	*September 24, 1957*
	56	CABELL PHILLIPS *"Dilemma of the Southern Moderates"*	*October 20, 1957**
	61	HOMER BIGART	*October 12, 1957*
	63	*Transcript of Mrs. Jorunn Ricketts' conversation*	*October 14, 1957*
	67	JAMES RESTON	*August 29, 1958*
5	72	WAYNE PHILLIPS	*February 23, 1956*
	76	A.P.	*December 21, 1956*
	77	GEORGE BARRETT	*December 22, 1956*
	79	GEORGE BARRETT *"Jim Crow, He's Real Tired"*	*March 3, 1957**
6	86	U.P.I.	*February 3, 1960*
	88	CLAUDE SITTON	*May 22, 1961*

CHAPTER	PAGE	AUTHOR/TITLE	DATE
6	89	CLAUDE SITTON	May 24, 1961
	91	CLAUDE SITTON	November 30, 1961
	93	HEDRICK SMITH	August 16, 1962
	95	DR. MARTIN LUTHER KING, JR. "The Case Against Tokenism"	August 5, 1962*
	101	HEDRICK SMITH	July 13, 1963
8	135	CLAUDE SITTON	March 2, 1964
	137	WILMA DYKEMAN & JAMES STOKELY "The Big Cure for Segregation"	September 24, 1961*
	141	CLAUDE SITTON	July 27, 1962
	148	CLAUDE SITTON	July 10, 1963
9	157	"Man in the News"	November 3, 1960
	160	CLAUDE SITTON	November 17, 1960
	162	CLAUDE SITTON	December 5, 1960
	166	HEDRICK SMITH	September 5, 1962
	170	CLAUDE SITTON "Atlanta's Example: Good Sense and Dignity"	May 6, 1962*
10	175	HARRISON SALISBURY	April 12, 1960
	178	JACK RAYMOND	April 14, 1963
	179	FOSTER HAILEY	May 3, 1963
	180	FOSTER HAILEY	May 4, 1963
	181	CLAUDE SITTON	May 7, 1963
	184	HEDRICK SMITH	May 13, 1963
	185	CLAUDE SITTON	May 13, 1963
	187	ANTHONY LEWIS	May 19, 1963
	197	CLAUDE SITTON	September 16, 1963
	197	JAMES RESTON	September 20, 1963
11	205	CLAUDE SITTON "Inquiry into the Mississippi Mind"	April 28, 1963*
	209	MARGARET LONG "A Southern Teenager Speaks His Mind"	November 10, 1963*
	211	CLAUDE SITTON	January 4, 1960
	214	"Man in the News"	September 21, 1962
	216	A.P.	October 1, 1962
	219	CLAUDE SITTON	October 2, 1962

CHAPTER	PAGE	AUTHOR/TITLE	DATE
11	222	CLAUDE SITTON	*January 17, 1963*
	224	"Man in the News"	*June 1, 1963*
	226	CLAUDE SITTON	*June 13, 1963*
	227	CLAUDE SITTON	*June 16, 1963*
	229	HODDING CARTER "Mississippi Now—Hate and Fear"	*June 23, 1963**
	231	CLAUDE SITTON "Inquiry into the Mississippi Mind"	*April 28, 1963**
	232	JOHN HERBERS	*January 30, 1964*
	233	JAMES W. SILVER "Mississippi Must Choose"	*July 19, 1964**
	239	JAMES BALDWIN "A Negro Assays the Negro Mood"	*March 12, 1961**
	245	WILMA DYKEMAN & JAMES STOKELY " 'The South' in the North"	*April 17, 1960**
	253	E. W. KENWORTHY	*August 29, 1963*
	254	RUSSELL BAKER	*August 29, 1963*
	256	E. W. KENWORTHY	*August 29, 1963*
	257	JAMES RESTON	*August 29, 1963*
	259	LAWRENCE E. DAVIES	*March 19, 1964*
	262	PAUL L. MONTGOMERY	*July 20, 1964*
	268	DANIEL BELL "Plea for a 'New Phase' in Negro Leadership"	*May 31, 1964**
	276	JOHN OLIVER KILLENS "Explanation of the 'Black Psyche' "	*June 7, 1964**

INDEX

Aaron, John, 67
Abernathy, Ralph D., 73, 95, 177, 178, 184, 282
Africa, emergence of, 242, 243
Afro-American Association, 260
Agitators, professional, 37-38, 39, 42, 48, 50
Alabama, 44, 87-93, 117, 119, 128, 131-33, 147, 173, 175-203, 287, 292-93, 304; *see also* Birmingham, Alabama; Montgomery, Alabama
Alabama, University of, 107-08, 121, 169, 190-91, 300
Albany, Georgia, 93-95, 97, 100, 103, 178, 288
Albany *Herald*, 93-94
Albright, A. D., 250-51
Alcorn A. & M. University, 225
Alford, T. Dale, 69
Allen, Ivan, Jr., 153-54
Allen, Jo Ann, 38-39
Allen, Ralph, 142-43, 145
Almond, Governor J. Lindsay, 298, 299-300
American Dilemma, An (Myrdal), 3
American Revolution, 279
Americus, Georgia, 290
Anarchy, 14, 78, 81, 100-03, 120, 184-89, 195-203, 258, 262-67, 287, 294-95
Anderson, J. W., 111
Anderson, Margaret, 7-8
Anniston, Alabama, 87
Anti-Semitism, 176, 249
Arizona, 32
Arkansas, 47, 59-60, 128
Arkansas *Gazette*, 47, 60
Ashmore, Harry, 47

Associated Press, 216
Athens, Georgia, 169-70
Atlanta, Georgia, 100, 153-54, 167-168, 170-74, 291, 300, 302
Atlanta *Constitution*, 95, 154, 173
Atlanta Crackers, 173
Atlanta *Daily World*, 172
Atlanta *Journal*, 154, 173
Atlantic, The, 258

Bachman, R. W., 213
"Backlash," the, 4, 13, 100, 261-62
Bacon, Kay, 63-66
Bagley, J. H., 77
Bailey, Melvin, 183, 197
Baker, Russell, 254-57
Baker County, Georgia, 148-51
Baldwin, James, 238-45, 251-52, 257
Baltimore, Maryland, 33
Bank of America, 259
Barnett, Governor Ross R., 120, 208, 216, 217, 218, 219, 221, 233, 284
Barrett, Don, 209-10
Barrett, George, 37, 77-78, 79
Bates, Daisy, 50, 51
Baton Rouge, Louisiana, 155, 159, 164
Beavers, Louise, 277
Beckwith, Byron de la, 232
Belafonte, Harry, 252, 278
Bell, Daniel, 268-76
Bevel, James, 181
Beyond the Melting Pot (Glazer and Moynihan), 273
Bickel, Alexander M., 9, 10, 47
Bigart, Homer, 61-63
Bilbo, Theodore G., 208
Birmingham, Alabama, 11, 87, 120, 121, 175-89, 195-203
Birmingham *News*, 182

Thompson, Allen, 227, 228
Till, Emmett, 211, 278
Timmons, Luther, 149
Transportation demonstrations, interstate, *see* Bus-terminal desegregation demonstrations; Freedom riders
Triborough Bridge demonstration, 258
Troops, federal, *see* Federal troops
Tuition grant plan, 43-44
Tuscaloosa, Alabama, 190, 195
Tuskegee, Alabama, 195, 304-05
Tuskegee Civil Association, 132
Tuskegee Institute, 81, 132
Twelve Million Black Voices (Wright), 282
Twenty-fourth Amendment, 128
Tyler, Harold R., Jr., 113
Tylertown, Mississippi, 126-27

United Nations 239, 245, 280
United Press International, 86
Urban League, *see* National Urban League

Vandiver, Governor Ernest, 168-69
Vardaman, James K., 208
Vinson, Chief Justice Fred M., 12, 22, 28
Violent resistence, 91-93, 100-03, 121, 175-79, 184-89, 195-203, 218-224, 227-29, 233, 294-95
Virginia, 32, 43, 119, 128, 255, 298-300, 301
Voluntary desegregation, 46
Voter Education Project, 151, 207
Voting in the South, Negro, 122-23, 126-52, 172, 206-07, 225
Voting registrars, corruption of the law by, 290

Wade, Virgil, 197
Wagner, Emile F., Jr., 159

Walker, Maj. General Edwin A., 55, 220-21
Walker, Mardon, 291
Wallace, Governor George C., 13, 121, 183, 184, 187, 189, 190, 191, 195, 196, 197, 198, 261-62, 293, 300
Waller, Bill, 232
Walthall County, Mississippi, 126-128, 130, 290, 295
Warden, Donald, 260
Waring, Judge J. Waties, 23
Warren, Chief Justice Earl, 28-29, 30, 68
Washington, George, 55, 279
Watkins, Robert, 34
Wells, Houston, 226
Wesely, Cynthia, 197
Weswego, Louisiana, 166
Whiskey Rebellion, 55
White, Byron R., 87, 88, 89
White, Governor Hugh, 236
White, W. Wilson, 113
White America, Inc., 34
White Citizens Councils, *see* Citizens Councils
White primary, 18, 21, 129, 131, 172
Williams, J. A. (Josh), 149
Wilmington, Delaware, 297
Wilson, Lucius, 126-27
Winona, Mississippi, 288-89
Wisconsin, 262
Wofford, Harris L., Jr., 115-16
Wood, John Q., 126-27
Woods, Robin, 63-66
Woodward, C. Vann, 207-08
World's Fair demonstrations, 258, 261
Wright, Judge J. Skelly, 155, 156-57, 158, 159
Wright, Richard, 282

Yoder, Gordon, 220
Young, Thomas A., 226
Young, Whitney, 269, 271

About the Authors

The joint byline of Portrait of a Decade *includes more than the reporters and writers actually named: the book is the work of a score of journalists who have filed millions of words about civil rights during the past ten years. In addition to those who covered and commented on the civil-rights story along with other assignments, the* Times *relied particularly on Claude Sitton, who since 1957 has been its southern regional correspondent. Based in Atlanta, where he was born in 1925, Mr. Sitton has traveled thousands of miles each year, and the datelines of his stories reflect almost every major episode of the struggle in the South for civil rights.*

Anthony Lewis, the author-editor of Portrait of a Decade, *wrote for it three special chapters dealing with the law and civil rights. He has for the past nine years been the* New York Times Washington *correspondent covering the Supreme Court and the Justice Department. Born in 1927 in New York City, Mr. Lewis has won two Pulitzer prizes and is the author of* Gideon's Trumpet.